PRAISE FOR
THEY CALL ME "SWEET LOU"

"As an undrafted free agent from Northern Iowa who played for eleven years in the NFL, I know the dedication it takes to suit up for a game. But that virtue doesn't pertain to just players and coaches. Just ask any football official. Better yet, just read about the career of Sweet Lou, and you'll discover the domain of tryouts, training camps, clinics, chalk talks, and film sessions does not belong exclusively to players and coaches.

"For over fifty years, Lou has been officiating football at every level. To last that long, you simply have to love the game. Having played in Baltimore before and after the Colts moved, I know about the love affair between the fans and its team. Having grown up in Baltimore, Lou was one of those fans. His passion for the game is unparalleled! It's a love story worth reading!"

—Steve Wright, author of *Aggressively Human*, entrepreneur, NFL veteran with the Dallas Cowboys, Baltimore/Indianapolis Colts, and Los Angeles Raiders

"Despite playing seventeen years of organized football, including six in the NFL, I learned so much about the intricacies of officiating that I had never realized. People don't know how difficult it is to become a respected official and the time and effort that has to be invested from the sandlots to the NFL. Lou has embodied all the traits that go into being a successful official, husband, and father. My only wish is that I had met him sooner. His story is an easy and entertaining read!"

—Sam Havrilak, NFL veteran with the Baltimore

Colts and New Orleans Saints, Super Bowl V champion, first player in Super Bowl history to complete a pass, catch a pass, and take a handoff

"When Lou Hammond states that he came from the sandlots, correction. He earned his stripes on the dirt lots just like his childhood hero, Johnny Unitas. This book gives you the other angle of pro sports, the side of the officials who work their way up to the bigs to be loved or hated. Going back over fifty years, it's a sports history lesson on how the game has changed and those who changed it. Lou is a true professional who has heart and pride in his job. If you want to witness the game from the field to the press box, then I highly recommend *They Call Me Sweet Lou*."
—**John Ziemann, Band President Baltimore Colts' Marching Band/Baltimore's Marching Ravens**

"As a football coach, I have always had a great relationship with the officials. With Lou, I had a great relationship with a great official. This is evidenced by the fact Lou issued me my only penalty in my thirty-six years of coaching. It was well deserved as I was making my point past the hash mark. I've always found Lou to be a referee who was knowledgeable about the complicated rules of football. Our friendship remains despite that one penalty."
—**Gordy Combs, head football coach for seventeen years at Towson University, commentator with Towson Football Network for ten years**

"This remarkable book is a heartfelt tribute to football officiating and the legacy of semipro and minor league football. Sweet Lou's vivid recollections and insightful commentary provide a rare and authentic glimpse into the world of semipro and minor league football. His stories highlight the unique blend of passion, perseverance, and community spirit that defines this level of the game. His reflections on memorable teams and the colorful personalities that he encountered are a powerful reminder of the impact and importance of the minor leagues in the broader landscape of American football.

"*They Call Me Sweet Lou* is not just a book; it's a celebration of the spirit and heart of minor league football. I highly recommend it to anyone who loves the game and wishes to understand the profound impact of football at this level."

—Dave Burch, President of the American Football Association

"The book offers a fun insight into the unique world of football officiating. I'm always amazed at the high-character people and the 'true' characters that are in college football officiating. Sweet Lou checks both boxes, a character with character!"

—Chris Smith, supervisor of officials, Coastal Athletic Association

"Since my teen years when I picked up spending money doing baseball and basketball games, I've always had a soft spot for umpires and game officials. Seldom a home game and never a standing O, officials are like long-snappers. The only time they're noticed is when we think they've screwed up.

"Sweet Lou spent most of his life dedicated to the stripes he wore with pride for over fifty years. He gives us a great peek behind the curtain from JV games to iconic rivalries like Harvard–Yale, and to the NFL, where he tells us about a quarterback who loved his in-game snacks. *They Call Me*

Sweet Lou will make you smile and just maybe make you like the officials so many fans love to hate."

—Scott Garceau, Baltimore sportscaster for the Baltimore Ravens and Baltimore Orioles, among others, and five-time Maryland sportscaster of the year

"Sweet Lou is a character that you just might like. I know because I crewed with him during my first year in the Atlantic 10. He takes you on his journey through the world of football officiating, from his humble beginnings to the highest echelons. It's a fascinating trip with many stories about places and people he met in his career. The ups and downs of life in the sport that you love are here for you to enjoy."

—Bruce Williams, retired supervisor of officials, Colonial Athletic Association, and side judge, Bowl Division, National Championship 2010

"Every football fan should read this book and see how some very normal people helped make the sport great. When we were on the football field, we were just enjoying the game that we loved. We didn't realize that we were making lifelong memories and friendships. In this book, he has memorialized them for all of us."

—The Honorable Lance J. Garth, retired circuit court judge, former Division I football official and technical advisor

They Call Me "Sweet Lou" :
The Life and Times of a Football Official
by Lou Hammond and Paul Travers

© Copyright 2024 Lou Hammond and Paul Travers

ISBN 979-8-88824-424-1

NON-FICTION

All rights reserved. No part of this publication may be reproduced, stored in a retrieval system, or transmitted in any form or by any means—electronic, mechanical, photocopy, recording, or any other—except for brief quotations in printed reviews, without the prior written permission of the author.

Published by

◂köehlerbooks™

3705 Shore Drive
Virginia Beach, VA 23455
800-435-4811
www.koehlerbooks.com

THEY CALL ME
"Sweet Lou"

THE LIFE AND TIMES OF A FOOTBALL OFFICIAL

LOU HAMMOND
PAUL TRAVERS

VIRGINIA BEACH
CAPE CHARLES

CONTENTS

Dedication
Chapter 1............................Goodbye, Sweet Lou!
Chapter 2..................... Fourth Down and Forever
Chapter 3........................Back to the Garden(ville)
Chapter 4............................Saturday in the Park
Chapter 5..Sandlot Rookie
Chapter 6......................................High School Daze
Chapter 7...Flags Unfurled
Chapter 8........................These are the Champions
Chapter 9................................Life in the Minors
Chapter 10...................................Semipro Heroes
Chapter 11......................................O' Canada! Eh!
Chapter 12......................................The Gunslinger
Chapter 13....................................Pinball Football
Chapter 14...A Fan Club
Chapter 15......................College Entrance Exams
Chapter 16...................................Finding a Home
Chapter 17.......................To the Head of the Class
Chapter 18.................The Game: Yale vs. Harvard
Chapter 19..Instant Replays
Chapter 20...Roll the Tape
Chapter 21....................................The Chain Gang
Chapter 22...................Sidelines and Snack Lines
Chapter 23...The Call
Chapter 24.......................Undercover in Chicago

Chapter 25..........................Welcome to the NFL
Chapter 26............................Officially an Official
Chapter 27...............................America Attacked
Chapter 28......................Push Bottom, Press Box
Chapter 29..My Favorites
Chapter 30..........................Finding Your Calling
Acknowledgments

DEDICATION

To my dad, Walter Dane Hammond, the man who taught me how to ride a bike, shoot marbles, roller skate, build a skateboard, ride a pogo stick, and play baseball. Together, we fished and crabbed along the Chesapeake Bay and its tributaries. Together, we attended everything Baltimore: Colts football, Orioles baseball, Bullets basketball, and Clippers ice hockey. During my football career, he was my number one fan who cheered for me every step of the way. Without him, my dream would not have been possible.

To my mom, Nancy Hammond, who guided me along the right path during my adolescence. Throughout my life, she was always there for my sister and me. While my father often accompanied me during road games, my mother would always pack homemade desserts to keep us well fueled during those journeys.

To my wife, Kelly, and daughter, Kathleen, who supported me with unwavering love. Most weekends in the fall, I was away for games. I missed weddings, birthdays, family get-togethers, school functions, to name a few. They sacrificed tremendously so I could chase my dream.

Thankfully, after my college career, the best was yet to come.

CHAPTER 1
GOODBYE, SWEET LOU!

I can feel his hot breath on my neck. A shadowy figure is tugging on the back of my jersey and calling my name. Without looking, I know who it is. Father Time has been chasing me for the last two years. It's a race that can't be won. All I can do is step aside gracefully and let him pass. In the spring of 2008, I decided this would be my last year on the college football field. After over 230 DIV I games, numerous DIV II and III games, and 1,000 high school games, it was time to give my feet and legs a break. Many of my colleagues doubted my sincerity because I had told the supervisor of officials that I would be retiring a few years ago. "Yeah, Lou, you retired yesterday, today, and tomorrow," they would joke in unison with a hearty laugh.

"Guys, I lost a step out there today," I would woefully lament after the game. While sprinter's speed wasn't a prerequisite to be a football official, you had to be able to move swiftly to the proper position to see and call the play. I wasn't as swift as I used to be. I still had some *swift*, but I never had any speed. In

November 1967, my freshmen year, I severed parts of two toes on my left foot in a lawn mower accident. That swiftly ended my short-lived high school career.

Over the ensuing years, I felt those lost steps as if I was running in sand. And with age, I didn't have the eagle eyes to compensate for reduced mobility. What most sports fans don't realize is that officials between the lines are on the field more than the players. We are athletes, the third team on the field. To inconspicuously glide up and down the field in the shadows of the players, they have to be in peak physical condition. The next time you watch sports such as soccer, ice hockey, basketball, or rugby, take a few seconds to focus on the officials and referees. They are always on the move and don't seem to miss a step. If you're an official focusing on catching your breath, you're not going to be able to focus on catching the play.

"Lou, you never had a step to lose," James Maconaghy, commonly known as Jimmy Mac, coordinator of football officials for CIP (acronym for the Colonial Athletic Association, Ivy League, and Patriot League consortium) chuckled when I made my announcement. If I had any doubts about retiring, they were quickly erased. "Sweet Lou, go out on top of your game," he added with a knowing smile. I respected that comment because I had witnessed too many legendary athletes who hung around the game after their talents had vanished. I didn't want to be in that category.

When Jimmy Mac spoke, you listened, especially if you were an official. To me, he was the godfather of officiating, a mentor, role model, and most importantly a cherished friend. In 2019, he was presented with the David M. Perry Award as college football's most outstanding officiating coordinator for exemplary professionalism and leadership. In addition to assigning officials for all CIP games, he coordinated clinics to educate officials and coaches on the intricacies of collegiate officiating, selected the top officials for the Football Championship Series (FCS) football assignments, and worked with coaches and schools to evaluate the game performances on a weekly basis.

During his career, he worked the 1997 Army vs. Navy game, the 1999 Eddie Robinson Football Classic (Kansas vs. Notre Dame), and the 1999 Independence Bowl (Mississippi vs. Oklahoma). In addition to serving as a coordinator of officials at the high school and college levels, he served as the game-day coach/quarterback coordinator for the NFL's Philadelphia Eagles for ten years. In 1996, he was named the National Football Foundation Collegiate Official of the Year and four years later inducted into the Pennsylvania Sports Hall of Fame.

I first met Jimmy Mac in 1986 at Franklin and Marshall College when we were assigned to work the ECAC (Eastern College Athletic Association) Southern Division II championship game. Like me, he had worked numerous high school and lower division college games. As fate would have it, the following year we were both promoted to DIV I and became the best of friends on and off the field.

To be honest, I had to admit there was a preponderance of legitimacy in Jimmy Mac's comment regarding my foot speed. All I had to do was remember my short-lived sandlot baseball career and my one year of JV football in high school. Add that to my foot issue, and the writing was on the wall. While I was never one of the fastest players, I always thought myself to be one of the smartest. Whatever I played, I knew the rules and how to play the game.

I was not only a precocious student of the game but also an astute technician. Little did I know as an eight-year-old Little Leaguer that those skills would get me to the big leagues in another sport. Just a few years later, I realized that I wasn't born to make the plays; I was born to make the calls.

Now that Jimmy Mac knew about my decision to step aside, it was time to go public. At the annual summer clinic for CIP officials, I told my crew that this would be my last year. No more timed runs or rule tests for me. No more road trips and Holiday Inns. In the future, I would enjoy the games from the comfort of my favorite lounge chair with an ample tray of my favorite snacks and beverages. My crew, which had been together for five years, grudgingly accepted my decision. They nodded in unison with solemn grins. In their hearts, they knew that one day they would be announcing goodbye. We had been in the trenches of college football, weathering great battles on the gridiron.

In early July, we were given our schedules for the upcoming season. It was always exciting to see where we would be traveling. To me, it always felt like winning an all-expenses paid vacation up and down the East Coast. As usual, assignments were complete except for the last week of the season. That weekend was held open to assign the higher graded crews to the more important games, such as rivalries, playoffs contenders, and championships.

As the season progressed, I was getting anxious about my last couple of weeks on the field. The end of my career was now on the near horizon, and I was squeamish about looking in that direction. It seemed that the older I got, the faster the season rushed by me. This season had been a blur. Despite my apprehension, I did the job to the best of abilities. In late October after another season successful, I finally got the call that I had hoped would punctuate my career.

"Sweet Lou, where do you want to go for the last week of the season?" Jimmy Mac asked as if I had won the grand prize in the CIP sweepstakes.

"Lehigh and Lafayette on November 22," I responded without hesitating. That game had been on my bucket list for a number of years. For me, it was the grand prize.

"You got it. Just keep it under your hat until the assignments are released," he whispered as if the FBI had been eavesdropping.

◆ ◆ ◆

In early November, assignments for the final week were released. My crew and I were headed to Lafayette College in Easton, Pennsylvania, for what is known as The Rivalry. Played between the Lafayette Leopards and the Lehigh Mountain Hawks, the game was the most-played and longest uninterrupted rivalry in the nation. It was so old that it predated the awarding of an iconic trophy. The winner only received the coveted bragging rights and a game ball painted with the final score. That was enough to keep the victorious alumni happy. While the game didn't have the pomp and circumstance of the Army and Navy rivalry, it was college football at its finest. In 2014, the 150^{tth} version of the game was played at Yankees Stadium in front of a sellout crowd of 48,256. It was that big.

This game was special for the crew because it reflected our outstanding performance during the season. After every game, we were graded and evaluated on rules application, physical appearance, handling situations under pressure, and communications with fellow officials, coaches, and players.

Some crews didn't get a game the final week because of questionable calls or behavior during the season. That's not because they weren't trying to do their best. Fans have to realize that officials take pride in their performance on the field just like the players. One crew didn't make the cut because they missed a couple of obvious fouls that could have impacted the outcome of the game. I say *could have* because you never know what *would have* happened if the correct call had been made. On another crew, the referee had a verbal confrontation with a head coach during the game. That crew was not handed any post-season games.

Fans have to realize that calls on the field by the officials are part of the game. That great unknown keeps the fans glued to their seats and TV screens. Fans get to replay and argue about questionable officiating until the next season. As for the crew, those responsible must live with a bad or missed call for the rest of the season and suffer the consequences, such as getting passed over for post-regular season games or great rivalries.

There was only one downside to our selection to the Lafayette-Lehigh clash was that our umpire John Shigo was a Lehigh alumnus. The All-American linebacker, who later played professional football for the Philadelphia Stars in the USFL, could not work the game. If John was disappointed, he didn't show it. He knew the league rules, and we knew that he was one of the reasons why we got the assignment. On the flipside, he could enjoy the game from the stands and cheer for his two favorite teams, one of which was dressed in black-and-white stripes.

Our referee for the year was Jack Winter. I first met Jack in 1998 during our rookie season in DIV I. Working his way up from DIV II and III, he developed the skills to be a leader of seven field officials. Respected by his peers, coaches, and administrators, he later became a replay official in the American Athletic Conference (AAC). Upon retiring from the field, he received the Outstanding College Football Official Award from the Philadelphia Chapter of the National Football Foundation and College Hall of Fame. One of my best friends, we would spend ten years together on the same crew.

Our line judge for the season was Ed Mokus. Ed was the perfect fit for our crew that was known throughout the league for its camaraderie and cohesiveness. My move from linesman to line judge opened up the position, and Ed found a home for the rest of his officiating career. After retiring from the field, he became an associate athletic director at Yale University.

The side judge on our crew was Chris Garth. I worked with his father, the Honorable Lance Garth, during my first year in DIV I in 1986. Chris often traveled to games with his father and mother Kathy. Like father like son, college football coursed through his veins. After retiring, Chris held various teaching positions in Massachusetts and Virginia.

Our back judge for the year was rookie Gary Powers from Columbia, Maryland. Gary developed into an outstanding official and later officiated in the Big 10 Conference. As district sales manager for Under Armour, he ensured that we always had the proper base layer clothing during the season. Rounding out the crew, was our field judge Jack O'Keefe, nicknamed JuJu. A dental equipment sales representative from Albany, New York, he became the communication specialist on the crew, always talking with folks to get us things that we needed. He possessed the gift of gab and gift of getting.

◆ ◆ ◆

The final weekend of my career began with a Friday dinner at a restaurant in South Bethlehem. The giant video screen in the restaurant proudly proclaimed, *Congratulations Lou Hammond on your retirement. 40 years of officiating 230 Division I games. Last game 11/22/08, Lehigh & Lafayette. Saved the best for last.* Despite not being an overly sentimental guy, especially when it came to football, I wiped my tears. I hadn't been this emotional about football since Johnny Unitas of the Baltimore Colts died in 2002. Father Time had finally caught me, but he had the decency to buy me a good meal.

Other than relax and enjoy myself, my only duty for the evening was to order appetizers. That culinary exercise was actually a running joke among the crew because I had a penchant for over ordering appetizers, especially calamari. By the time dinner arrived at our table, everyone was usually too stuffed to eat.

During dinner, we swapped stories from the past. Following dessert, my crew presented me with a gold watch, a golf jacket with the Yale Bulldogs logo (more on that later), and a handle—1.75 liters of Tanqueray gin. That was my drink of choice and was affectionately and effectively known as the *weekender* because it had to last the entire weekend. And in most cases, it did.

After dinner, we didn't retire to the bar and watch football as most people would have presumed. Instead, we returned to the hotel conference room for our evening film session with plays from the previous week. We also had a weekend crew exam that had to be retuned to the crew supervisor the following day. Answers to each question were extensively discussed. Agreement on a procedure had to be unanimous. As always, I had question seven, part of the crew tradition, to ensure that I had to only answer one of the ten questions for the evening.

Here's a typical question on the exam in the language of football officials:

Third-and-Five on A6. Team A trails 17-14 with 0:04 remaining in the game. QB A1 attempts a handoff to Back A2 but they muff the exchange and the ball rolls into the end zone. A88 bats the ball in the end zone over the end line to prevent B7 from recovering the ball (0:00). Immediately after the snap Nose Guard B5 head slapped Center A5 at the LOS.

Here's the translation in layman's terms: It's third down and 5 yards to go for a first down. The ball is on the 6-yard line of the defense. The offense is losing 17-14 with four seconds to go in the game. The quarterback attempts to hand off the ball to his running back, but the ball hits the ground and rolls into the end zone. The tight end hits the ball into the end zone to keep the defensive linebacker from recovering the ball with no time on the clock. After the center snapped the ball to the quarterback, the defensive lineman slapped the center in the head at the line of scrimmage.

How would you rule on this play? There are two penalties on the play, one by each team. The tight end hit the ball in the end zone to prevent the linebacker from recovering it, and the defensive lineman hit the center in the head. Answer: Offsetting penalties, replay the down.

Following the meeting, I settled into my pregame routine that included a call to my wife, Kelly, and a gin and tonic nightcap. Kelly, ever thoughtful and caring, didn't want to attend the game because she felt it would be a guys' bonding weekend. She was right, but it would have been reassuring to see her smiling face. Even with the nightcap, I couldn't relax my mind as I wrestled with the tendencies of both teams and the possible scenarios that I might encounter. Like my colleagues, I wanted my last game to be perfect.

For hours, I rolled back and forth across the bed with intermittent bouts of sleep. In this torpid state, hundreds of plays from past games flashed before me like a movie projector on fast-forward. Mindful of my mechanics, I carefully positioned myself to chase after each play. With each step, I ran slower and slower until the players faded like ghosts. Looking at my feet, I saw that I was running in sand and wearing a pair of baseball cleats. I was a powerless spectator for my entire football career. Finally the whir of the projector fell silent. It seemed that just as I drifted off to a deep sleep, the alarm clock sounded. Mercifully, it was Saturday and time to play college football in America. Despite the turbulent night, I awoke calm and confident.

Almost football heaven!
Kidd Brewer Stadium in the Blue Ridge Mountains.

CHAPTER 2
FOURTH DOWN AND FOREVER

I awoke at 6 a.m. and immediately started to prepare and pack for the game. After a shower and a cup of coffee, I met the crew in the hotel lobby for breakfast. Most of the guys had a light breakfast of cereal and fruit, but that was not my pregame routine. I was a firm believer that breakfast was the most important meal of the day. As always, I sampled the breakfast buffet to include an egg omelet, waffles, sausage, and bacon.

Maybe, it wasn't too healthy by today's standards, but there were a lot of calories to be burned off during the game. I always joked to my crew that I was old school, following in the footsteps of the players from the 1950s and 60s who put the *pro* in protein. They usually dined on steak and eggs for breakfast.

Over the years, I had watched officials eat some of the strangest concoctions imaginable. A back judge on one of my crews would go into the kitchen and request an omelet with hot chili peppers, hot sauce, and onions. I don't know how he could eat it, but he never had an upset stomach. I'd get an upset stomach watching him eat. A linesman on one of my crews didn't like to eat with us because of a prank. Whenever we went to a Cracker Barrel or similar establishment, we always told the hostess that it was his birthday which it wasn't. On cue, the staff would gather around our table to sing "Happy Birthday." If it was me, I would have also skipped breakfast. Another frugal linesman would always bring a loaf of bread and a jar of peanut butter for his breakfast and lunch. He even saved a few more dollars by not buying jam. For me, the buffet was just fine.

We left the hotel at 8:30 and headed to Lafayette College. On the way to the game, I called Kelly for a final pep talk to calm my nerves. Always good Samaritans, we parked in our assigned spots across from the Allan P. Kirby Sports Center and gave our parking passes to friends who were attending the game.

Waiting for us at the entrance to the field house were the locker room attendant and a campus security guard. They escorted us to the locker room where a game program, a towel, and bar of soap had been placed on our stools. With hot water in the showers, we didn't need anything else. A food platter would have been nice, but we were well aware this was not the NFL. After our pregame conference, which consisted of discussing each team's tendencies, such as pass versus run, types of passes (long, short, screen, shovel), special teams, on-side kicks, long or short punts, it was time to suit up.

Opening my game bag, I found my father's black officials hat, the one he wore when he attended my games, and a card from Kelly wishing me a happy retirement and a great game. Those love notes, which always found a mysterious way into my bag, never failed to put the game in perspective. No matter what happened on the field, there's was always somebody waiting at home who loved me. On this day, it was comforting to know that my home crew would be on the field with me in spirit, if not in person. I was ready for the kickoff.

Jimmy King, our technical adviser, stopped by with some last-minute advice for the crew and to wish me well. In all the hoopla over the rivalry and my retirement, it was relaxing to see my old friend before my last game. Jimmy and I worked together for a number of years before he came off the field. Today I just wished that he was with me on the field one last time. That would have been a special treat.

In addition to grading our performance on the field, his job was to watch the game as an impartial observer for the coordinator of officials and report any unusual plays or controversies that could impact the level of officiating.

For example, the quarterback is hit late on the play and the defensive player is ejected for unnecessary roughness. Was the penalty correct and was the ejection warranted? Another one of my favorite scenarios was the weather. The officials may have the power of God on the field, but they cannot control the weather. One game started thirty minutes late because the grounds crew had to remove the snow from the field. Could the referee have better a job of coordinating snow removal or should the officiating crew have been issued snow shovels? Just kidding about the shovels, but the example shows the extent of officiating duties and responsibilities.

On Monday morning, the TA would grade our performance using game film, television video, or plays sent in by the coaches. Each official was given a grade of 1-10, and these ratings were used in assigning post-season games.

After Jimmy left, we checked ourselves in a mirror and headed to the field for our pregame babysitting session. Due to a number of altercations during warm-ups over the past few years, officials were now required to patrol the field to ensure proper football decorum and etiquette. I simply filed that under "other duties as assigned."

During the pregame warm-ups, each team is assigned a designated area for calisthenics, offensive/defensive line play, passing/kicking drills, and uniform inspections. Rarely do the two teams jaw at one another, but we were present to prevent any unnecessary penalties. The game is physical enough without a pregame boxing match. Two officials were required to be on the field while the teams warmed up. The field judge and the side judge would do the first twenty minutes and the line judge and head linesman would do another twenty-minute segment. Fifteen minutes before the game, the entire crew would be patrolling the field and performing other pregame field duties.

As I stepped into the bright sunshine, the side judge called me over and told me that the sideline reporter for the TV broadcast wanted an interview. After forty years, I was finally getting my ten minutes of fame. I was immediately peppered with questions that caught me off-guard. Where I was from? How long have I been officiating? Why so long? What am I going to do now? Thankfully, the interview was edited to a few minutes and played during the telecast of the game. That's entertainment! I could only imagine how players dealt with the media after the game, especially if it was a loss.

As the teams readied for the kickoff, the referee walked over to where I was standing. "Sweet Lou, I want you to toss the coin at midfield," Jack said excitedly. I followed him to midfield where he introduced me to the team captains.

"Gentlemen, this is Mr. Lou Hammond, and he is officiating his last college football game. He has worked over two hundred and thirty Division I football games."

After shaking hands with the captains, I overheard one of them say, "Lou who?" Being a Baltimore Colts fan, I was instantly reminded about Alex Hawkins who was the first special teams captain in the NFL. When introduced before the coin toss for a preseason game against the Chicago Bears, Dick Butkus, the Bears' infamous linebacker, responded, "Captain who?" Dick had no problem recognizing John Unitas and Gino Marchetti, the other two captains. I was in select company.

I just chuckled at the thought and trotted to the sideline where Lehigh Coach Andy Coen congratulated me. That sign of respect was another special moment, especially coming from a coach. Sadly, one of the classiest coaches I ever met, a true gentleman in all aspects, stepped away from the game in 2018 after a diagnosis with Alzheimer's disease. During his thirteen seasons, Coach Coen was a two-time Patriot League Coach of the Year and led his teams to five Patriot League championships in thirteen seasons. With Andy, respect on and off the field was earned. Sadly, Coach Coen passed away in April 2022. College football lost a giant of a man.

◆ ◆ ◆

Finally, it was time to play football. On a cold, blustery afternoon, the overflow crowd of 16,000 fans at Fisher Stadium was buzzing with excitement. As the kickoff sailed gracefully into the end zone for a touchback, a wave of deafening noise rolled over the field. A shot of pure adrenaline! I looked at my crew. Everyone was smiling. *If they could only bottle this stuff*, I thought. Like fans and players, it was impossible for the crew not to get caught up in the emotion of the moment. However, we were the ones who had to maintain control and keep calm heads in the midst of chaos.

I had a chance to catch my breath during the first TV commercial timeout. Still floating on a cloud, I walked over to the chain crew who offered their congratulations and made some small talk about the weather. That had the calming effect that I needed. I was back in my zone, completely focused on the play in front of me, and oblivious to the crowd noise. While the game on the field slowed for me, the game clock seemed to be racing ahead as if the timekeeper forgot to take his finger off the button. Before I knew it, we were running off the field for halftime.

In the locker room the crew asked how I was doing. Right before heading back to the field, the referee addressed the room. "Let's go guys. Don't fuck up Sweet Lou's last half of football," he barked with a grin. I nodded approvingly. The message was clear. Come hell or high water, today the brotherhood had my back on the field.

On the field, the wind was whipping, and the temperature was dropping rapidly. All I could think about was windblown passes and kicks that could affect the game. Before the second half kickoff, I glanced in the end zone stands where John Shigo was waving at me with a big cigar in one hand and a big cup of beer in the other. "See you after the game. I'll have a *taste* (gin and tonic) waiting for you," he shouted above the wind. The brotherhood also had my back off the field.

The third quarter proved to be a hard-hitting defensive battle as the Lafayette Leopards scored the only points on a 22-yard field goal. At the end of the third quarter, the Lehigh Mountains Hawks were clinging tenaciously to a 17-15 lead. I was excited, but not as nervous as the fans. With the pads popping, the game had all the ingredients to be one for the record books, and I was there to witness it.

When teams switched ends of the field at the end of the third quarter, my mind began to wander as if I was having an out of body experience. In all of my years on the field, this had never happened to me. From a dark corner in the back of my mind, it finally dawned on me. This really was the last time that I'd be in uniform. There would be no more patrolling the sidelines while talking to coaches and listening to them bitch and moan about a penalty or the spot of the ball. Oh, the ties that bind!

In a flash, I remembered my father taking off from work to accompany me to my first DIV I game at Bucknell University. I could see the pride and delight on his face when I handed him a black officials hat. I remembered Kelly flying up to Boston to be with me for her first-ever college game at Harvard. After the game, she met Teddy Kennedy while waiting for me to come out of the locker room. All great memories!

My sweet daydream ended abruptly when the players lined up for the first play of the fourth quarter. To finish the perfect game, I still had to stay focused and in the zone until the final whistle. The question now was could I meet the challenge with my mind going haywire.

With 7:11 left in the game, Lehigh scored a touchdown to take a 24-15, but Lafayette was not deterred. On their next possession, they hurriedly marched down the field to the Lehigh 10-yard line when disaster struck. On the next play with just under five minutes remaining, Lehigh linebacker Al Pierce intercepted a pass and raced ninety-four yards for a touchdown to seal the victory.

As the play unfolded, one question in my mind remained. Did I have one last gallop in my step to get to the goal line and cover the play? Instantly, I remembered my dream from last night and thought I was doomed. No need to worry. As I looked up, the referee, who had the goal line covered, raised both hands above his head. The well-oiled machine was running on all cylinders. At the commercial break, I breathed a sigh of relief as if I had been holding my breath for forty years. The perfect game was within reach. A classic game in a classic rivalry was guaranteed. The all-important big *M*, momentum, had shifted on one play. The dejection of the Lafayette offensive was a death rattle while the jubilation of the Lehigh sideline was deafening.

With about thirty seconds left in the game, the fans rushed the field and stole umpire Eddie Keefer's hat. Eddie was John Shigo's replacement. During the stampede, the game clock mercifully wound down to zero. Thank goodness we didn't have to clear the field to run another play. My last game was over in seemingly the blink of an eye. As the crew ran to the safety of the locker room, I stopped to take one last look at the game of football from my vantage point.

I stared hard into the stands and remembered my first college football game at Ursinus College. At that time, I never envisioned the moment when it would end.

If only I could go back and play all the games again, I pondered as my mind drifted off to a favorite Hollywood movie. *If only someone could make that wish come dream*, I mused further. What I needed was for Ray Kinsella from the *Field of Dreams* to walk up to me and say, "Lou, what if I could make that dream come true?"

◆ ◆ ◆

Stepping off the grass and onto the track, I realized that I had crossed that cosmic boundary like Moonlight Graham in the movie. There was no turning back the hands of time. I was humbly thankful there had been a Ray Kinsella at every junction in my career. At various crossroads, these special people took a wide-eyed rookie official under their wings and helped him make the right decisions. They made my dream come true. At that moment, I felt like I was the luckiest man on earth.

My crew and other field personnel were waiting impatiently for me in the locker room. After an endless barrage of hugs and handshakes, it was back to business as we filled out its final game reports. After the reports were handed to the technical assistant, he went around the room to critique each individual performance.

"Sweet Lou, I have nothing to say about your performance today. You were outstanding. I just want to thank you for all you have done over your career, especially with helping newer officials become better officials."

Teary and dry throated, all that I could do was nod in agreement with a tight smile. That's the ultimate compliment for anybody in any profession. I had paid my dues to join this exclusive fraternity and now had paid it forward.

I thanked the crew for sharing this special day with me. I gave my hat to Ed who had filled in for Shigo. I gave my beanbag to Jack and told him that in all my years it had never been used to enforce a penalty or mark a spot for a possession change. I gave my whistle to JuJu and penalty flag to Chris. In return, the crew presented me with a signed game ball to commemorate my final game. *A more than fair exchange to say the least*, I thought.

Back at the hotel, I called Kelly to give her a replay of the day's events. That was my normal postgame routine, a kind of football therapy to get the game off my chest without an inquisition from the press or coaches. On a somber note, I only wished my father was still alive to see it. My family had sacrificed so much in their own lives so I could chase footballs on Saturday afternoons. I only hoped and prayed that I had given them even more in return.

After the phone call, I headed down to the hotel lobby where drinks and food had been set up. It was customary to celebrate the end of the season with a party. In the background, college football games blared from a bank of TV screens. What else would you expect from a group of football officials whose livelihood was their hobby?

Before wrapping up the postgame party, I presented my crew with parting gifts to thank them for keeping me on the field in good standing. Each member received a vase with the inscription: *Thanks for the memories, Sweet Lou*. Short and sweet, there was nothing more to be said.

Back in my hotel room, I had a late-night phone call from the supervisor of officials congratulating me on a great career and asking me if I wanted to join his staff of technical advisers next year. I immediately said yes.

"Oh, and one last thing. Don't put away your uniform just yet. No promises, but you may be getting a call from me tomorrow evening." Could the season be even sweeter? I kept my fingers crossed.

That Sunday night I got the call at home. My crew and I were headed to Appalachian State University (ASU) for a first-round playoff game with South Carolina State. I had met another Ray Kinsella. Now all I needed was a new hat, a whistle, a penalty flag, and a beanbag.

Situated in the Blue Ridge Mountains in the town of Boone, named after frontiersman Daniel Boone, ASU was one the highest-altitude campuses east of the Mississippi River at 3,333 feet. It's a place where country entertainers rival athletes as notable alumni. One of the top schools in the country for outdoor enthusiasts, it also boasted an exceptional football program that won three consecutive FCS national championships (2005 through 2007) and six consecutive bowl games (2015 through 2020) as an FBS member.

As I pulled into the parking lot of the Sleep Inn, I was ready for mountain football. The ninety-minute ride to Boone from the airport had been stunning. Like a rolling ocean of green, mountain vistas stretched to the horizon. Cradled in those mountain depressions were the legendary hollers where moonshine and country music were distilled for general consumption. Any minute I expected to see Robert Mitchum behind the wheel of a 1950 Ford sedan careening around the next curve with a load of white lightnin'.

In a tight battle, ASU finally broke open the game with two touchdowns in the fourth quarter for a 37-21 win. Despite the cold rain after halftime, the crew enjoyed another thriller. What a great way to end the season and a career!

In the locker room, there was a sense of deep satisfaction as crew members peeled off their uniforms. "Great way to end the season, maybe your best game of the year," the technical adviser bellowed with delight. He was right. Despite the lop-sided score, the crew had remained focused on every play. Officials as well as players get psyched for the playoffs. As we changed into civilian clothes, the crew razzed me about my next step.

"Lou, don't forget your friends once you cross over to the dark side," someone shouted across the room. The dark side translated to a position as a technical adviser/observer.

"Nah, you guys aren't friends, you're family," I joked, but I wasn't joking.

"Hey, Uncle Lou, don't forget about your cousins," someone quipped. I merely smiled and nodded. The comment was very close to the truth. He should have said brothers.

After the locker room emptied, I sat in silence and once again thanked my lucky stars—more accurately my long line of mentors who guided from that first game at Radecke Park to this last stop at Kidd Brewer Stadium. I couldn't have ended my field career in better fashion. I went out on top of my game.

All I could think about was the next step, or the dark side as my colleagues joked. In hindsight, there was no dark side to my career. This transition was merely a rebirth, a reinventing of oneself. I was moving from one stage to another literally and figuratively. Little did I know at the time, but past the darkness was a bright light that would lead to the blinding spotlight of the National Football League.

Mom and Dad at an awards dinner.
In reality, I should be posing with a portrait of them.

CHAPTER 3
BACK TO THE GARDEN[VILLE]

Sunday morning after a trip to the breakfast buffet, I headed home to share my farewell game with family and friends. As soon as I turned onto the main highway to the airport, my thoughts started to wander. I instinctively tightened my seatbelt for a voyage down memory lane. After forty years of weekend road trips, I knew why Americans loved the open road. The hypnotic effect of a deserted interstate was spellbinding.

Gazing through the windshield at the endless concrete ribbon flanked by the majestic Blue Ridge Mountains, I pictured myself standing in the end zone after the Lehigh game. *"Whir click, whir click,"* I heard the camera in my head replaying the Kodak moments from my life. For a few seconds, I thought that I heard Paul Anka singing "Times of Your Life." It wasn't exactly rock 'n roll, but the sweet, schmaltzy, soppy lyrics struck a nerve. I couldn't believe the moment. Here was Sweet Lou, Gardenville's rock 'n roll legend, under the spell of a cabaret singer.

I instinctively reached for the radio dial. Seconds later, I was cruising down the highway listening to an oldies station playing hits from my favorite band, the Beatles. Recognizing the throbbing bass guitar and the twangy guitar riffs at the beginning of "Get Back," I cranked up the volume. Without warning, time imploded and collapsed around me. No big boom, blinding light, or cloud of smoke, just a faint feeling that raised goose bumps on my arms. I was reaching down for the volume knob of my first car, a 1969 gold Chevy Nova SS (nicknamed Goldfinger after the James Bond movie) with a black vinyl top and mag wheels.

In the blink of an eye, the memory of my first game as an official washed over me like sacred water from the river of life. The riptide of that receding tsunami carried me back to a ten-acre island of grass and compacted dirt. It was fall of 1969 and a place called Radecke Playfield. Instead of standing on a shoreline, I was standing along the sideline of a football field. I could see, hear, and smell it. If I wasn't driving, I could have reached out and touched it. For me, that day in that year was a seminal event that ranked up there with Apollo 11 and Woodstock.

I grew up in a Baltimore suburb enchantingly named Gardenville. Perhaps, Garden of Eden or Elysian Fields would have been seen as an exaggerated marketing ploy, but there would have been some truth in advertising. To my dismay, when I was nine years old my parents moved from my beloved Hampden, a community of aging row homes north of the city originally built for mill workers. We weren't sailing across the ocean or crossing the country in a covered wagon, but it felt like it to me. How could we move? The Hammonds were a Hampden trademark. We were deeply rooted, and I wasn't quite ready to plant my feet in new dirt.

For over fifty years, my grandfather Winfield Hammond owned Hammond's Barbershop on the corner of Falls Road and

Union Avenue. He knew every male head by touch. Patrons often joked that with a blindfold he could identity anyone sitting in the chair by massaging their scalp. I had no doubt that he could.

On the weekends, business was always brisk. If you weren't there for a haircut, you were there for the latest gossip. The barbershop was the place to hang out instead of the corner tavern. Later in life, I learned that barbers and bartenders have a lot in common. Like a bar stool, a barber's chair was a confessional, a place to unburden your soul. It helped if the barber was a great listener, and my grandfather ranked as one of the best.

He always listened with rapt attention as patrons excitedly divulged the latest family lies, secrets, foibles, and indiscretions. Nothing was too trivial to be aired. Absolution was often a word of encouragement and an appropriate barbershop anecdote. With decades behind the chair, my grandfather had a voluminous library of tales.

As a Hammond, I was fortunate to bear witness to my grandfather's sagacity. My father built a shoeshine box for me, and on Saturdays I would shine shoes for ten cents a pair. With a haircut and a pair of glistening shoes, patrons high-stepped in the street feeling good about their lives. Generous tips were routine for barber and bootblack.

I literally plied my trade at the foot of the master and his barbershop disciples. "Hey, Lou, give my good buddy a good shine today," my grandfather would exclaim to my sheer delight as I opened a tin of polish and grabbed my rags. With blazing hand speed that ended with a sharp slap like a bullwhip, I could bring any pair of shoes back to life. I liked feeling grown-up and being one of my grandfather's buddies. It was such a sweet memory that I subconsciously incorporated the phrase *good buddy* into my vocabulary. If you were a friend of mine, you were a good buddy.

A decade later, I realized the barbershop was a classroom that shaped my character. My grandfather's lessons in the art of effective listening proved invaluable. The skill advanced my career in football where listening became synonymous with communicating.

On the football field, I was an astute speech detective. When a player or coach shouted or screamed at an official, I could discern who, what, when, where, and why. Emphatic to a point, I didn't take the abuse personally as long as the comments weren't personal. When that time arrived, it was resolved with a flag and a fifteen-yard penalty. On the field, officials, at least one with highly polished shoes, won every argument.

Decades later, the blue-collar village of Hampden would find fame as the quintessential Balwmer neighborhood where Bawlmerese was proudly adopted as the native tongue. HonFest (just picture beehive hairdos and John Waters movies) and *Miracle on 34th Street* (a Christmas light show extravaganza) became national tourist attractions. However, during the time my family lived in Hampden, there was no blueprint on the horizon for an urban rebirth. For better neighborhoods, better schools, and hopefully a better life, you had to move to the exotic suburbs.

◆ ◆ ◆

For the Greatest Generation in Baltimore, the clarion call was to head northeast where the urban wilderness had been tamed. Families were going "up the country" (cue to the band Canned Heat at Woodstock) and leaving the inner-city blues far behind. In essence, they were simply replacing what they left behind.

When they arrived at their promised land, they were not disappointed. The fertile farmland that had once been the domain of truck farmers supplying vegetables for Baltimore's dinner tables, was now being harvested for the American Dream. Endless rows of crops were being replaced by seemingly endless rows of red brick row homes and duplexes, which are now called townhouses.

The new money crop was not corn but kids, hundreds and hundreds of Baby Boomers in all shapes and sizes. Fortunately, real estate developers and city planners recognized the need for these kids to play someplace other than backyards and alleys. To meet the demands of the rambunctious youths who crowded every inch of grass, Radecke Playfield, commonly known as Radecke Park, was born from a cornfield, just like in the movie *Field of Dreams*. A new chapter in Baltimore's illustrious park history, certainly not envisioned by the Olmstead family who pioneered greenways for the city's grand Victorian parks, was waiting to be written. If you build it, we will come, and we came in hordes as families expanded.

Comprised of ten acres, the complex featured four ball fields, one in each corner of the postage-stamp sized lot, a three-room recreation center where everyone gathered in the winter, a wading pool, a basketball court, and a pavilion that was used as the local hangout throughout the year. In the fall, the outfield space between the ball diamonds became a football field and a soccer pitch. The park was where you first played organized sports. It was an initiation into the rules of the game and the rules of life.

If you had a sport that didn't fit the current configuration, you simply improvised. When a few of my friends discovered the game of golf, the park became their Augusta National Golf Course. Overnight, they dug five gopher holes around the fields to serve as ersatz greens. Adding the four pitcher mounds, they had a nine-hole pitch-and-putt course. The links were open to everyone. All you had to do was surreptitiously borrow an iron from your father's golf bag and a few golf balls. After a few rounds, you were on your way to a green jacket.

In the winter, the steep hillside on one edge of the park offered sledding. Moore's Run, a narrow creek that that ran alongside the other edge of the park, became an ice rink for figure skaters and hockey players.

The park was our home away from home. During summer vacation, it was where we seemingly spent every waking hour playing games. Parents didn't worry about your whereabouts. You were simply at the park. The two basic rules were to be home for supper and be home when the streetlights came on. All bets on your arrival and departure were off the table when you became a teenager.

For most kids, the park was the place you first experienced the ultimate truth of organized sports. Not everybody, and mostly like nobody, was going to be a professional athlete. The subliminal message was to enjoy your games while you can because in a few years you'll be punching a time clock.

After sports dreams faded into the harsh reality that playing alongside Brooks Robinson and Johnny U at Memorial Stadium was not in your future, the park became the place of your first cigarette, first beer, first kiss, and other firsts that were considered immoral or illegal at the time.

Park patrons, including myself, seemed to be driven by the mantra, "Growing old is mandatory; growing up is optional." Dreams weren't retired, they were redefined. When softball supplanted baseball in the career progression, the dreamers (The Gardenville Guys) were undaunted. They confidently packed up the balls and bats and relocated to the next ball diamond in the far corner of the park away from prying eyes. No one cared that the ball was bigger and the base paths shorter. To hydrate, forget the water fountain. There were now coolers beneath the benches filled with beer.

To enhance the game with tape measure home runs, the home team *borrowed* materials from a nearby construction site for a fence. To round out the beer league schedule, they solicited equally thirsty opponents by posting an article and a team photo in the community newspaper. The fact that most of the team was under the legal drinking age at the time was not a factor in arranging games.

After the game, the beer and the stories continued into the summer nights that seemed timeless. There was never anywhere else in the universe that you wanted to be until someone got restless. "Anybody feel like some exercise?" someone would announce in a bored and intoxicated voice. That statement resulted in a phone call to the local police precinct to report underage drinking and disorderly conduct at the park.

Thirty minutes later a police sedan would arrive, turn off its headlights, and then race across the park, using only the side mounted spotlight for illumination. Players with six-packs in hand would scurry like rats to the edges of the park and well-known hiding places. Once the police vacated the area, drinking resumed and another story was added to the anthology.

"Too bad Barry Levinson wasn't born in Gardenville. We could have been Hollywood legends," was the frequent lament that aired annually at neighborhood reunions. Being a kindred soul, I had to agree. The Gardenville guys and gals deserved a movie. In the late '60s and early '70s, they dressed and partied like rock stars. Often the sartorial splendor resulted from substantial discounts offered by those who worked at a shoe store or shirt factory.

In his 1982 comedy drama *Diner*, Barry portrayed his salad days while hanging out at the Hilltop Diner in Northwest Baltimore. The coming-of-age movie was about growing up in Baltimore. Set against the background of Christmas 1959, the movie was hilarious, outrageous, and realistic. If you were a native son or daughter, you could readily relate to the characters on the screen. But Barry was not alone.

Barry had the diner; we had the park. While the movie *Diner* symbolized life in '50s and '60s, Radecke Park epitomized the late '60s and early '70s, the dawning of the Woodstock generation and all the craziness that flower power evoked. Ever conscious of social norms and fads of the day, the guys would proudly remark, "We're not hippies. We're just hip." It was easy to define the generational differences. Barry had Elvis; we had Hendrix.

During Christmas 1969, Gardenvillers would have been drinking beer or whiskey in the park before heading to a local dance or the bars in Fells Point with fake IDs. If the mood was right, and it usually was, the evening would be accompanied by a cappella singing, ironically, songs from the late '50s and early '60s. Barry probably would have enjoyed the impromptu concert.

Often the choir would huddle around a fire in one of the metal trash barrels to stay warm and keep the beer from freezing. If you're picturing the neighborhood scene from the movie *Rocky*, you have 20/20 vision. At the conclusion of the evening, usually around midnight, revelers convened at the local sub shop for more hijinks.

My teenage years in Gardenville impacted my life immeasurably. The park was a living classroom. When the episodes of drunken revelry continued into adulthood, I pled not guilty. I was a product of my social and cultural environment. Unknown to me at the time, I was also training for life as a football official.

Ragtag and rugged sandlot team at Radecke Park in the 60's. Number 12 seemed to be a popular among players.

CHAPTER 4
SATURDAY IN THE PARK

Years after moving away to start families and search for careers, the Gardenville Guys, these icons of terminal adolescence, would occasionally visit the park. They returned to relive the magic as if the dirt fields were covered in a sheen of fairy dust. Unlike my contemporaries, I didn't drift away. I kept returning as if pulled by some supernatural force or the tracker beam from *Star Trek*. For me, the park was truly a promised land, a journey, and a destination. It will always be remembered as the place where I worked my first football game, the start of my officiating career. No doubt, there was magic dust on the field that glorious Saturday long ago.

It was a cold, blustery late morning when I walked over to the park to hang out with friends and catch up on neighborhood news. In the age before cellphones and the internet, the park was a communal bulletin board. If none of your friends were there, you were guaranteed to find someone from another neighborhood who was willing to share the latest teenage headlines.

The park was deserted except for some peewee football players, ages eight to ten, warming up for their game. With nothing else to do, I decided to watch the game from the sideline and wait for the inevitable arrival of some friends. I always enjoyed watching the little guys play because they performed with unbridled enthusiasm. Simply put, they were entertaining. They really didn't know the game or the rules, and that resulted in some hilarious plays. It was always a great way to kill time.

I was standing on the sideline with my hands in my pockets when I got the call. It was not a voice from heaven or a whisper in the wind, but a shout from the lone official on the field.

"Hey, pal, you want to give me a hand. My partner didn't show, and I need help. Really appreciate it," the man in the striped shirt implored in a friendly tone. The gap between the Greatest Generation and the Woodstock Generation was about to narrow.

"Yeah, sure, just tell me what to do," I responded eagerly, ready to assert myself in a position of authority at the tender age of eighteen.

After assuring the official that I knew a little about the rules of the game, I was immediately assigned to the line of scrimmage as a linesman while my partner lined up behind the linebackers. Even though I had no striped shirt, whistle, or black cap, I had no problem being identified as the other official. Wearing a dark blue pea coat, bell-bottom blue jeans, and blue Jack Purcell's, and looking more like a baseball umpire, I was the biggest kid on the field. I could relate to the players. As they said in the '60s, "Oh, man, I can dig that," and I did. It was a groovy scene.

"Just the more obvious penalties. If you see one, just wave your hands over your head after I whistle the play dead. I'll confer with you before I call the penalty. Most of all have fun out there today," my partner advised. His last words were prophetic.

Being introduced as "Mr. Lou" at kickoff was hilarious but heady. I was an instant role model to the next generation of park users and abusers. More than anything, I was on the field with the sport that I loved. I had fun, the prerequisite for any sport.

Football at this level was more about teaching than officiating, an outdoors classroom for players, coaches, and officials. Preventive officiating was the popular term that would be used at all levels. I spent most of the game ensuring that players were in the correct positions prior to the snap of the ball. On almost every play, I had to chase a few extra players from the field. At times, it seemed like there were thirteen or fourteen players on each side of the ball, and there probably were on a number of plays. Eavesdropping on the huddle, I knew what play was called. As for direction, that was anybody's guess.

Once the ball was hiked, the players buzzed around me like a swarm of excited bees. This was old-school football, three yards and a cloud of dust, or in the case of a wet field, three yards and a glob of mud. Lined up close together, players bumped, pushed, and shoved in one general direction before the ball carrier was finally wrestled or trampled to the ground by a horde of defenders. Tackles looked like predator/prey scenes from Marlon Perkin's *Wild Kingdom* TV show. Pop Warner and Woody Hayes would have enjoyed the spectacle. The biggest yardage gains came when the ball was fumbled and unintentionally batted or kicked forward.

With both sides of scrimmage surging toward the ball like a rugby match, I felt as if I was standing in the middle of twenty-two plastic football figures on the metal field of an electric football game. Any second I expected to feel my feet vibrating on the ground.

After the game, my partner walked over to shake my hand. "Lou, great game. You looked like a natural out there. If you're not doing anything next Saturday, stop by. Maybe I can put you to work again. And if you can, find a whistle somewhere."

"I'll try to work it in my schedule," I replied casually. *What schedule*, I thought. Other than work, the band, and a few beers on the weekend, I had no schedule. Still a teenager, I was already falling into a middle-aged rut. All I needed was a wife and two kids to fully assimilate into the American Dream.

A few of the parents thanked me for lending a hand with a pat on the back. The rest were busy customizing plastic bags with scissors, a most curious postgame ritual. As soon as their young warrior exited the field in his dirty, muddy, grass-stained uniform, a plastic bag with a cut out for his head was placed over his body. He was then duly escorted to the family sedan. On rainy days, plastic bags made excellent rain parkas. "Plastics," the mantra from the movie *The Graduate,* was thriving in G-ville. Now, if they could only get plastic bags with team logos, money could be made.

The following Saturday I was back on the sideline with my hands in my pockets when I got another call.

"Hey, Lou, you ready to officiate. I'm short again," my new coworker proclaimed excitedly. I reached into my coat pocket and pulled out a whistle. Smiling and shaking his head, he walked off the field, opened his small duffel bag, and tossed me a striped shirt. As I pulled the shirt over my jacket, I chuckled to myself with pride. A baby zebra had his first stripes. Geez, it almost sounded like the title for a children's book. I was unofficially an official.

◆ ◆ ◆

While Radecke Park was the place where dreams were auditioned, my home address a few blocks from the park was the place where my parents officiated, unknowingly creating a template for my professional life as a football official. Mom and Dad interpreted the rulebook of life and instilled the values of faith, family, and flag that hopefully would guide us for the rest of our lives. Infractions didn't draw a flag but there were penalties just as in football. Instead of loss of down, we had loss of allowance. Intentional grounding, the harshest of penalties, didn't result in the loss and down and yardage. It meant you were grounded as incarcerated in your home with the loss of all privileges previously afforded you for good behavior.

Hard work, honesty, and humility were the building blocks for a happy and productive life. As with every child, parents at times needed help in lifting and cementing those blocks. Unknowingly, parents in Gardenville had help in molding the future of America from one of the most unlikely sources on the face of the earth.

♦ ♦ ♦

Role models come in all shapes and sizes, but no one in the city of Baltimore suspected it would be a professional football team named the Baltimore Colts. Arriving in 1953, this ragtag bunch of castoffs, previously known as the Dallas Texans, was the perfect fit for the city. The downtrodden, sooty, sweaty, and smoky industrial burg between the trendy villages of Washington and Philadelphia needed to polish its image. Luring a professional sports team was far easier than enticing a white-collar industry to relocate.

The players were welcomed with open arms, a marching band, a fight song, cheerleaders, and a young lady atop a white pony who circled the field after every score. In a few short years, the love affair with the city and its football team blossomed. The Baltimore Colts became Baltimore's Colts. They were us, and we were them. The Colts didn't win or lose on Sundays. We won or lost. When you talked about the players, it was on a first-name basis because after all they were family. You rooted for them on and off the field through the good times and the bad. Like our parents, the players proudly embraced the blue-collar attributes that meshed with the psyche of the city. The only difference was they donned blue jerseys for work when they were home on Sundays.

Living in the city year-round, players hustled to make a buck just like our family members. Many of them worked alongside our uncles or cousins at the steel mills or shipyards. Johnny (Unitas) and Gino (Marchetti) worked at Bethlehem Steel in Sparrows Point. Artie (Donovan) sold liquor while Jim (Parker) sold cemetery plots. Big Daddy (Lipscomb) and Don (Joyce) became professional wrestlers.

After work, practice, or a game, you could find them at a neighborhood watering hole having a shot and a beer. If you weren't old enough to drink, you didn't worry. There were other ways to meet your gridiron heroes. When Alan (Ameche) and Gino broke into the fast-food business, you had to stop for a burger, shake, and fries. *Everybody goes to Gino's* and *Meetcha at Ameche's* were more than advertising slogans. They were invites to dine with your football family, and you went without question.

In a stroke of marketing genius, the Colts front office had the players headline in the community. Street carnivals, sports banquets, bull roasts, crab feasts, the latest Colt-owned fast-food store; wherever there was a social gathering, you could find a Colt. They were accessible and amiable with a stack of action cards or photos in one hand and a pen in the other. Want an autograph, no problem. How about two? That was name recognition at the grassroots level. Imagine professional athletes doing that today?

My first exposure to Colt fever came in December 1959. Talk of back-to-back NFL championships filled the air with every Christmas greeting. Every Baltimorean had a second championship on their Christmas wish list. Leafing through the Sears Christmas catalog that year, I expected to find it under sporting goods where you could order a replica Colt uniform. Like everyone in Baltimore, I wished for that championship to bring the good will of men and peace on earth to the citizens of Baltimore. But if the Colts didn't win, then I'd be satisfied with that uniform.

In 1958, the Colts won the NFL championship against the New York Giants in the league's first sudden-death overtime game against the New York Giants. At the age of seven, I really didn't pay much attention to the contest that was billed as the *Greatest Game Ever Played*. Now a year later, I was afflicted with Colt fever because that meant being part of my family and the Colt family. That year my father and I were Team Hammond, the twelfth man on the field for the Colts. However, two weeks before Christmas, our partnership nearly dissolved.

On that Sunday, the annual assembly of the train garden was postponed because the Colts were on TV. *Just freakin' unbelievable*, I thought. My father was abandoning family tradition for a football game. *What the hell is going on here?* Christmas without trains was like Christmas without baby Jesus. While I was apoplectic, my dad was politely apologetic. "Lou, this will give me a few more hours to plan the layout for this year," he sheepishly advised. I nodded with a frown and prayed that the game would end quickly, win or lose. For me, being a Colts fan had its limits.

◆ ◆ ◆

I was upset for a good reason. Christmas in Baltimore was synonymous with trains. Baltimore was home to the Baltimore and Ohio Railroad, the first commercial railroad in the United States, and the world-famous B&O Museum. Trains were part of our DNA. The annual trip to the museum was a slice of railroad heaven. Next to the Sears Christmas catalog, the Lionel catalog was the most cherished book in the neighborhood. Who needed *Playboy* magazine when you had Sears and Lionel? If kids couldn't grow up to be a Baltimore Colt, they wanted to be an engineer on the B&O. Lionel put you in the engineer's seat.

Train gardens sprouted up not only at nearby firehouses but in nearly every Baltimore basement, including the Hammond house. I was not ashamed to say that I loved my Lionel trains. Every year I couldn't wait to have them up and running. Lionel was alive with electricity. With my father being an electrician, he had the power to bring the train garden to life with circuits, wires, and light bulbs. This annual resurrection of metal and plastic was an intoxicating mixture of sight and sound.

Gatemen, signalmen, switchmen, and yardmen moved to the rhythm of the rails as trains chugged along the tracks and belched smoke. Workers loaded and unloaded freight from mechanical rail cars while bells and whistles sounded. Passengers shuffled in continuous circles around train stations under the haze of muted streetlights. Who was in charge of this make-believe world? None other than me! I was the chief engineer at the controls of the dials, levers, and push buttons that directed the men, the machinery, and the motion. I embraced the feeling of power.

During those early Lionel years, a seed had been planted. Later in life, I became an action junkie and followed the path from steel rails to the gridiron. Railroad men became players and coaches. Machines became instant-replay cameras, radio headsets, and electronic clocks. Motion became the game of football. Like my train garden, I was in the center of the action and loving every minute. To this day, I love Lionel. While there aren't any *Playboy* magazines around the house, you can always find a Lionel catalog.

What stuck in my mind at the time and remains to this day is a 1959 magazine advertisement for Lionel. It featured Chuck Connors, ABC TV's *Rifleman*, with the caption that read, *How A Family Grows ... Together.* I liked the idea of working with my dad. On that memorable Sunday, the father-son bond had been briefly interrupted by a football game. Ironically, years later it would be football that continued that bond with more sweet memories that would last a lifetime.

◆ ◆ ◆

On December 27, 1959, we won another championship convincingly, 31-16, over the same New York Giants. Once again, we showed those uppity New Yorkers that blue-collar was blue blood in the NFL and the city of Baltimore. The Hammond household was in ecstasy. After a dinner of Christmas leftovers, we prepared to ring in the New Year with even more football and another lesson in life.

That year we celebrated New Year's at my grandmother's house. Two televisions were lined up so we wouldn't miss overlapping major bowl games. At that time, the Cotton, Sugar, Rose, and Orange Bowls were played on January 1. Following the lead of my dad, I cheered the good plays and booed the bad.

Whenever a penalty was questioned by any of the Hammond clan, my dad would always respond, "Just part of the game. The refs are only human. They're giving it their best." I liked that attitude. Those words have stayed with me throughout my life. However, I didn't remember him saying that when the Colts were playing for the championship only a few days earlier. Then the officials were as blind as bats and dumb as rocks. "Bunch of turkeys," he would utter in disgust with calls against the Colts. Oh, how I loved being a football fan.

Over the next few years, I attended every home game and shared in the passion play that was Baltimore football. My dad, a season ticket holder, would buy me a student ticket for a dollar so I could enter the stadium. I would then stand, kneel, or sit with him in his seat. That's how fathers and sons bonded in Baltimore back then.

That Christmas I didn't find a Colts jersey or helmet under the tree (NFL merchandise was in short supply and short demand in those days), but I didn't need one. I knew in my heart that one day I would be suited up in a blue jersey and a white helmet with the horseshoe logo. I gleefully pictured myself running onto the field at Memorial Stadium in front of 60,000 rabid fans. I could hear Chuck Thompson, the iconic Hall of Fame voice of the Colts and Orioles, proudly announce, "Starting at halfback, from Gardenville, Maryland, Sweet Lou Hammond."

The world's largest outdoor insane asylum, as dubbed by a Chicago sportswriter, would erupt with deafening cheers that could be heard back at Radecke Park. "Lou, Lou, Lou," they would yell at the top of their lungs in a hypnotic frenzy. When the decibels decreased, they would nudge each other in acknowledgment. "The hometown boy did good," they would chuckle with Baltimore pride. That would have been heaven on earth for any Baltimore youngster.

But the more I thought about it, the notion became more problematic. Every block in Gardenville had a pubescent Johnny U, Raymond Berry, or Lenny Moore waiting in the wings. The odds of making the team were minuscule. If I was ever going to be on the field in uniform, I would have to find another way. For certain, I wouldn't be wearing pads and a helmet for a living. It would have to be as a cop on security detail, an usher, or an official.

Until that autumn in 1969, I had no idea how that was going to happen. Over the next couple of years, my game plan gradually unfolded as a football official. In the background, my childhood gridiron heroes became unsung guides to a career between the lines. Their honesty, humility, and hard work exemplified the traits that I would need to be successful. From that prescient first Saturday, every time I ran out onto the field at the start of a game in my striped shirt, I knew my Colts were running with me. Johnny U and the rest of the boys would give a wink and a nod. "Yeah, the hometown boy did good," they would say with pride.

Peace, love, and football!
I'm just a singer in a rock and roll band.

CHAPTER 5
SANDLOT ROOKIE

After my second sandlot game, I spent the winter months deciding my football fate. There's nothing like being at the crossroads of my life before reaching twenty-one. *What happened to my teenage years*, I wondered. I was still upset that I had missed the Woodstock Music Festival that August. Nevertheless, a decision about my future was imperative. There was only one certainty in my life. I loved the game of football and wanted to be part of it. My best option, especially if I wanted to be on the field, was to officiate. I knew the apprenticeship would be arduous and protracted, but time was on my side. In retrospect, it was probably one of the easiest decisions in my life.

Youth would be my only advantage at this point in my career, and I had to leverage it. I viewed myself as a hot prospect. Who wouldn't want an eager neophyte official to educate and indoctrinate? I was football clay, or as my friends joked "football silly putty," ready to be molded. I readily admitted that with just two games under my belt, I was addicted to the game. "You're wasting your time," some of my peers lamented. "Nothing ventured, nothing gained" was my mantra.

Naysayers be damned, it was full speed ahead. Officiating was in my DNA. Physically, mentally, and emotionally, I was ready for a new challenge. On the horizon, there was a void in my life that would need to be filled. In my case, it was not a romantic one, although that would have been nice. It was a musical one. The band, which had been my career since the mid-60s, was breaking up.

◆◆◆

In 1963, Herring Run Junior High School had a talent show, and I wanted to perform. While I could carry a tune decently, I didn't want to appear on stage by myself, so I concocted a plan. After some arm-twisting, I finally convinced several of my classmates who owned musical instruments to join me on stage.

"Hey, guys, we'll be babe magnets," I confidently proclaimed. That's all it took for them to decide. The result was Eric and the Wall of Sound, a rhythm-and-blues band heavily influenced by the British invasion groups like The Animals and the Rolling Stones. The original group consisted of Chuck Huber, lead guitar, Carl Frock, rhythm guitar, William "Butch" Hensel, bass guitar, Ronnie "Froggy" Gershive, drums, and me (Eric) on lead vocals. What we lacked in talent, we made up in tenacity and pomposity. We didn't win the show, but the babes crowded the dance floor for our two songs. It was a musical high. Rock n' roll was a proven teenage aphrodisiac, and we were dealing it out with the latest Top 40 hits. Life was sweet.

In 1965, the group went through a few personnel changes as we honed our musical skills. In 1967, we appeared on the *Kerby Scott Show*, a Baltimore TV dance show that aired on Friday afternoons. The show, a successor to Baltimore's legendary *Buddy Deane Show*, regularly featured local bands and big-name acts passing through the city. To be invited to perform on the show was like being asked to perform at The Fillmore.

Competing against Dick Clark's teen dance party *American Bandstand* in Philadelphia, Kerby's show struggled in the ratings. Unfortunately, music fans overlooked our TV debut, but we didn't care. We had our moment of rock n' roll fame and played in the TV studio where some of the all-time greats strutted their stuff. Over the short life of the show, Kerby's guest list included The Temptations, The Four Tops, James Brown, Paul Revere and the Raiders, The Cowsills, and my all-time favorite—The Jimi Hendrix Experience. The thought of Jimi Hendrix on stage with Kerby still blows my mind. In 1967, the Jimi Hendrix Experience opened for the Monkees during their US summer tour. To us that proved anything could happen in the music business. We still hoped something like that would happen to us.

In 1968, we reformed the band and became the Sand Pebbles, a rock and soul group. Cashing in on our local fame, we made guest appearances on TV shows hosted by Jack Alix in Washington, Johnny Dark in Baltimore, and back again with Kerby Scott. In May 1969, we opened for national recording artists Peaches and Herb. We had reached the apex of our musical careers. There was nowhere to go but down.

In 1970, the group disbanded to pursue other interests that included going to college, getting a job, being drafted, and avoiding the draft. Hard to believe that my bandmates and I were becoming too old to rock and roll. Forget the adage about "never too old to rock and roll, only too young to die." In our late teens, we were over the hill, a prescient garage band too old to play CYO dances, pool parties, and teen centers. As for Kerby, his show folded a few years. In 2002, Buddy's show became the hit Broadway musical *Hairspray*, which later became a cult film classic that broke box office records. Music was a fickle bitch for sure.

As for me, I was gone but not totally forgotten. Decades later, the faded liner notes of my career would be etched into music history. In his book *Baltimore Sounds*, author Joe Vaccarino listed every Baltimore band and solo artist from 1950 to 2000. Included under the letter *E* was Eric and the Wall of Sound. I was going to miss the music, the camaraderie, and, of course, the girls, but I now had football. *Did officials have groupies like rock bands, even neighborhood bands*, I wondered. No, not really, I found out.

♦ ♦ ♦

As whispers about "time to move on in life" grew louder from my parents, I decided I wasn't going to fade into Gardenville history at such a tender age. I wanted to be remembered as more than a rock and roll singer. Although, if you ask any Gardenville Guy, the musical highlight of their teen years was listening to the Wall of Sound at the Twin Willow Swim Club, which was adjacent to Radecke Park. Don't believe a word of it! Like the band, they came to watch the babes in bikinis on the dance floor. Some of the swimsuits left little to the imagination, or maybe it was a lot of imagination, and that's just the way we liked it.

In the spring of 1970, I received a call from the Maryland Independent Football Officials (MIFO) asking me if I was interested in becoming a full-time sandlot official. "Lou, would like you to join our team of officials? You come highly recommended," the supervisor of officials cordially exclaimed. My name had been submitted with a recommendation from Ron Daiker, my officiating partner at Radecke Park. I immediately answered "yes." Like being in a band, I liked being part of a team. With one phone call, the void in my life had been filled.

That summer, boot camp for rookie officials started with an annual meeting that included a two-page sheet of instructions about the league, a rule book, and a clothing list. Purchasing uniforms was the responsibility of each official. The only item not on the clothing list was shoes.

Before my first game that year, the referee pulled me aside. "Lou, you look great, but the shoes have to go. We don't have anyone to stitch up these kids," he wisecracked as he stared looking at my feet.

My games shoes were actually a pair of baseball cleats. With a fresh coat of black polish (Winfield Hammond would have been proud), the low-cut shoes were quite stylish but definitely a threat. I could see peewee players being rushed to the emergency rooms with apparent knife wounds as parents shrieked in horror.

Although there were teams named the Jets and the Sharks, Radecke Park not *Westside Story*. I had made my first rookie mistake, a bad judgment call, before the teams had lined up for the kickoff. However, in my defense, the cleats were worn to a metallic nub, nothing like the razor edges on Ty Cobb's baseball spikes.

Other than my shoes, the one thing that I didn't need to learn was how to dress. I learned early in my athletic career that if you couldn't play like a pro, look like a pro. I always looked good in black and white. In front of my mirror, I looked even better as a football official. Black hat with white stripes, a zebra shirt, white knickers, and ringed black-and-white stirrup socks gave the air of authority and formality. All I needed was a badge and gun to complete the ensemble.

♦ ♦ ♦

In the early 1900's, officials dressed like tennis players of the era, minus tennis shoes. After reading an article about my predecessors, I wondered how I would look in white pants, a white, long-sleeve shirt with a black bow tie, and a white floppy newsboy cap. When I started my football career, it would have been quite stylish. For some inexorable reason in the late '60's and early '70's, there was a brief nostalgic rush for the Roaring Twenties among my cultural contemporaries.

The novel *The Great Gatsby* became the fashion guide as one decadent decade briefly found new life. Gardenville Guys were trading their suede Beatle boots for spats, basically two-tone leather Beatle boots with white uppers and snaps. The New Vaudeville Band had a No. 1 hit with "Winchester Cathedral," a Rudy Vallee knockoff that featured a vocalist with a megaphone instead of a microphone.

My band had missed the chance to cash in on the fad. Forget R&B. The Wall of Sound could have been the Vallee (Valley) of Sound, the most popular dance and wedding band in the city. Instead of a state-of-the-art Shure microphone, I could have saved a few bucks and simply swiped a rubber traffic cone along the highway.

But baseball cleats! What was I thinking? That was like wearing tennis shoes with a tuxedo. The adage that "life's journey is not about the shoes we wear, but the steps we take" didn't apply to me. If I wanted to take any more steps as an official, I had to find the right shoe, or my journey was finished. This was not the time to be shopping for a new pair of Beatle boots or spats.

That following week, I took my hard-earned football money and invested in a pair of Riddell football shoes for coaches. They were expensive but I was looking for a shoe that would pay dividends down the road as fellow officials commented on my sartorial splendor. With kangaroo leather, rippled soles, white shoelaces, and a white snug tie at the collar, I instantly became the debonair official that I had seen in my bedroom mirror. Money aside, they were the most comfortable shoes that I had ever worn, and they held the shine like a pair of imported Italian loafers. And I certainly knew about shoeshine.

While known more for football helmets than shoes, Riddell at the time was the number one shoe for football officials. To expand their market share, I was tempted to share with them my marketing genius. They needed to manufacture high-top instead of low-cut shoes for officials. I easily saw myself sporting a pair of Johnny U signature models. In Baltimore, the shoes would have crossed into the teenage market in an avalanche of sales. What kid who grew up with the Colts wouldn't want a pair of Johnnies? John Riddell with Johnny U at his feet would have replaced Jack Purcell as the fashion leader in Gardenville. The ubiquitous blue-toed tennis shoes would have been on the fashion bubble and in the trash. It was a nice pipedream that entertained me with riches beyond my wildest dream. If someday I made it big as an official, maybe there would be a Sweet Lou model.

My informal shoe survey conducted that winter revealed that John and Jack were both victims of the fickle finger of fashion. Chuck (Converse) and the Dassler brothers (Puma and Adidas) were taking over their turf as everyone strived for the bohemian soccer shoe look. At least bell-bottoms were still in vogue. As for me, I was now a Riddell man, but bucking my own personal fashion statement.

For Beatles fans, such as myself, the fashion dilemma was bewildering. George Harrison was photographed wearing both Jacks and Chucks. What do I wear to adulate my favorite band? In the end, I kept the Jacks and thought about buying a pair of Chucks. If only the Beatles had been photographed wearing Riddell referee shoes. Sports and music would never have been the same.

◆ ◆ ◆

Back on the field that first full season, I worked two to three sandlot games every Saturday for teams that ranged in age from eight to fourteen. It was an ambitious attempt to gain as much grass time (game experience) as I could. The heavy workload ruined my Saturdays, but I wanted to be an official who wasn't surprised by any situation on the field. I firmly believed that good judgment came from experience, and experience came from bad judgment. At this point in my career, who was I to judge anybody on the field, be it players, officials, or coaches.

Like the players, I was learning about the game of football and perfecting my craft. Unlike the players, I had to get it right the first time. I did not have the luxury of running the play again. Calling the perfect game was always the goal. If mistakes occurred, which I referenced as learning experiences, I wanted them out of the way early in my career. I always remembered the quote from NFL legendary official Jim Tunney. "In officiating you have to be perfect the first game and get better the second and each game after that." That was my creed.

For each game, there were normally three officials: a referee, an umpire, and a linesman. The referee, the only official in a white hat, was positioned behind the quarterback and responsible for the area around the quarterback. He also was the head of the crew who announced and explained the penalties.

The umpire, a black hat, was positioned on the defensive side of the scrimmage line and responsible for the interior line, linebackers, and the defensive backfield.

The linesman, another black hat, straddled the line of scrimmage where the chain crew was located. Watching for infractions along the line of scrimmage, such as offside, false start, illegal shift, illegal block, linesmen were also responsible for marking the line of scrimmage, and the conduct of the chain crew. He ensured the proper placement of the rod men (persons holding the ten-yard rods or "sticks") and the box man (person holding the rod or "stick" with down indicator that marks location of the ball).

With only three officials, sometimes only two, we had a lot of ground to cover. We had to be quick on our feet and ready to move at the snap of the ball to cover our area of the field. This was my introduction to the world of mechanics, the art of properly officiating a football game.

Good mechanics involved proper positioning before the play, reading keys (players) at the snap of the ball to identify the play (run, pass, kick), moving with the play to a designated area, knowing the location of your crew on the play, and a sense of field awareness until the whistle ended the play. I quickly learned there was a lot more to officiating than blowing a whistle and throwing a flag. Like coaches who emphasized technique to their players, crew supervisors did the same with their officiating teams.

By the end of 1970, I officially became a sandlot official. Being paid the princely sum of six dollars per game, I was now a professional, or maybe semiprofessional. The money was a pittance, but I was in good company. In 1956, Johnny U was only making six bucks a game quarterbacking for the semipro Bloomfield Rams when he received a call from the Baltimore Colts general manager Don Kellett for a tryout. The "eighty cent phone call" became legendary.

After his tryout, John was invited to the Colts summer camp and the rest was NFL history. From a dirt lot filled with glass and grass at Arsenal Middle School, he moved to the manicured fields at Western Maryland College in Westminster, Maryland, located thirty-six miles north of Baltimore. John's journey to the pros proved that fields of dreams came in all shapes and sizes.

I was starting on a barren stretch of compacted dirt that hurt at Radecke Park, hoping my next stop would be a high school field where they watered the grass at least once a month. As for my infamous phone call, I only hoped that MIFO got their money's worth. Local phone calls in 1970 cost about ten cents. I knew that I wasn't going to be a once-in-a-lifetime bargain like Johnny U. However, I hoped that in the end I would be worth more than ten cents, the price of a shoeshine at Winfield's Barber Shop.

◆ ◆ ◆

In my first full season, I immediately noticed football was getting more dramatic and detailed on and off the field. While the emphasis was still on instruction, there was a broader interpretation and stricter enforcement of the rules. Of course, both issues required guidance from the league in the form of meetings and memos.

Those meetings and memos from the league's hierarchy provided a peek at the administrative machinery that foreshadowed later stages in my career. If I desired to advance to the next level, paperwork would be as important as footwork. This was especially true at the college level where the job wasn't done until the paperwork was finished. Fans have the misconception that after a game, officials go to the locker room, change into street clothes, grab a few beers, and go home. We could only have wished for such a luxury.

I continued honing my craft for three years on the sandlots until I became a Saturday fixture around Baltimore. "Hey, Lou, what's new?" was the common refrain when I arrived for a game. I was on a first-name basis with coaches, parents, and fans. In hindsight, the relaxed setting was the perfect environment to develop the communication skills that would be essential at higher levels.

I quickly learned to walk the walk and talk the talk. Fans don't realize all the talk that takes place between the lines, especially along the sidelines. Officials talk to the players (the play is over, the runner is down, roll off the pile, nice job playing the whistle, etc.) and talk to the head coach—and the head coach only.

To the head coaches you explain penalties and game situations, but also tip them off for possible infractions. "Coach, your offensive tackle is holding on pass plays," or "Coach, your tight end is too far off the ball," or "Coach, next time I see that I'm going to have to call a penalty." That last comment always garnered immediate attention with the offending player being pulled out of the game for a couple of plays to correct the error of his ways. The key was to show respect and maintain a professional demeanor. Hopefully, it was a two-way street, and it was with some minor exceptions.

The rapport with players and coaches wasn't difficult for me. I was more of an extrovert. I liked to talk but wasn't one who enjoyed hearing his own voice for the sake of being heard. I was an elegant storyteller, a balladeer not a bullshitter. And don't forget, once upon a time I was a singer in a rock n' roll band. I had learned to communicate with any and all audiences.

In those freewheeling days of sandlot football, sometimes we had a regulation field of 100 yards in length, rarely the regulation 53.3 yards in width. At times, a soccer pitch was used. Sometimes we had two goalposts, many times only one or none. Sometimes we had chalk lines to mark field boundaries and yardage increments (hash marks). Most of the time we forgot about end zones. We were lucky to have goal lines and goalposts.

Sometimes we had an unblemished, regulation peewee football (the small ball). Many times we had a heavily scuffed, oval-shaped, air-filled bladder that vaguely resembled a regulation rugby ball. No chains, no scrimmage marker . . . no problem. We used anything that could be picked up and carried to mark the field. Many times honest fans were recruited to become human yardage sticks and first down markers. Small plastic orange cones became essential survival gear. I never left home without them.

A lot of credit for my initial success belonged to my fellow officials, especially the Baltimore Gas and Electric (BGE) cadre who were fellow coworkers. Ron Daiker, Buzz Stallings, and Dick Rosenberger mentored me in the early stages of my BGE and officiating careers. All three men lived in the Gardenville area and started their officiating careers at Radecke Park. Another gentleman, Frank City, took me under his wing and assigned me games in the eastern part of town.

We traveled to Herring Run Park and the northeast suburbs of Overlea, Rosedale, Putty Hill, Sparrows Point, Dundalk, Lutherville, Timonium, Essex, and Perry Hall. Our first game was Saturday morning, followed by an afternoon game, and at times a night game. There was a lot to learn, and I was cramming for the next test every time I took the field. On a good day, my take home pay was eighteen dollars when gas cost thirty-six cents a gallon and a six-pack of Baltimore's own National Bohemian Beer, Natty Boh as it was commonly called, cost around a buck. There were no complaints from me.

Another step forward. Working a high school game early in my career.

CHAPTER 6
HIGH SCHOOL DAZE

Like any athlete, I craved the challenge of competition at the next level to prove that I belonged. After 1973, I felt ready to start officiating high school games. Boot camp for a boot (neophyte) official was about to enter its next phase, a type of advanced combat training. With the price of gasoline and beer inching up by pennies, a bigger payday was needed.

In 1974, I joined the Maryland Board of Football Officials (MBFO), the governing body who supplied officials for all high school games in the Baltimore area. After taking a rules test, I was accepted as an applicant. That was the easy part. Before proving myself on the field, I had to prove myself in the classroom. I was grossly mistaken when I thought that I was done with school after high school.

Every Monday from July to November of that year, I attended evening class from seven to nine. All classroom materials, such as rule books, case studies, handbooks, and game officials' manuals, were sanctioned by the National

Federation of High School Football. With this more intensified instruction, I felt like a freshman in high school. And, yes, quizzes were given weekly. If you didn't make the grades, you washed out of the program.

During the season, the training continued for all officials. Every Monday, there was an MBFO meeting to discuss rules, mechanics, and events of the previous week. Later field clinics, where officials were on the field and walked through plays and positioning, were added to demonstrate the mechanics for punts, kickoffs, or whatever odd formation was schemed by coaches. Any negative feedback for mistakes by game officials, or *critique the technique* as I called it, was conducted off to the side. That deep-rooted professionalism was a trait that I tried to instill in my crews during my career. We were literally the third team on the field. If we were to be successful, teamwork was essential. We didn't want to air our dirty laundry. Memories needed to be short. Criticism was to be considered training. *Don't take anything personally* was the golden rule. Of course, that's unless you really screwed up on the field.

My first year as an applicant, I worked two freshman and two junior varsity games. At the high school level, there were now four officials on the field. In addition to the referee, the umpire, and the lineman, there was now a line judge. Unlike my sandlot career, I was being graded during every game by my crew, all full-fledged members of the MBFO. They carried rating cards that were completed after the game and forwarded to the membership chairman. In addition, there were MBFO observers in the stands evaluating my performance.

At times, I felt like the only official on the field with everyone staring at me. The process could be intimidating; dealing with pressure was part of the learning process. You couldn't afford the luxury of second-guessing yourself on the field. Whether right or wrong, good or bad, the play was called, and you had to move on. Not only did I have to be fast on my feet, I had to make speedy decisions.

I was now making twenty dollars per game, the bottom rung. Since freshman teams played on Wednesday afternoons and junior varsity teams on Thursday afternoons, I had to use a full day of vacation time from work to officiate these games. Unless there was a family emergency or other mitigating circumstance, requests for half days were not company policy. I was the low man on the totem pole in MBFO and at work.

A few weeks after high school in 1969, I had started my career as a draftsman with BGE. Working my way up the corporate ladder, I strived to be a team player and create the image of a company man. I did so willingly, knowing that I was being watched by my peers and evaluated by my superiors. I carefully treaded the line between *vocation* and *avocation*. Four years later after accumulating some seniority, I was finally able to take a half day of leave. Also for the first time in my life, I had time to take an extended vacation and do something that was not football related. That was a problem. For over five years, I lived and breathed football. My avocation was becoming my vocation. At the time, I didn't see that issue as necessarily bad, even though it could have been a prescription for career burnout.

Did I need to expand my horizons beyond the goalposts? Of course. However, the challenge was finding places to go and something to do. So what did I do? I did what that any dedicated official and football junkie would; I attended football clinics in the Mid-Atlantic region. These were opportunities to meet other officials and develop a network of contacts. The Bahamas could wait unless there was a tropical clinic on the schedule.

◆ ◆ ◆

After being on the sandlots for nearly four years, I was comfortable with the rules and mechanics at the freshmen/JV level. In many instances, it was only a small step from the ten to twelve-year-old sandlot players. For me, the game was slowing down. I was seeing and hearing more on the field. Likewise, my decision making quickened. All positive signs that I was advancing.

While sandlot mechanics and the rules were applicable in high school, expectations were far more demanding. Attention was now focused on football hardware, namely the field, the equipment, and the uniforms. Standardization and uniformity became buzzwords. Sandlot exceptions were no longer tolerated.

"Is that regulation?" I frequently asked the crews.

High school officiating required more equipment. We had stop watches to keep game time (most schools back then didn't have electronic scoreboard or if they did, they didn't work), bean bags to mark fumble spots or penalty enforcement, adhesive tape to mark the five-yard spot on the chains, a game card to record the score and timeouts, and rubber bands for our fingers to keep track of downs and ball location between the hash marks. Despite the gadgets, officials still improvised.

There was one high school official who kept stones in his pockets to keep track of the timeouts. Another official filled a gold sock with sand to use it as a penalty flag. Very clever but not all officials had gold socks to spare. For uniformity, a group of officials absconded with gold table napkins from a restaurant for use as penalty flags.

At the high school level, we tried to ensure that players on the team with the same numbers were not on the field at the same time. Many public schools simply didn't have money in their athletic budgets to buy new uniforms every year. Another tough regulation to enforce was having jersey numbers correspond to positions. Rules stated single digits and teens numbers were for quarterbacks; 20s, 30s, 40s were for backs and linebackers; 50s for centers; 60s for guards; 70s for tackles; 80s for ends. Such infractions were rarely called, but it was always a good time to practice your communication skills with coaches. If a penalty flag was tossed for a jersey infraction, it was usually for delay of game as players frantically changed jerseys on the sidelines.

My second year in the program was my first year on probation, officially known as P1. Again, I worked mostly freshmen and JV games. However, the real motivator, the brass ring, was the opportunity to step on the field for some varsity games. Again, I had to take leave from work because varsity games for public schools were played on Friday afternoons. The trade-off didn't faze me a bit because I wasn't working at BGE to earn a vacation and wasn't officiating to make money.

Varsity games paid forty-five dollars, but you had to earn your money as the intensity of players and coaches increased dramatically. On the field, the more talented players were focusing on college athletic scholarships. On the sidelines, the more goal-oriented coaches were hoping for a successful season that would be the ticket to college football as an assistant coach.

For the first time, there was also media coverage that rarely existed for freshmen and JV teams. Media hype meant closer scrutiny of calls by the officials. As for me, my main goal was to work private school games played on Saturdays. My hope was to be invited to work one of the big high school football rivalries played on Thanksgiving Day.

I worked my first homecoming game on a sun-drenched Friday afternoon in early October. As the home team ran through the spirit banner at the ten-yard line, the quarterback, leading the charge, tripped and fell. The rest of the team toppled like dominoes to the delight of the frenzied crowd.

"Lou, if you hear the police over the air. Run for your car. This is a tough place for zebras, especially all white ones," the referee intoned with a bemused grin. We were at an inner-city school, and I was the only White official among the four-person crew. Another crew member joked that I should run if I heard police sirens. Just then I heard the piercing static of the police radio. I turned my head and saw a patrol car parked at the thirty-yard line, flashing its emergency lights.

"Ladies and gentlemen, please rise," the officer instructed, standing next to his vehicle with a microphone in his hand. With those words, I was ready to run but nervously held my ground while looking for the quickest exit. The officer then handed the microphone to the homecoming queen for a soul-stirring rendition of the national anthem that brought tears to my eyes. At midfield, the crew laughed, and I smiled.

"Hey, Lou, welcome to ghetto football. This is a school tradition," the referee joked. All I could do was smile and shake my head. The initiation prank was priceless. On the field, the brotherhood of officials was colorblind.

◆ ◆ ◆

My third year in the program was my second year on probation, officially known as P2. Except for the fact that I was working more varsity games, there was no noticeable difference between my second and third years. Meanwhile, I worked as many freshman and JV games that I could fit into my schedule.

Finally after three years as a neophyte, I was a full-fledged, card-carrying member of the MBFO. During my fourth year, I was getting varsity games at schools with established programs. They were always highly ranked and noted for sending players to the next level. While I didn't tout myself as God's gift to officiating, I was getting better games because I was becoming a better official. To that end, I made sure that no one worked harder than me.

Hard work paid off when I was assigned a game in the state playoffs. Officials didn't get plaques or trophies for an all-star season. They got a playoff game in the state championship. That was the ultimate goal of every high school official. To work a playoff game, you had to be certified by Maryland Public Secondary Schools Athletic Association. Certification required a minimum score of eighty-five on a written test, favorable reports from game observers, and a favorable recommendation from the supervisor of your group. During my high school football career, I was fortunate to officiate over ten state playoff games and three state championship games. I was obviously doing something right.

While the much-desired playoff games were exciting, the early Christmas gifts for MBFO officials were Turkey Bowl games on Thanksgiving Day. Two games were played at Memorial Stadium, later at M&T Bank Stadium, both among the oldest high school football rivalries in the country. At ten in the morning, Calvert Hall (Cardinals) squared off against Loyola Blakefield (Dons) in the annual battle of the Catholics. At one, the public-school powerhouses Baltimore City College (Black Knights) and Baltimore Polytechnic Institute (Engineers) lined up for the rivalry that dated to 1899.

These crosstown rivalries had all of the tradition and pageantry of the Army-Navy game. Marching bands, alumni reunions, tailgating parties, and bragging rights for the year resulted in crowds averaging ten to 20,000 fans. If you lived in Baltimore, the games became part of your Thanksgiving tradition along with a turkey dinner. If you didn't attend any of those schools, it didn't matter. Everybody had a family member who did. You were automatically a surrogate or subway alumni.

For players, coaches, and officials, it was memorable because the games were televised. That always got the adrenaline pumping for everyone involved. During my career, I worked six Turkey Bowl games, three as the referee. When the game was played at Memorial Stadium, the crew dressed in the locker room for the NFL officials. The dank and dark cell-like room with no windows and located in the bowels of a concrete bunker was depressing, but it was a taste of the big-time. Every time I jogged out onto the field through the dugout, I was running with the Colts and fulfilling part of my childhood dream. I never tired of that feeling.

For me, the clash of the Catholics provided the most highlights. My most memorable experience was the 1991 game at Memorial Stadium. A snowstorm the previous night dumped five inches of snow on the city. The start of the game was delayed twenty minutes while prisoners from the Baltimore City Jail shoveled and swept snow from the field.

After the snow was cleared, the stadium grounds crew began prepping the field. Prior to kickoff, my crew and I inspected every inch of the field. As the referee, the white cap, it was my responsibility to ensure the field was playable and the players would not be at risk of injury. Thankfully, the field was in excellent condition. The snow, which acted as a blanket for the grass, hadn't melted into the ground. I could only imagine the controversy if I had to call the game because of unplayable conditions. That was the good news.

The bad news was that my decision to delay the start of the game had profound repercussions. Television coverage by WMAR TV started at 9:30 a.m. with a 10:05 kickoff. The play-by-play announcer Scott Garceau and his color analyst Tom Matte, the former Baltimore Colt running back, had to fill time twenty minutes of airtime. No problem there. With the rich history and tradition of the game, the duo could talk for hours.

If pressed for subject matter, Tom could have told stories about his playing days from sandlot to the pros. The viewing audience would have been delighted. Someone would have probably asked me to delay the game further.

As I was inspecting the field for a final time, Calvert Hall Coach Bill Mackley approached me. "Lou, I'm in a bind and need a favor," he pleaded with a worried look. "Band parents are in an uproar because the band can't perform the pregame show." The award-winning hundred-member band, which years later would be crowned national champions and play at the Sugar Bowl, was being pre-empted by the weather. The coach, *sotto voce*, reminded me that half the fans on the Calvert Hall side were here to see and hear the band.

I didn't need to be reminded about the metaphysical connection between marching bands and Baltimore. I knew the soul of the city was at stake. Seemingly every citizen knew the words to the Colts fight song long before they could recite The Pledge of Allegiance. When the Colts snuck out of town in March 1984, the Baltimore Colts Marching Band spearheaded the movement to obtain another NFL franchise.

Their relentless campaign was dutifully rewarded to the ecstasy of every Baltimorean when in 1996 Art Modell announced he was moving his Cleveland Browns to Baltimore. With new uniforms and new lyrics to the fight song, the band became the Baltimore Marching Ravens. Producer and director Barry Levinson (the *Diner* guy had deep roots) explored the band's amazing journey in his ESPN documentary *The Band That Wouldn't Die*.

With that in mind, I was not going to be responsible for the Thanksgiving Day the music died. I quickly and quietly looked around the field and pursed my lips. Workers were still drying a few wet patches near the sidelines and in the end zones. There was no way that I could let the band interfere with the grounds crew. It would be a disaster waiting to happen. If anyone was injured, all fingers would point at me.

"Coach, it's not going to happen, but let me call the press box and see if I can work something out for you," I replied worriedly, not wanting to raise any hopes. I definitely needed a second opinion, and the TV producer was the only man who could grant Mackley's wish.

To my surprise, the producer was sympathetic and eager for a solution. I always wondered if he was a Calvert Hall alumnus. "Yeah, Lou, I can make this work, but it's going to be a compromise. We only have so much airtime."

About ten minutes before kickoff, I conferred with both coaches. "Gentleman, due to television constraints, there will be only twelve minutes for halftime." They both nodded in agreement.

As they turned and headed to their respective sidelines, I called out to Coach Mackley. "Coach, tell the band they have twelve minutes and not a second more. If you can't get them off the field, it's going to be a fifteen-yard penalty for delay of the game and unsportsmanlike conduct," I stated with a grim look.

I didn't know if it was legal, but the TV people were breathing down my throat. I had to save face for my crew and me. In the end, it proved to be one hell of an acting job on my part. The band played an abbreviated show to a standing ovation and exited the field in a timely manner. In the dressing room after the game, I was sitting in front my locker with a silly grin. In my head, I could hear Scott and Tom ad-libbing the lyric from Don McLean's "American Pie" as they described the action on the field. "Tom, it looks like the players tried to take the field, but the marching band refused to yield."

"You're right about that Scott," there's a lot of commotion at the fifty-yard line," Tom would reply excitedly. "Looks like the referee Lou Hammond has thrown a flag and called a fifteen-yard penalty for trespassing. Never heard of that before. By the way, Scott, do you recall what was revealed the day the music died."

"Well, Tom, I think the call should have been only five yards for offside or illegal motion."

In what would be my final varsity high school football, I was assigned to the 2012 Calvert Hall vs. Loyola Turkey Bowl at M&T Bank Stadium, home to the Baltimore Ravens. One of the things on my football bucket list was to use the referee microphone to address the fans in the stands and television audience. Unabashedly, I took full advantage of the opportunity. My voice boomed over stadium's state-of-the-art PA system as I deftly announced the coin toss, time outs, and penalties. Like any great showman, I saved the best for last. "Hey, Scott, a Happy Thanksgiving to you, Tom, and our viewers," I exclaimed cordially at the conclusion of the game.

"Hey, Lou, a Happy Thanksgiving to you and your crew," he chuckled. I waved to the press box and walked off the field to a smattering of applause. Once again, everybody left the stadium in a joyous mood. That was the essence of sports and high school football at its finest.

♦♦♦

After my career on the field, I continued my involvement with high school football in the Baltimore area as an administrator. I served on the board of directors of the MBFO for six years. In 1986, I was elected president. During my tenure, I initiated several changes to upgrade the quality of officiating. We watched game films whenever we could cajole coaches to send in their reels. We produced a video to help members learn the proper techniques for field mechanics. We wrote a new mechanics manual for five-member crews. And lastly, we cut expenses by reducing printing and mailing costs. In addition, I appointed committees to develop strategies for a public relations campaign and recruitment/retention of officials.

My hard work did not go unnoticed. In 1986, I was presented the Paul Menton Award. Menton, the longtime sports editor for *The Baltimore Evening Sun*, was the founding commissioner of the MBFO in 1922. The award was presented annually to the official "best exemplifying those humanistic qualities of self-discipline loyalty, cooperativeness, fairness, so characteristic of A Paul Menton." I was honored and humbled to be included with some of the best officials who had ever worked a game. In the end, going back to high school proved to be a step in the right direction for my football career.

CHAPTER 7
FLAGS UNFURLED

The phone was ringing as I headed out the door to another game. *Should I answer it or not? Ah, what the hell,* I thought. *Could be a chance to pick up another game this week or next.* As soon as I picked up the phone, I realized that I had made a mistake. The caller was John Carrigan, football official, football entrepreneur, and all-around football junkie. Boy, he reminded me of someone I knew; I felt as if I was talking to myself on the phone. I had to think quickly on my feet before the phone call turned into an hour rant about the state of everything in the world, especially football.

"Hey, Lou, I'm going to make you an offer you can't refuse," he mumbled in a raspy voice like Marlon Brandon in the movie *The Godfather*. He quickly detailed his latest venture and invited me to join him in changing football, or at least the world of flag football. It was an offer that I couldn't refuse. John's Irish charm, Irish temper, and Irish stubbornness were made for selling a new version of football.

I considered the offer because John was a role model for officials and a football father figure to me. His background in professional football taught me game management and how to deal with coaches. An ex-marine who prided himself on loyalty and teamwork, he demanded respect for the game and game officials. If you didn't get it and give it, you were gone, or as John used to joke, "dishonorably discharged" from the game. On the field, he was always impeccably dressed as if standing for inspection. His uniform was always pressed, his shoes shined, and his hat sharp and blocked.

"John, why is it, you always come to me when you need a favor," I responded slowly in my best *Godfather* imitation. After we both stopped laughing, I told him that I accepted his generous offer. "Just tell me when and where," I added. It didn't take long for the answer. I was immediately appointed supervisor of officials for the United States Flag Football Association. This was the only time in my career when I started at the top with the opportunity to work my way to the bottom as both supervisor and an official.

In a city noted for its share of colorful and lovable characters, especially in the sports world, John found a niche in Baltimore. What I immensely enjoyed was his connection to the old Colts. When I first met him, he was a good friend of Colts Hall of Famer Art Donovan, not surprising since both men were marines from the Old Corps. Following his retirement in 1961, Artie and his wife remained in Baltimore. They opened the Valley Country Club in Timonium, and Art became the most popular raconteur in the city. He never refused a speaking engagement or autograph session as long as there was plenty of cold Schiltz beer and kosher bologna. The mortal sin was for the host to run out of beer because Art never ran out of stories.

It was John who finally convinced Artie to follow the lead of current players and start getting paid for personal appearances.

That was nearly impossible because Art felt he was forever indebted to the city of Baltimore, a debt he could never repay. With John acting his unofficial agent, Art earned a lucrative second income, becoming a fixture on commercials and late-night television shows with David Letterman and Johnny Carson. His hilarious stories about his life in football eventually resulted in a book titled *Fatso: Football When Men Were Really Men*. America couldn't get enough of Art, and neither could Baltimore. Every bookcase in the city had a copy of Art's book, including mine.

At this time, I was moving up in the world. I was now living in an apartment in Gardenville (yeah, family and community roots ran deep in Bawlmer) and was now working as a senior draftsman at BGE. The money was good, and the living was easy in the *Land of Pleasant Living*, the slogan given to Maryland by advertising executives at National Brewing Company. To top it off, there were more than enough football games for all the officials in the area.

At the end of 1976, the country was winding down its bicentennial with an extravagant, outrageous, yearlong party that bathed the country in red, white, and blue. I was now celebrating, or maybe second-guessing, another career move as a football official. *Was flag football a step up or a step down in my career*, I wondered. Either way, I was committed to John. In 1976, I became an official in the fledging United States Flag Football Association (USFFA) whose logo just happened to be red, white, and blue.

Founded in November 1976, the USFFA unified independent leagues into state associations that operated under a constitution with standardized by-laws, rules, and tournament standards. This was a radical change for many of the free-lance leagues around the country that operated independently on shoestring budgets. The scenario resembled the early freewheeling days of the National Football League. There needed to be standardization and organization, and John was the man to do it.

The response to a national organization was overwhelming. The USFFA consolidated nearly 12,000 teams and 250,000 players. Each state purchased a franchise in the association and served as the parent body for leagues in that state. The selling point for the players was a national championship tournament held in conjunction with a national convention. Every flag team in America wanted to play in its version of a Super Bowl. With John, they were going to get that chance. However, when considering the backgrounds of the players, it really wasn't a hard sell.

The USFFA mission statement boldly declared that its goal "was to strengthen the physical, moral, and competitive fiber of American men by expanding opportunities for participation in autumn flag football leagues." The league's aim was to "contribute positively to American society by helping create associations in every state of the nation so that all men might reap the benefits of physical fitness, wholesome recreation, brotherhood, and leadership and spread that ethical code to other segments of society."

I didn't know whether to read it or salute it. The future of America was now in the hands of flag football. Of course, the mission statement was pure John, pure bullshit, and I loved it. The clarion call to embrace those of old-fashioned red, white, and blue values was a marketing gem. On paper it was the American Legion meets the Civilian Conservation Corps meets the American Christian Temperance Movement meets the American Olympic Committee with Teddy Roosevelt as the commissioner. It tugged at the heartstrings of every patriotic man, woman, and child in America.

In reality, it was *Animal House* meets *The Replacements*. Instead of John Carrigan, my pick for commissioner would have been Rodney Dangerfield. I had been around the game of football for some time and knew the leagues' idiosyncrasies would not disappoint its players or fans.

If anybody could get the association off the ground, it was John. He had the marketing skills of Ray Kroc and the guts of General Patton. I couldn't wait to get started. The time was ripe to put a new face on flag football.

The teams in the Baltimore metropolitan area were an eclectic and eccentric mix of former high school and college football players. A few teams had former players with professional experience. Heroes and villains, saints and sinners, and has-beens and wannabes joined forces to burn off the combustible mix of middle age testosterone and adrenaline. While tempers frequently flared on the field with an occasional fight, team brawls were rare. No one wanted to see their football career end with being banished from the league. Even in flag football, dreams died hard.

Once the game ended, players shook hands and retired to a local watering hole to rehash the game and replenish lost fluids. Since games were played on Sunday mornings, the celebration usually lasted from early afternoon into the late night. Depending on what shift you worked at the steel mill, shipyard, or assembly plant, the revelry could extend into Monday morning. *Play hard, drink harder* could have easily been the league's motto.

One of the funniest quotes I ever heard at one of these postgame bacchanals was from a fan. Siding up to the bar with a beer in one hand, probably a Miller Lite, he bellowed in a Rodney Dangerfield voice with spastic hand and body movements, "Hey, guys, I got to tell ya', I get no respect. Today I went to a fight and a flag football game broke out." The punch line drew a ton of laughs, but it was not entirely accurate. What happened at the games was that an argument broke out, guaranteed as if it was written in the contracts.

At the coin toss before kickoff, you could cut the tension with a knife. Everybody seemed to have an attitude problem. Maybe it was because they had a rough week with the boss at work or with the wife and kids at home. On some days, players would argue about everything from the size of the field to the size of the football. To me, they argued for the sake of arguing. But all it took to quell an uprising was a verbal warning from one of the officials. "If you don't shut up, you'll be watching the game from the stands," I would declare sternly. That threat always worked wonders. Even though I was friendly with a number of players, having met them at bull roasts and crab feasts, I enforced the rules to protect the integrity of the game. I played no favorites, and the players respected that.

Unlike high school, and college later in my career, I had some leeway in ensuring the players behaved themselves. I could chew their ass out and threaten them with expulsion under USFFA Rule 9. It dealt with deliberate flagrant fouls, unfair acts, personal fouls, and use of hands and arms to ensure that flag football remained a limited contact sport. It empowered officials to be judge and jury. We joked about it as our *John Wayne* clause. It was like patrolling the field with a six-shooter at your side instead of a rule book.

Since there were no game evaluations for officials in flag football, officials did whatever it took to maintain law and order. As long as the game didn't make the police blotter in one of the newspapers, leagues could have cared less. They were just happy to find officials willing to work for twenty dollars a game. Forget the money, I did it because it was fun. Plus after the game, there was always free food and booze. There was no better way to spend a Sunday afternoon in Baltimore during the NFL season, especially when the Colts were on TV.

Each game was sixty minutes with four quarters. The field was 100 yards divided into 20-yard zones. Each team fielded nine players. Every game began with a kickoff. The ball carrier was down when the flag was removed. The official flag belt was a ball-and-socket design. The offense had four downs to advance the ball into the next zone for a first down. All players except for the three interior linemen were eligible to catch a pass. A first down was achieved when the offense advanced into the next 20-yard zone.

What you had was a basic NCAA template with a few major exceptions. Obviously, you could not tackle opponents. You also could not obstruct the ball carrier by grasping, blocking, or holding when removing a flag. Blocking was allowed with restrictions. Blockers could not leave their feet or throw hands, elbows, or forearms.

Blocking below the waist and two-on-one blocks beyond the line of scrimmage were illegal. The ball carrier could not deliberately run into a defensive player or obstruct an opponent with an extended arm or hand to impede attempts to grab a flag. The key to success was for the ball carrier to dance, swirl, twirl, twist, and turn around the defenders.

The most obvious connection between flag and tackle football was the officials. We wore the standard black-and-white striped shirt, white knickers, black stirrup socks, and uniform caps. Although we looked like NFL officials, we always had to keep in mind that we were officiating flag football. *Improvise to survive* was our mantra.

A crew of game officials consisted of a referee, umpire, and linesman. The referee was responsible for the quarterback and offensive backfield. The umpire watched the line play and short passes across the middle. The linesman, who worked the opposite side of the field from the umpire, covered linebackers, defensive backs, and long passes. During the state and national tournaments a line judge was added to the crew. For those games, the umpire would move to the defensive backfield and the line judge would work opposite the linesman. Regardless of the number of officials, you had to be quick on your feet and keep your head on a swivel to avoid being run over.

In the immortal words of Michigan State football coach Duffy Daugherty, "Football isn't a contact sport, it's a collision sport. Dancing is a contact sport." In the immortal words of John Carrigan to league officials, "Gentlemen, flag football isn't a collision sport, it's a contact sport. Ensure that it remains just that." It certainly was good advice to control the game, but John had no comment about dancing.

What everybody liked about John was his ability to produce memorable but enigmatic quotes, in many ways like baseball's Yogi Berra. While flag football was designed as a gentlemen's game betwixt and between touch and tackle football, there was enough latitude in the rules to ensure a fair amount of physical contact. I often described the game as "football in a straitjacket." There were enough restraints to keep the violence in check.

On the field, the play was fast and furious. Most players were in their mid-twenties and early thirties and could still run, some even faster without pads and helmets. Basically, there were two types of teams—blazers and bruisers. Teams lacking bulk were blazers. They stocked their roster with runners, in many cases former trackmen. Their game relied on speed and stamina. Plays would be either short runs or passes toward the sideline quickly followed by a series of downfield laterals resembling a rugby game.

As for the bruisers, they simply filled up the field with their size and strength making it difficult for blazers to find open space. They churned up and down the field like a stampeding herd of buffalo.

Still have doubts that flag football isn't real football? Think again! In 2022, Troy Vincent, NFL's executive vice president of football operations, told the press that the NFL was working to include flag football in the 2028 Olympics. According to Vincent, the game had international appeal due to its emphasis on athletic skills from other sports that could easily be transferred to the gridiron. After being involved with the game, I heartily agreed. In October 2023, the International Olympic Committee announced that flag football would be included in the 2028 Summer Olympics.

Tim "Bulldog" Brannan with the Florida Blazers of the World Football League before becoming saloon owner.

CHAPTER 8
THESE ARE THE CHAMPIONS

No team personified the Wild West image of flag football more than Wilkens House, a pub in northeast Baltimore. Owned by former Curley High School and University of Maryland star Tim "Bulldog" Brannan, the team became a USFFA legend, winning five consecutive championships from 1979 to 1983.

A journeyman guard for several NFL teams, Tim finally found a home in the nascent World Football League (WFL) with the Florida Blazers and San Antonio Wings before the league went bankrupt. After being cut by the Denver Broncos in 1977, Tim returned home and used his life savings to buy the bar. Eager to find an outlet for his competitive juices, he teamed with his old friend Frank Culotta, a former middle guard from Villanova, to form a team.

His gregarious personality and outrageous behavior set the tone for the team and the season. He routinely showed up for games dressed in costumes more suited for professional wrestling, such as a ten-gallon hat, a cape, and Speedos. Not too unusual for someone who wore a T-shirt, shorts, and shower shoes to make money drops at the local bank in the dead of winter with snow in the air.

In 1982, his team featured seven players with NFL or WFL experience. Most of the remaining roster had pro tryouts somewhere in their career. The roster read like a Who's Who in local football history: Mike Creaney, second team All-American tight end, Notre Dame; Lou Carter, running back, Maryland, five years with the Oakland Raiders and Tampa Bay Buccaneers; Vince Kinney, wide receiver, Denver Broncos; Frank Russell, wide receiver, New York Jets; Greg Schaum, defensive end, Dallas Cowboys, 1978 Super Bowl champions; and John Ricca, defensive end, Florida Blazers.

They were the ultimate blend of blazers and bruisers. They were fun to watch and even more fun to officiate. Critics claimed the team was too physical. Even their coaches admitted that players had a hard time adjusting to grabbing an eighteen-inch vinyl flag. While physical, they weren't cheap-shot artists. They readily admitted they had their day in the sun and played merely for the love of the game. Too often they were the recipients of cheap shots from opposing players testing their manhood against former professional athletes.

Commissioner John Carrigan came to their defense. "Wilkens House isn't too rough. They're physical. When you have a 275-pound lineman going against a 195-pound guy that's an eighty-pound difference, and it's going to get physical. They play hard and clean. Any other flag football team can go out and recruit this kind of talent if it wants to," John commented to *Sports Illustrated* in an article written about the Wilkens House dynasty. Somehow, John never mentioned anything about a 275-pound former NFL pro lining up across a 160-pound high school second stringer. Yes, the league had some lop-sided matchups.

Tim and his team were good publicity for the association and the league. Games routinely drew overflow crowds eager for exciting football and autographs after the game. His pub became Baltimore's version of Boston's Bull and Finch, the bar that inspired the TV show *Cheers*. Like the old Colts he worshipped as a kid, Tim never forgot his Bawlmer roots with his local philanthropy. He was the better man for it, and the city was a better place to live in.

On the field, I enjoyed watching players that I had officiated during sandlot and high school games. There were even a number of Gardenville Guys scattered on the rosters around the league. Opposite the former pro and college players, there were athletes like Gardenville's Mike Trott. Just a few years younger than me, I had the pleasure of watching his career in a number of sports. He was one of those big kids in sandlot football who simply bulldozed would be tacklers or carried half the opposing team on his back into the end zone. Starring in other sports, I often called him the Jim Thorpe of Gardenville. He excelled at everything he played. Like the Bulldog, he was an affable guy who would shake your hand and buy you a beer after the game.

Unlike the Bulldog whose life was football, Mike's passion was baseball. He starred at every level from sandlot to college. He topped off his baseball career as a member of Johnny's 19 and under national championship team. The perennial powerhouse sent scores of players to the majors, including Hall of Famers Al Kaline and Reggie Jackson.

With his quickness and coordination, his baseball skills were well suited to flag football. Like many other local athletes who didn't major in football, he found a competitive outlet in flag football as a standout for the Highlandtown Moose Lodge.

After watching Mike play, I realized the mission statement of the USFFA wasn't so far-fetched after all.

◆ ◆ ◆

Just as there were memorable players, there were memorable events. For me, they occurred at the national championship games when I was the referee. In 1979, my first championship game almost became my last.

The championship game had ended, and fans gathered on the field at Utz Twardowicz Stadium to congratulate the players. I was walking along with them to the winner's sideline for the presentation of the championship trophy when John Carrigan stopped me.

"Where's the goddamn football?" John screamed at the top of his lungs.

"John, I don't have it," I replied calmly with a smirk. That answer wasn't good enough.

"For Christ's sake, you're the referee. You're supposed to keep track of these things."

"John, I'm not the ball boy," I quipped.

"I know you have it. Now where's the fucking football. I need to present it to the game MVP," he shouted, the veins in his neck bulging.

The ruckus attracted a number of curious onlookers to include members from the Wilkens House who had just been crowned this year's national champion.

"Here's a football for you, John," Tim Brannan, owner of the Wilkens House, shouted as he tossed a football in John's direction.

John caught the ball and spun it in his hands. "Jesus Christ, I need a Wilson not a Spalding. They're the official football of the league."

"How about a Johnson? I got one right here in my pocket," someone from the crowd shouted. The off-color, humorous remark struck a nerve. John just shook his head and mumbled in feigned disgust before laughing.

"Hey, John, start a new tradition and give the MVP a fifth of Jack Daniel's," Tim bellowed as the crowd roared with delight.

"Hey, Tim, you cheap bastard. Why don't you start another tradition and donate a fifth of Jack Daniel's for the MVP," John grinned.

"Hey, John, you cheaper bastard. Why don't you buy the first round at the pub," Tim roared to the delight of the thirsty fans who were ready to party. The lost football had been forgotten. A ball boy wiggled through the crowd and handed John a genuine Wilson football.

It was a heartwarming scene to see the beloved commissioner and one of the most beloved sponsors congratulate each other with such endearing words. The USFFA mission statement was working its magic. It was now time to celebrate the success of another national tournament and toast the victors. All had been forgotten between John and me, or so I thought.

As we headed for the parking lot at the conclusion of the awards ceremony, John continued bitching about the missing Wilson. "Lou, I know you. I know you have it somewhere," he whined.

After a few more steps in silence, I had my fill of John's rant. "You're absolutely right, John. I have it here in my game bag," I barked angrily.

"Well, I want it back. It's league property," he shouted.

"Not so fast, John. The reason I picked it up was to give it to you. I wanted you to have something to remind you of your first national tournament in Baltimore. Yeah, I got it for you." I replied meekly.

John looked at the sky, lost for words, a rare occasion, indeed. For a second, I thought I saw a tear in his eye. "I taught you well, Grasshopper," John whispered, impersonating Master Po from the TV series *Kung Fu* as he placed his arm on my shoulder.

The relationship between mentor and student was sealed. I never told John that I secreted the ball in my game bag to take home. But as we were walking toward our cars, I thought about what John had done for flag football and decided it would make the perfect gift. My conscience got the better part of me. Besides, there would be many more games and many more footballs in the future. I just had to keep perfecting my sixth sense of finding things before they are lost.

Before I got into my car, I looked back at the field and smiled with satisfaction. I had officiated a national championship as the referee. Even though it was only flag football, it represented a milestone in my career. Once again, I owed my success to John.

◆ ◆ ◆

My second most memorable game was the national championship in Akron, Ohio. It was only early December, but the temperature was hovering around zero before the kickoff. The ball felt like a cinder block and the field looked like a green concrete slab. In the stands, fans, dressed in fur like Eskimos, passed around bottles in brown paper bags to ward off the Arctic chill.

Everybody was bundled in layers except for the officiating crew and the players, but the players had the advantage. They ran plays and then ran off the field to a warm parka or a sideline heater. We weren't so lucky. Once again, we were the only team on the field for the whole sixty minutes. With only a minimal base layer in the age before thermal synthetic fabrics, we were cold. While we were cold, our whistles were frozen.

After the opening kickoff, the back judge waved his heads over his head to signal a timeout and came running over to me with a worried look. "Lou, my whistle is broken," he shouted excitedly.

"What in the hell are you talking about?" I responded incredulously. "Whistles don't just break. Here, I'll prove it to you." I quickly lifted my whistle to my lips and blew. *Phew!* Nothing but the sound of air coming out of the top hole! *Phew!* I blew again. Still nothing! I quickly huddled with the crew and had them test their whistles. I inspected each whistle and shook it. No rattle! "What the hell happened to the peas?" I mumbled in disgust. Either the pea was frozen to the metal sides, or it had shrunk and fallen out due to the extreme temperatures.

We were like gunslingers without our six-shooters. It was time to improvise. I called over to the head coaches and explained the situation. "Gentlemen, we're going to use verbal commands to signal the end of a play. Tell your players to be listening for a command instead of a whistle." A crisis was averted, but I couldn't stop thinking about what would have happened if a whistle had frozen to our lips. I would have loved to read the postgame report to the supervisor of officials. On the bright side, it would have created one of the funniest moments ever seen on a football blooper film. I did mention the whistle malfunction in my postgame report.

A few years after the whistle debacle, technology came to the rescue. Ronald Foxcroft and Charles Shepherd developed a pea-less plastic whistle that they called the FOX 40. This was truly one of the greatest inventions in the world of officiating and coaching. It also became very popular with lifeguards. Next time you want to impress someone who uses a whistle at work, ask them, "Hey, is that a FOX 40 you got there?"

◆ ◆ ◆

By 1980, the USFFA was firmly established as the governing organization for flag football. However, to remain viable, there had to be some tweaks in the system. A glaring weakness was the lack of standardized rules and regulations. Some renegade leagues were using local rules in officiating that resembled touch football. Another hot-button item that always caused controversy was downfield blocking. Every league seemed to have a variation on the theme that would require separate rulebooks.

Unfortunately, these discrepancies usually surfaced around tournament time and gave the association a blackeye. Bickering among the leagues ran contrary to John's code of good housekeeping, and he wasn't shy in expressing his feelings at the annual convention. "Gentlemen, this behavior is unacceptable and will not be tolerated. We are trying to garner positive national media attention, not tear the association apart. If you want to play by your own rules, you can leave now and form your own league," he proclaimed adamantly. Silence filled the room as if all the oxygen had been sucked out in a vacuum. No one dared to call his bluff.

John was on the mark with his comments. The rules and regulations of flag football needed to be coded for all leagues. We needed a national rule book, but who could John turn to? As always, John was quick with the fix. He quickly surmised that no one was better qualified to write that book than the supervisor of officials. The job was mine. It was another offer I couldn't refuse.

In 1982, I began the arduous task, in addition to conducting a national rules clinic for the national tournament and assigning officials to work those games. To start the project, I requested a list of rules used by the various leagues around the country. Then I interviewed the various league coordinators to discuss the pros and cons about the variations they were utilizing. After receiving their comments, I discussed the proposed rules with Commissioner Carrigan who had the final say. We worked meticulously through three drafts of the new rulebook before it finally went to press in 1983. In keeping with the tradition of newly published authors who were football officials, I hosted a publishing party at a local tavern.

By the time I left the association in 1987 to officiate college games, there was a lot to celebrate. John's offer in 1976 proved to be a springboard for my officiating career. It offered me opportunities in all functions of officiating and allowed me to bolster my football resume. I was beginning to look as good on paper as I did on the field.

CHAPTER 9
LIFE IN THE MINORS

In 1977, a year after becoming a flag football official, I took another step. Forward, backward, sideways, who knows? The important thing was that I kept moving to avoid becoming complacent. I had to faithfully hone my skills to a razor's edge. Once again, the latest strategic move started with a phone call from my gridiron godfather, John Carrigan.

"Hey, Lou, I got another offer you can't refuse. Are you ready for the next step?" John exclaimed enthusiastically.

"Yeah, sure John, as long I don't step in it," I joked. *Here we go again*, I thought excitedly.

"The pros are calling. Well, more like semipro, but it's a taste of big-time football. Are you interested?"

Of course, I was interested. It was another offer that I couldn't and didn't refuse.

Only a year earlier, I received a similar call that was definitely a step in another direction. However, the problem was figuring out what direction that was. At a minimum, flag football honed my skills and expanded my network of contacts. In a worst-case scenario, the semi-pros would do the same. *What the hell, I have nothing to lose*, I thought. I had to keep moving, no matter what direction. If anything, football with John was an adventure. I was definitely along for the ride.

Only this time, it was a two-step move, a definite step forward and a step back to the basics. I was moving to another level of tackle football that mirrored the rules and regulations of the NCAA and the NFL. If officiating was a video game, I was playing at level four. I had advanced from sandlot to high school to flag and now to the semipro/minor league. If the league was a TV series, Rod Serling from the *Twilight Zone* would have hosted it because it was a surreal mix of sport.

In my mind, I could hear Rod with his weekly introduction to the games. "There is a football dimension beyond which is known to fans. It is a dimension as vast as multi-year, million-dollar contracts and as timeless as the Jets victory over the Colts in the Super Bowl. It is the middle ground between the bright lights of Monday Night Football with Frank, Howard, and Don and the lengthening shadows of a high school field after the senior season. It's a dimension not only of sight, sound, and salaries but of reality, comedy, and fantasy. That's the signpost up ahead. Your next stop . . . the world of Minor League Football."

The prologue would apply to owners, players, officials, and fans. All of us were on a journey to the football unknown, and we couldn't wait to get started. It was time to line up for the kickoff and blow the whistle, as long as it wasn't too cold outside.

What was the difference between semipro or minor league football? To fans in the '70s, it was a blurred line as teams came and went like clouds in the sky. The titles *semipro* and *minor league* were fluid and often used interchangeably. I simply solved the dilemma by lumping both brands under the heading

The Minor Football League or the MFL as opposed to the NFL. No matter what I called it, whenever I mentioned minor league, football fans knew exactly what I was talking about.

To owners, players and officials, the differences were obvious. Part of the answer was skill level, name recognition, and attendance. However, the biggest was money. No surprise there to any football fan.

For the most part, minor league players were former college and pro athletes who received a small salary or game wage. Semipro athletes played for travel expenses and the love of the game. In response to any questions about salaries, owners and players agreed with a wink and a nod that perceived wages were strictly travel expenses. Any money under the table was dismissed with another wink and nod as the fantasy of sports writers.

Ownership was another variable that defined minor league and semipro. Minor league owners were usually established businessmen with deep pockets. Semipro owners were usually a consortium of local businessmen with shoestring budgets. Regardless of the number of employees and sales figures, the size of a company's bank account did not guarantee success. Owners had to sell their team to the public by any means available. It was rumored that some owners sold more than football at their games, proving they could mix business and pleasure.

Such was the case with two semipro teams, one in Baltimore and the other in the District of Columbia; both were reportedly owned by drug dealers. Since both teams were local, I officiated many of their games, always keeping my head on a swivel on and off the field. At this level of play, the unexpected was the expected.

I never knew if the nefarious owners were legitimate businessmen but getting paid before the game always felt like a sting operation. The clothes, the lingo, and the setting suggested a Blaxploitation movie from the '70s. It was a good thing that I liked soul music.

At times, I expected to see Fred Williamson or Jim Brown, both former NFL stars and subsequent Hollywood actors, appear at midfield for the coin toss. Isaac Hayes singing the "Theme from Shaft" before the kickoff wouldn't have surprised me either.

In DC, one owner, who looked like a former defensive lineman and dressed in black like a backwoods preacher at a camp meeting, would suddenly emerge from the crowd and appear along the sideline. Surrounded by an entourage that resembled mobsters, he would approach the referee (the good guy in the white hat who was frequently me) and ceremoniously hand him a Bible.

"Would the congregation please turn to the following pages," he would bellow as if standing at the pulpit. "The wicked shall perish. The righteous shall triumph. And the high priests in this sanctuary shall preserve the law to avoid the wages of sin." After his invocation, he would gently hand over the book to the referee. Secreted at the announced pages were hundred dollar bills, usually a Benjamin for each official. No change was given because crews didn't carry money in those neighborhoods. No comments were directed at the generosity of the home team or the manner in which we were paid. Likewise, no questions were asked about the passages in the Bible.

There was another stylized payment method in Baltimore with the setting and characters eerily similar to those in DC. Only this time, the team owner pulled out a thick money clip and counted out the bills to the referee.

"Is that enough, Mr. Official? Are you sure that's enough 'cause there's plenty more where that came from. You know we're just striving for equal opportunity on the playing field," he would cackle in a shrill, staccato voice to the delight of his entourage.

Forget playing the national anthem before any professional games. It would be more appropriate to play Pink Floyd's

"Money," which has a line about buying a football team. Everyone always wondered why I was laughing before the kickoff. I just kept the joke to myself and enjoyed the moment.

I was certain that my "money anthem," the ode to capitalism, would be a hit. Players and owners would love it because they lived it. I loved it because now I was making seventy-five dollars a game, a substantial raise from the twenty-five bucks I had been getting. In addition, we received legitimate travel expenses without any winks or nods. As for myself, I would have bought a ticket to the games just to witness the crews getting paid. It was that entertaining. I never understood how some of the owners never made it to the silver screen or the bestseller list.

Like minor league baseball, minor league football was a collection of teams scattered around the country that featured a varying caliber of play. Unlike minor league baseball, minor league football was not a progression to a career in the NFL, but rather an extension of a career that already peaked.

◆ ◆ ◆

While some players at the minor league level unrealistically harbored the NFL dream, there were exceptions. Most notably was Vince Papale who became the real-life Rocky Balboa of the football world. After graduating from St. Joseph's University, which didn't have a football team, Papale began his football career with the semipro Aston Green Knights of the Seaboard Football League. After a successful try out, he spent two years with the Philadelphia Bell of the WFL as a wide receiver.

In 1976, at the age of thirty, he signed with the Philadelphia Eagles and became the oldest rookie non-kicker in the history of the NFL. After three productive years as special-teams standout, he retired due to a shoulder injury. His remarkable football journey was chronicled in the acclaimed Disney film *Invincible*. That movie poster had to be taped onto the bedroom wall of every player in the minors.

Papale validated the dream and gave hope to those in his footsteps. I related to his story because I was in a similar situation. To pursue my dream, I had to keep taking steps forward. No doubt, it was easier for me than the players. They insidiously knew there would be no steps forward. Eventually, they would step down to flag or touch football, equivalent to having one foot the football grave. In the MFL, the road to glory was littered with broken bodies and crushed dreams, but there was always Vince Papale to inspire. It was those rags-to-riches stories from the sports world that kept me moving forward. Thank you, Vince!

◆ ◆ ◆

Think about minor league football and the first team that comes to mind is the legendary Pottstown Firebirds, which ruled from 1968 to 1970. Featured in the 1970 NFL documentary *Pro Football, Pottstown, PA,* they were originally a farm club for the Philadelphia Eagles. The Eagles provided equipment and helmets (with Eagles wings) for a team comprised mainly of former NFL and college players. At the time, the Firebirds quarterback was Jim "The King" Corcoran, former quarterback at the University of Maryland. Described as the poor man's Joe Namath, Jim was an unforgettable and unapologetic playboy who scored off the field more than on. His success in all things football eventually landed him in the MFL Hall of Fame.

Back home in Baltimore, we had our version of the Firebirds ironically named the Eagles, though not affiliated with the Philadelphia Eagles. They started as a semipro team in the

Mid-Atlantic region with a roster of college and high school athletes. In 1976, they were national champs after beating the Southern California Rhinos 33-13 in the semipro Super Bowl at Las Vegas on December 18.

The game was broadcast back to Baltimore on WFBR radio with Chuck Thompson, the smooth as silk baritone voice of the Baltimore Orioles and the Baltimore Colts, and Charlie Eckman, Baltimore's irreverent and irresistible raconteur simply known as "The Coach."

The broadcast received high ratings, reaching out to an audience of thousands of football fans in the Baltimore area that included me. I simply couldn't resist hearing Chuck and Charlie on the radio. If there were any doubts about Baltimore being a football town, they were erased with this game. Too bad Bob Irsay, owner of the Colts before they snuck out of town in the middle of the night in March 1984, didn't listen to the broadcast. He would have learned an invaluable lesson about loyalty and integrity.

After the season, *Pro Football Weekly* recognized several players as semipro All Americans, to include Al Neville, hometown quarterback from the University of Maryland. Other players received try outs with NFL and CFL teams. Mayor Schaefer, the Maryland State Legislature, and the National Football Foundation also honored the team with proclamations. Baltimore loved its football team in all shapes and sizes!

At the HOF induction with my close friend and mentor, Lance Garth.
That's the ring in my right hand.

CHAPTER 10
SEMIPRO HEROES

Over the years, I was privileged to watch hundreds of players in the MFL as a fan and official. There were three players whose careers are permanently etched in my mind. Their triumphs and tribulations embodied the core values of football at any level. While never replicating their high school and collegiate success in the NFL, they eventually attained a degree of fame in the MFL. Guided by an unyielding "will to win," they courageously overcame the obstacles in their careers and endured the pathos and ethos of the sport. In the end, they accepted their fates with stoic dignity. That was the definition of a winner in my book.

In 1979, the Baltimore Eagles joined the Atlantic Football Conference and played a regional schedule with teams in Pennsylvania, New York, and Connecticut. No longer semipro, this was now minor league football at its finest with bigger crowds, more marque players, and better officials. The roster included eleven former college players from the Baltimore metropolitan area with professional experience.

The featured player, whose caricature graced the cover of the 1979 official program, was Joe Gilliam. In 1974, Gilliam beat out Terry Bradshaw, becoming the first Black quarterback named the starter before the season.

On September 15, 1974, at Three Rivers Stadium, Gilliam passed for 257 yards and two touchdowns in a 30-0 rout of the Baltimore Colts. He appeared to have taken his first step to the NFL Hall of Fame. The shellacking of my beloved Colts was probably the only thing that I didn't like about Joe. However, that game was one of the few bright spots in his NFL career. Benched mid-season for his erratic performance and failure to follow the game plan (more running and less passing), he served as a backup to Bradshaw as the Steelers won back-to-back Super Bowls.

His dream crashed and burned after four seasons as he battled the demons of cocaine, heroin, and alcohol abuse. After failed tryouts with the New Orleans Saints in 1976 and 1977, he found his way to the MFL after living in a cardboard box under a freeway for two years.

On the evening of October 13, 1979, Joe led the Baltimore Eagles to the Atlantic Football Conference championship with a 20-9 win over the Pittsburgh Wolf Pack at Homewood Field on the campus of Johns Hopkins University. Baltimore football fans finally had a measure of revenge as their former nemesis led a Baltimore team to victory over a team from Pittsburgh.

It was a heroic feat considering that a month earlier he had been savagely beaten after being robbed in an alleged drug dispute. He remained unconscious in the hospital for two days.

Straddling the line of scrimmage as a head linesman for Eagles home games, I observed Joe as if I was a wide receiver for the Eagles. Although he was an old twenty-seven, he still had a canon for an arm. Tall and lanky, I couldn't help but notice that some of his physical mannerisms on the field resembled Johnny U, most notably the way he cocked his head while barking out signals, his backward shuffle after the ball was snapped, and his standing tall in the pocket until the last minute.

His play exuded an air of confidence that rubbed off on his teammates. There was no doubt that he came from a higher league. Knowing that he was a reclamation project that could be excellent publicity for the league, I hoped he maintained sobriety for another shot in the NFL. It wasn't meant to be.

After his season in Baltimore, Joe played for the New Orleans Blue Knights of the Dixie Football League. After a brief stint with the Washington Federals of the USFL in 1983, he was out of football for good. In 1986, he was inducted into the American Football Association Hall of Fame. On Christmas Day 2000 at the age of forty-nine, he died from a drug overdose after being sober for three years. Only nine days earlier, he attended the Steelers final game at Three Rivers Stadium.

Throughout his life, he blamed no one but himself for his misfortune and was gracious for the opportunities he had been given. It was a pleasure and privilege to watch Joe play football. In the back of my mind, I filed his career as *what should have been* if he had only stayed the course.

◆ ◆ ◆

Many sports writers labeled Greg Hare from Fort Hill, Cumberland, Maryland, as the greatest college quarterback never to have thrown a pass in the NFL. Recruited by over thirty major college teams, which included Maryland and Penn State, Hare finally decided on Ohio State because he wanted to play in the Rose Bowl.

With pro size, (6'3" and 210 pounds), and speed, he became the main cog in Woody Hayes three yards and a cloud of dust offense. Midway through his sophomore year in 1971, he became the starting quarterback. In 1972, he led the Buckeyes to the Big Ten championship and the Rose Bowl where they lost to the top-ranked USC Trojans, 42-17. He lost the starting job in his senior year due to a hamstring injury and saw limited action in mop-up games.

Despite his lack of playing time, his skills, especially his arm, attracted NFL scouts. His fate rested with the Buffalo Bills who drafted him in the eighth round. After a failed attempt as a cornerback in preseason, he declined a position on the taxi squad as third-string quarterback. Disenchanted with pro football after a brief stint with the Calgary Stampeders of the CFL, feelers from Kanas City Chiefs and Baltimore Colts, and a tryout with the New York Giants, he returned to Cumberland. An NFL dream was shattered, but his love of the game remained intact.

Back home he launched a football career with the Chambersburg Cardinals of the Interstate Football League and pursued a business career with Xerox. Both were incredibly successful. He was the national Player of the Year three times and led the Cardinals to three national championships.

In 1990, he was inducted into the American Football Association Hall of Fame. In 2019, he was inducted into the Fort Hill Hall of Fame for his community involvement, which included working with high school quarterbacks and coaching in youth leagues.

Looking back on his career, he commented, "I think I had as good an arm as most of the quarterbacks in the NFL and the skills to play. Just nothing about it ever meshed. I sometimes wonder about what might have happened if I hadn't gone to Ohio State or if I had been drafted by the Dallas Cowboys. I have no regrets. I have my own successful business and I love living in Cumberland. I have had a great life."

Watching Greg from the line of scrimmage throughout his career with Chambersburg, I was always amazed at his athleticism. Unlike Joe Gilliam, he was in his prime and seemed a step faster and a second quicker than anyone on the field. While Joe Gilliam played like he came from a higher league which he did, Greg played as if should be in a higher league. Unlike Joe, Greg didn't falter when obstacles were thrown in his path. I filed his career under what *could have been* if only he had taken another road, maybe to Penn State where Joe Paterno promised to throw the football.

◆◆◆

My favorite player from the minors was Ron Meehan because I could relate to Ron's career in many ways. Both of us were local guys who experienced the game at every level possible: sandlot, high school, college, semipro, minor league, and professional. Those experiences became a common bond as Ron and I became friends off the field.

Ron attended Woodlawn High School in Baltimore County, not the high school from the movie *Woodlawn*, where he was an All-County and All-State quarterback. A four-year starter at Towson State University from 1977 to 1980, he earned All-American honors from UPA and All-American Honorable Mention from Kodak and *Sporting News*. In his senior year, he was named first team All-ECAC DIV II. Twice he won the Doc Minnegan Award as Towson's MVP. In 2006, he was inducted into Towson's Football Hall of Fame.

Signed by the Oakland Raiders as a free agent in 1981, Meehan impressed the coaches with his football savvy. While he wasn't the biggest or fastest quarterback, he knew how to play the game. With only fifteen minutes to the deadline for the final roster, he was informed by Al Davis that he had been cut. The timing couldn't have been worse. By that time, it was too late to catch on with another team.

Disappointed but not despairing, he forged ahead with his football career. In 1982, the Baltimore Colts signed him as a free agent. Before being released in preseason, he played against the Minnesota Vikings in the annual Pro Football Hall of Fame Game. The nationally televised game featured the broadcast team of Frank Gifford and Howard Cosell.

In 1984, after a brief stint with the CFL Winnipeg Blue Bombers, he had a final unsuccessful tryout with the USFL's Washington Federals. The dream of playing professional football had ended, but Ron was undeterred. He lived and breathed football. Playing the game was paramount regardless of where or when. Baseball had Crash Davis from the movie *Bull Durham*; football had Ron Meehan. In 1985, he began an eleven-year career that led to two championships with the Chambersburg Cardinals and four championships with the Frederick Falcons of the Continental Football League. He closed out his career with the Baltimore Bears, earning league MVP honors in 1990 and 1991.

Following his playing days, he coached football at the jayvee and varsity levels in Baltimore County before becoming passing coordinator/quarterback coach at Towson University. In 2008, he joined the coaching staff of the Baltimore Mariners of the American Indoor Football Association. In 2010, the team brought home Baltimore's first indoor championship. However, the joy of victory was short-lived. A few months later, the team owner was convicted of embezzlement and sentenced to fifteen months in prison.

After a hiatus, the team returned in 2014 with Ron as head coach. That year, the Mariners won the championship and Ron was named Coach of the Year. In 2015, the team folded due to financial woes. I filed his career under *what would have been* if only for those fifteen minutes.

◆ ◆ ◆

Time was of the essence in my career also. I couldn't afford the luxury of waiting for something to happen. As a result of my friendship with John Carrigan, I worked two championship games for the minor leagues. As supervisor of officials, John decided on the crews. It was nice to have friends in high places. The first game was the Baltimore Eagles versus the Wheeling Rockets in front of a raucous, redneck crowd of 15,000 West Virginians. It was a game to remember for what happened on and off the field.

The game was officiated by a split crew, three officials from Baltimore and three from West Virginia. Since we were using NCAA rules, the combined crew was comfortable with the mechanics. Not surprisingly, the biggest headache for the crew came from John. A few days before the game, John was removed from the crew after the Rockets filed a protest for possible conflict of interest. John felt slighted and slandered, rightfully so. While the old Marine was strongly opinioned at times, he never let his opinions sway his judgment or affect his emotions on the field.

At the pregame meeting for officials, John was still livid. "You guys go out there and just do your job. Show those hillbilly bastards what professionals we are." That's all that needed to be said. John had our backs. The perfect game by the crew would be the sweetest revenge. However, to be covered in glory was not to be cloaked in the traditional black and white of an official.

Before the national anthem, the crew lined up on the field and removed their caps. The referee looked down the line and shook his head. "For Chrissake, I don't whether to salute you guys, the flag, or both," he chortled.

We instantly knew what he meant. Instead of black and white, we wore red and white striped shirts, white knickers, and blue stirrup socks. While we were the sharpest dress team on the field, we had doubts about our non-traditional attire.

Officials wore black and white for a reason, and it's not to reflect the league's logo. It's to be recognized and easily identified. Black and white denoted formality and authority. Outfitted in red and white, we resembled candy canes. I knew that Lloyd Olds would readily have agreed with us. Lloyd who?

In 1920, while officiating a college game, Lloyd, dressed in a white shirt and bowtie, was inadvertently passed the ball after a player mistook him for a teammate who was wearing a white jersey. To avoid any future confusion, Lloyd recruited a friend to make a shirt that would separate players from officials. A year later, Lloyd debuted the latest football fashion, a shirt with black-and-white stripes. Although not an overnight success, it worked well. By 1945, the NFL adopted black-and-white shirts for its crews.

While I enjoyed being a trendsetter, I was a dedicated follower of traditional fashion. I was proud to follow in Lloyd's footsteps and wear black and white, or was it white and black? Of course, Lloyd's innovation had a major drawback. Zebras on the field were now recognizable and identifiable. Irate coaches and fans could now direct their wrath at the offending official. When numbers were later added to our jerseys, the stripes became a bull's-eye.

That championship game in Wheeling produced one of the funniest moments in my football career. After the game, I inadvertently became a celebrity at one of the local watering holes. Since the game was played in a dry county, the only way to get a drink at a bar was to join a social or veterans club, such as the Elks, Moose, American Legion, VFW, as a guest. For a one-time fee of five dollars, the crew and friends joined the local Moose for an all-inclusive one-day membership. Not a bad deal because this allowed us to enjoy big cans of Foster's Lager at a substantial discount. How Australia's best-selling beer became the house brew in the hills of West Virginia remained a mystery, but the beer was cold and plentiful. As expected, the jukebox in the corner played non-stop country music.

As out-of-towners who frequented local bars and restaurants, we were used to quirky glances from the clientele. Only in this club, it seemed everyone was looking our way at the beginning and ending of each song. Perhaps, people recognized us from the game. After all, it seemed like the entire population of Wheeling had filled the stands. Finally, one of the patrons made his move and casually approached our table. We just hoped it wasn't a drunk and pissed-off Rockets fan.

"It's a real honor to have you at our club," the man slurred, swaying slightly. "It would be the memory of a lifetime if you boys would sing us a song. Whatever you decide, gospel or county, it don't matter."

We sat silently for a few seconds with bewildered looks. *What the hell is this guy talking about*, I thought. Before anybody could say a word, the gentleman pointed a finger at me. "Sure as shit, you're Joe Bonsall. I'd recognize you anywhere," he proudly proclaimed as if he had grown up in Gardenville.

My second thought was, *Who in the hell is Joe Bonsall?* One of the crew came to my rescue.

"No, sir we're not the Oakridge Boys, we're the officiating crew from today's game."

"Ah, Jesus, you had me fooled for a minute. Sorry for the interruption, but I know you're Joe Bonsall. Yes, sir, you are," he laughed, looking in my direction along with the rest of the patrons who spied on our table.

We quickly finished our beers and headed for the door. I was expecting some of the club members to follow us and watch us file in the band bus after autographing a stack of glossy band shots.

On the way back to the hotel, the crew started razzing me. "Hey, Joe, sing us a song. How about the 'Old Rugged Cross' or 'Amazing Grace' for starters." I remained silent with a creased smirk on my face. These jokers didn't know the joke was on them. I wasn't Joe Bonsall, but I was the former lead vocalist for Eric and the Wall of Sound, the legendary garage band from Gardenville. Maybe, I should have said that to the drunk at the club. He'd be scratching his head and thinking, *Who in the hell is Eric and the Wall of Sound and where in the hell in Gardenville?*

Sometime later, I found a picture of the Oakridge Boys from the early '80s. Damn, I could have easily passed for Joe Bonsall with my droopy mustache and long hair. Maybe, I should have sung them a song to remember me. I just don't know how well my band's classic rendition of "House of the Rising Son" would have been received.

◆◆◆

My affiliation with semipro and minor league football lasted from 1977 to 2000. In 1998, my patience, perseverance, and professionalism paid off with another phone call from John Carrigan.

"Lou, we're going to Canton," he announced excitedly.

"For lunch or dinner," I replied under the impression that he wanted to dine at Baltimore's bohemian waterfront neighborhood.

"What the hell are you talking about?" he countered dumbfounded, not realizing that I wasn't thinking about football in another state.

"I'm talking about Canton. You know, the harbor."

"Hell, no! I'm talking about Canton, Ohio, and the Pro Football Hall of Fame," he howled deliriously. Mystery solved; I was heading to the Hall of Fame, or should I say a Hall of Fame. It didn't matter if it was the NFL or the MFL. I was being recognized for my contribution to the game of football. In addition to the American Football Conference, Interstate Football League, and the Continental Football League, I also officiated in the Mason Dixon Football League for a total of twenty-three years. I was more than qualified for the honor.

Although the American Football Association (ASA) was headquartered in Sarasota, Florida, their Hall of Fame induction was held at the Holiday Inn in Canton, Ohio. It was an enchanting weekend with all of the pomp and circumstance of the NFL induction ceremony. On that Saturday, July 22, 1989, there was a morning bus trip to the Pro Football Hall of Fame and later that evening a dinner where inductees were presented with rings.

My wife Kelly, my father's sister and her husband, my good friend Lance Garth, and two other friends accompanied me to Canton. Sadly, my parents couldn't make the trip. My father stayed home to care for my mother who was ill. Thankfully, the induction was videotaped so my parents could view the ceremony. If not, I was prepared to hire a videographer.

I was truly honored to have Judge Lance Garth as my presenter. We had been together in the officiating trenches through the good and bad times since my first year in DIV I. As Lance recalled my career to the audience, I sat holding Kelly's hand with an easy smile. In my mind, images of faces and places rushed by in a soft blur. At the time, I was only the seventh football official to be inducted in the ASA Hall of Fame. I was now in the select company of football legends, such as Johnny Unitas, Art Rooney Sr., Vince Lombardi, Otis Sistrunk, Tom Dempsey, Sam Wyche, Greg Hare, and John Carrigan. The roster of ASA past inductees read like a Who's Who in the world of football, a collection of great names who made indelible contributions to the sport. Every name had a fascinating story that deserved to be heard. It was humbling to think that I was now on the roles.

During my acceptance speech, I thanked my wife, my parents, and all the officials who helped me get to where I was today. A special thank you went to John Carrigan for getting me involved in minor league football. What an emotional moment! I felt like I was floating in space, slowly rising above the crowd. I kept the speech short to avoid blubbering. It was tough to fight back the tears and keep my voice from cracking, but somehow I graciously maintained my composure.

Also inducted that evening was a middle linebacker from Baltimore by the name of Mike Davidson. He was a tough and smart defensive player who played for the Baltimore Eagles and their 1979 championship team. He never played college football but played in the league until he was forty-six years old. I remembered him as one tough son of a gun who could have earned a spot on the Colts defense from the 1950s. Tough guys like Art Donovan and Bill Pellington would have loved him.

While it seemed the NFL and AFA were light years apart, this was not always the case. There were a number of players and coaches enshrined in both organizations. It just showed the thin line that separated fame and fortune. If not for a twist of fate, no one knew where his career would, could or should have taken him. That thought always brought to mind Joe Gilliam, Greg Hare, and Ron Meehan, my unsung mentors. I learned their lessons well.

Driving home from Canton, I pondered my good fortune and wondered how many more highlights were ahead and where I would find them. John promised a taste of the big-time and he delivered. I couldn't help but wonder if there was more to be tasted. Even the proverbial cup of coffee would taste just fine. I just hoped that John never lost my phone number when pouring.

CHAPTER 11
O' CANADA, EH!

Every couple of years, there seemed to be a fork in the road, namely my career path. By 1994, I was beginning to think Robert Frost was my career counselor. He didn't need to point out the road less traveled because it's the one that I always seemed to take.

As always, a simple telephone call provided directions. All I had to do was pick up the phone, then pick up my feet. This time the caller was Lance Garth, fellow official, and good friend from my first college DIV I crews.

"Hey, Lou, can you put me up for a night or two next weekend?" Lance asked expectantly.

"Sure, buddy, no problem. Passing through or visiting in the area?"

"Job interview with the CFL (Canadian Football League) at BWI (Baltimore Washington International airport) on Saturday. If you're interested, I can make a phone call to see if I can get you an appointment," Lance added.

"Anytime day or night, buddy. Just get me a name and number," I replied excitedly. Lance explained that the CFL would be expanding to a minimum of three teams in the United Sates for the 1994 season. That necessitated a pool of qualified officials in the US to work those games exclusively.

The odds for Lance looked favorable. He had a recommendation from a friend who was a CFL legend. Dave Ritchie, former head coach of the Winnipeg Blue Bombers, had won three Grey Cups and was elected to the CFL Hall of Fame. Like any business, it helped to be connected. Dave wasn't going to be our calling card. He was going to be our trump card, our ace in the hole, or so we hoped. It would be like applying for a job with the NFL and having a recommendation from Vince Lombardi. Time to stock my fridge with Molson Canadian. Lance and I were headed for the Grey Cup.

That following week before heading down I-95, Lance called with the good news. "Lou, you got an interview. Feel free to drop our names if you think it will help," he prompted. We knew this was just the first step with no guarantees. Just like any fledging player, we only wanted a tryout to prove ourselves.

That Friday night before our interviews, we prepped with basic information about the CFL, mainly the nuances between the NFL and the CFL. Canadian football evolved from Canadian rugby in the 1860s. At the time, it was distinctly separate from the American version that was a rugby-soccer hybrid. We wanted to appear knowledgeable about the Canadian game. We wanted to show the league officials that we did our homework before the big exam. While both the NFL and CFL featured tackling, blocking, running, and passing, there were enough differences that had us shaking our heads. Perhaps, the test was not going to be as easy as we thought.

The CFL field was longer and wider; 110 x 65 yards with a midfield at fifty-five yards and end zones twenty yards deep. The

NFL field was 100 x 53 1/3 yards with a midfield at fifty yards and end zones ten yards deep. The CFL's goalposts were at the front of the end zone like the early years of the NFL.

While there were seven officials on the field as in the NFL, mechanics would have to be adjusted to cover the larger playing surface that included two additional players. In the CFL, there were twelve players for each side as opposed to eleven in the NFL. All backfield players were allowed to move toward the line of scrimmage before the snap, regardless of their horizontal position. As in flag football where passing was paramount, there was going to be a lot of movement to track before and after the snap of the ball.

In the CFL, the offense had three downs per possession to gain ten yards for a first down (four in the NFL), and two timeouts per game (three per half in the NFL). The CFL game clock stopped for every play at the three-minute warning in the second and fourth quarters.

In the CFL, there were no fair catches or touchbacks. The kicking team was awarded a rouge, a single point, if the receiving team was unable to run a kickoff, punt, or missed field goal out of its end zone. Once a rouge was awarded, the receiving team got the ball at the 40-yard line as a result of the play.

On punt returns, the receiver could catch the ball in the air, catch it off a bounce, or pick it up off the ground after letting it fall. To protect the punt receivers from being bulldozed into the turf, the punting team had to provide a five-yard buffer zone. Infractions resulted in a ten-yard penalty.

The following morning as we drove down to the hotel, I had butterflies in my stomach. This was my shot at the big-time, and I was nervous. The CFL was professional football, just a smaller stage than the NFL. It didn't matter if the games were played in Canada or Casablanca.

In a few months, I wanted to be standing at the 55-yard line with my hat over my heart when they played both national anthems. Hell, I was ready to sing both anthems if that's what it took to get on the field. I could easily do it, but first I had to pass the audition.

On interview day, I met with Donald Barker, supervisor of officials for the CFL, emphasizing my NCAA experience at all levels, my ability to adapt to rules changes in different leagues, and my supervision of officials for the USFFA. For extra measure, I plugged myself as the author of the USFFA rulebook.

The interview delved into my background, covering marital status, finances, arrests, and substance abuse. The last question concerned travel, which to a football official was a required formality. At any level of the game, if you didn't want to travel, you didn't want to officiate. Barker advised that he was interviewing applicants from around the US and would respond in a few days. On the way back to my house, Lance and I talked about the different questions Barker had asked us. We were confident about our chances. At home I waited with my fingers crossed.

A week later Lance called with an update. "Lou, I didn't make the cut. So much for my miraculous connection," he grumbled in a bitter tone. "How about yourself?"

"I got invited to the clinic in Birmingham," I replied sheepishly almost apologetically. I felt bad for Lance, but he quickly realized he wasn't in the right place at the right time. That was the nature of the business.

◆ ◆ ◆

Things in the CFL were moving fast. The league wanted to expand to possibly five teams based on the success of its first US franchise in 1993, the Sacramento Gold Miners. The rumor was that four or five teams would be added for the 1994 season with a number of them located in the South. Since Birmingham was rumored to be the league headquarters in the US, it was the logical place to hold the clinic.

Two weeks later, I gathered with twenty-nine other CFL hopefuls for a weekend clinic. The agenda included interviews, seminars on CFL football, and a video rules test. I graded high on the rules test that had applicants watching video replays and applying CFL rules. Likewise, I thought my interviews went smoothly.

Back home, I was feeling confident that I would be offered a position. The phone was going to ring any minute and lead me down the less traveled road. A week later, I was notified by the league via the US Postal Service that my services as a field official would not be needed due to limited expansion. There would only be three new teams, the Las Vegas Posse, Shreveport Pirates, and the Baltimore Stallions.

What the hell just happened? I received a Dear Lou letter from the CFL. A phone call would have sufficed, I fumed in disbelief. Professional football was rightfully returning to Baltimore, and I was on the outside looking in. It was time to act.

A few days after I was waived by the CFL, I contacted the league office and asked if they needed help in recruiting a chain crew, commonly called the chain gang, for the Stallions home games. In the NFL, the crews were recruited and provided by the home team. In the CFL, those tasks belonged to the league. After one phone call, I was on my way to becoming the boss man on the chain gang. The league was happy to have a point of contact in Baltimore. Now I had to roll up my sleeves and roll out my Rolodex.

My first call was to Larry Yocum. For twenty years, he had been assigning chain crews and clock operators for the

University of Maryland Terrapins. He provided the contacts that I desperately needed and gave me invaluable insight into the inner workings of the chain crew. "Lou, I can surround you with some great people, but what position do you want?" he asked before hanging up.

"Let me think about that," I replied somewhat bemused. I had never seriously thought about working on the chain crew. I had always been a field official. That led to another dilemma. Did I really want to be on the field outside the white lines?

Being a member of the chain gang was technically part of the officiating crew. In reality, chain gangs were a separate team treated like second-class citizens by the league. You were on the field but not inside the white lines, invisible lines of a caste system not to be crossed. Not only were you carrying the chains, but you were also shackled to the sideline. No matter, I concluded it was still better than sitting in the stands.

That thought swirled around my head for a few days until I realized that it was bullshit. I was an experienced official with references and a resume to back up my claim as one of the best on the field. If the league wouldn't back me, maybe my hometown would support my cause. It sounded good, but I needed a plan. As always, I first made a phone call. That always got the ball rolling.

I called Lance Garth and asked if he was interested. "Nice opportunity, but too far to travel for one's day work," he chuckled. When I mentioned my angst about not being selected for the field, his voice took a more sober tone. "Lou, it's right in your backyard. Give it a shot and see what happens. You know how the game works. Anything can happen." I listened and acted. I now had a simple plan. Dial direct!

The next day I called the Baltimore Stallions front office. In football lingo, it was a Hail Mary pass, a desperate last-second throw in the end zone to miraculously win the game. One thing was in my favor. I was never shy when it came to dealing with strangers. When the front office opened, I picked up the phone, dialed the number, and asked to speak with Jim Speros, the team owner.

"Who should I say is calling?" the receptionist asked politely.

"Lou Hammond, CFL representative for field officials," I replied firmly without any hesitation. While it could have been a total bullshit story, part of it was true. I was in charge of the chain gang.

"Lou, what can I do for you?" Jim replied casually, much to my surprise and delight. Here was a man who took his own phone calls. I liked him already. I quickly explained the situation with the chain gang and asked for a point of contact in an effort to keep the conversation alive. "If there's anything else we can do just let us know," he added after giving me a name and number in field operations.

I quickly took the bait. "Well, Mr. Speros, as a matter of fact, there is something you could do," I countered. After explaining my situation with the CFL, I made my sales pitch, my Hail Mary pass.

"Jim, I'm a Baltimore native who grew up with the Colts and want to get on the field as part of the officiating crew," I pleaded politely. "Can you pull some strings for me?"

"Lou, as a new owner, I'm feeling my way with how things are done in the league. Let me see what I can do," he replied cordially. "Someone will get back to you." My pass fell incomplete. I knew no one would contact me; my gambit was over. It was time to put the finishing touches on the chain gang.

That task involved asking Larry if he would select and assign the chain crew for the home games. Eager to be part of professional football in Baltimore, he readily agreed. Although the pay was minimal as expected, we were an integral part of the game, marking the down and the line of scrimmage, tracking the line-to-gain for a first down, recording penalties called by the on-field officials, and marking the start of the drive by the offense for use by media.

As the supervisor of the crew, I even managed to get my father a job as a grip man. He held the cable used for the game clock on the scoreboard. While I had reservations about being outside the lines, my dad was thrilled to be part of game day. For all the support he provided over the years, he deserved a Super Bowl gig, if not that than a Grey Cup.

Pro football returns with the Baltimore CFL Colts.
Owner Jim Speros in center with helmet.

CHAPTER 12
THE GUNSLINGER

With one exhibition game under our belts, the chain gang was ready for opening day. On Saturday, July 16, 1994, the Baltimore Stallions and the Calgary Stampeders took the field at Memorial Stadium in front of nearly 40,000 fans. Although the Stallions were easily herded and lassoed in a 42-16 loss, the game proved that summer football could compete with the summer baseball, namely the Baltimore Orioles.

Once again, it was exhilarating to be on the field at Memorial Stadium for a professional football game. The air was charged as the crowd emitted a deep buzzing noise like a swarm of agitated bees. After both the Canadian and American anthems, the stands erupted with deafening cheers that lasted through the player introductions. The largest outdoor insane asylum was once again open for business and accepting new patients. For a minute, I thought the Beatles had taken the field for a reunion concert.

When the Baltimore Colts Marching Band played the Colts fight song, people screamed at the top of their lungs. For a second, I thought the fans were going to storm the field. The sight of Johnny U and other Colt legends on the field blessed the event and revved up the crowd another notch. I had goose bumps on my arms as I surveyed the unfolding spectacle. Standing on the sidelines, I remembered with a smile those Sundays sitting in the stands with my dad as the Colts were introduced.

Opting not to participate actively in the chain crew, I became a gunslinger by default. The actual title of the position was pistol mechanic. *What in hell was a pistol mechanic?* I mused. I would soon find out. In the CFL, the pistol mechanic was the official who fired the gun at the end of each quarter. It didn't sound too dangerous for someone whose marksmanship was limited to water pistols and cap guns, but it proved to be a daunting task for a novice.

In the 1920s, the CFL and NFL used starting pistols to end each quarter at a time when the stadium clock, if there was one, was not the official time on the field. With its loud and piercing crack, the pistol shot also served to avoid confusion with whistles that were used to end plays and air horns that indicated penalties. Eventually flags replaced air horns, but whistles and the starting gun remained. In 1994, the NFL discontinued the use of starting pistols when officials were prohibited from carrying guns on airplanes.

However, the CFL did not follow suit. To avoid any travel restrictions, they simply had the home team provide a pistol. While I was in the locker room with Larry and the crew, the Stallions director of field operations approached me, carrying a large wooden box under his arm.

"Lou, here's your piece," he stated calmly as he opened the box and handed me a pistol. Hell, it wasn't a pistol; it was a cannon. I was startled by the size and weight of the weapon.

It immediately reminded me of Inspector Harry Callahan's .44 Magnum from Clint Eastwood's movie *Dirty Harry*. According to Harry in the opening scenes, it was the most powerful handgun in the world. To me, it looked and felt like it.

As if on cue, the crew jumped up from their stools with their hands in the air. "Please mister, don't shoot. Just take the money and leave peacefully," one the crew screeched in a fake Texas drawl. The room erupted in laughter.

"Hey, Lou, welcome to the CFL . . . Carrying Firearms Legally," someone yelled from the back of the room. The joke was on me, and all I could do was laugh with them. Not only was it one of the funniest pranks that I ever witnessed, but it also helped to relieve some of the pregame tension. Why the nerves? This was our debut in Baltimore, and everybody from owners down to the vendors wanted it to be perfect.

"Do I get a holster to go with this thing?" I asked nervously with sweaty palms. For God's sake, I was a fisherman, not a hunter.

"Lou, relax. Here how it works," the director advised cautiously. "A minute before the end of each quarter, someone will hand you the gun. Stand close to the sideline away from people and slowly squeeze the trigger when the game clock winds to zero. After that, hand back the gun. Whatever you do, don't hold the gun in the air or above your head. You'll go deaf. Keep it at your side at an angle away from your body."

At the end of the first quarter with gun in hand, I nervously watched the clock wind down to zero. Stepping to the sideline, I slowly squeezed the trigger. Boom! The gun jerked violently (I didn't know if it was the gun or me) and thundered like a cannon from a Fort McHenry reenactment. I quickly looked around to see if any bodies had fallen to the ground. The last thing Baltimore needed was another homicide, especially at a football game. But I had to admit, that scenario would have been a great plot for Barry Levinson's TV series Homicide: Life on the Street. The drama about homicide cops was currently being filmed in Baltimore. Maybe, I could make my acting debut on the show.

I handed back the gun nonchalantly and thought that my first shot went rather well. Nobody was killed or injured. Perhaps, this was the perfect job for me. I only had to work four times a game and keep track of the chain crew. Of course, easier said than done. In my heart, I instinctively knew that nothing comes easy, whether be the game of life or the game of football. *No surprises. I've seen it all*, I thought, echoing the comment from my sandlot days. What could possibly go wrong on a day like today? I would soon find out.

Other than the heat and humidity, the game proceeded without any incidents until late in the second quarter. That's when I noticed a ball boy running in my direction.

"Lou, your balls are soft," he frantically squealed as he caught his breath.

I quickly looked around to ensure that I wasn't part of a practical joke. Nobody was giggling but everyone was looking in our direction. "Hey, buddy, what the hell are you talking about?" I asked incredulously.

"The game balls are losing air. The ref keeps throwing them to the sidelines. They said I should see you," he added nervously, handing me a leather ball that felt like a day-old birthday balloon. I had no idea who *they* were, but somebody had to do something before a disaster occurred.

"You have the gauges and the pumps. Check the pressure. If it's low, pump it up. Keep the balls rotating until halftime, then I'll talk with the referee," I advised calmly, standing there with a gun in my hand. After the ball boy left, I chuckled. He must have been scared to death when he saw me ready to shoot.

Expect the unexpected was a creed for all football officials. I had seen under and over inflated footballs in high school but never at this level. In the pros, the referee or his designee routinely and regularly inspected game balls. It was just one of the many duties that officials had to perform outside the white lines.

The CFL football, made by Spaulding, was slightly larger than the NFL ball with white stripes at the tips. It was a professional grade football that shouldn't have been losing air. To my relief, I never saw the ball boy again. Nobody bothered to follow it up with me, and I didn't press the issue because it wasn't my responsibility. The problem could have been defective materials, the weather, or even tampering.

For those who doubt the latter, check out *Deflategate*, the 2014 AFC championship game between the New England Patriots and the NFL team from Indianapolis. What was their name again? Hmm, I always seem to forget. The bottom line is that deflated footballs are easier to deform and grip. Following the ballyhooed incident, the NFL instituted more stringent rules for the inspection, authentication, and distribution of game balls before, during, and after the game.

To my delight, I thoroughly enjoyed my time with the chain crew. Although I had no feelers from the league about becoming a field official in 1994 or 1995, I was content to wait and see what happened. Most importantly, I was having fun and meeting a lot of wonderful people who would become lifelong friends.

But all good things must end, and the good times for me ended on November 6, 1995.

◆ ◆ ◆

On that historic day in Baltimore football, Art Modell, owner of the Cleveland Browns, announced that he was moving his team to Baltimore at the end of the current season. Hooray! Huzzah! The NFL was finally returning to Baltimore after a twelve-year hiatus. Pour out the Molson and crack open up a Natty Boh to the Colts fight song!

On the flipside, pass me a box of tissues. Sadly, the Baltimore Stallions instantly became a footnote to football history. They would be the only CFL team in North America to win the Grey Cup, and Baltimore would be the only city to have won championships in the CFL and NFL.

Like all Baltimore football fans, I was jubilant, but also out of a job. If anyone deserved sympathy, it was Jim Speros, Baltimore's unsung hero. At a steep price, he erased any doubt in the minds of NFL owners that Baltimore deserved an NFL franchise. During its two-year existence, the franchise appeared twice in the Grey Cup. Most importantly, they were a box office hit. In 1994, they drew a league high average attendance of 35,000 fans for home games. In 1995, they were second best with an average of 30,000 fans per home game. Not bad figures when visiting players were as recognizable as the prime minister of Canada. In comparison, the Colts in 1984 averaged 38,336 fans for home games, a generous figure for fans who found themselves floundering in a sea of empty seats.

When the cash register rings, the owners sing. As soon as Modell made this announcement, registers around the city choired a mellifluous tune. Ravens apparel with the winged shield was literally flying off the shelves. Meanwhile, Jim Speros was singing the Baltimore blues. For the two playoff games that year at Memorial Stadium, the team literally had to give tickets away to draw respectable crowds of 21,040 and 30,217.

On November 19, 1995, the Grey Cup headed to Baltimore as the Stallions defeated the Calgary Stampeders 37-20 at

Taylor Field, Regina, Saskatchewan, in front of 52,564 fans. No TV crews from Baltimore were dispatched to cover the game. A week later the scheduled Grey Cup celebration at the Inner Harbor went largely unnoticed by the media and the fans. Only a couple hundred die-hard football fans attended. Jim and the Stallions deserved a better fate.

Although I never met Jim Speros, I frequently watched him along the sidelines and tried to eavesdrop on his conversations. Like Johnny U, Jim was a man of the people. He mixed easily with strangers and was always quick with a smile, a handshake, and a kind word. Too bad Jim wasn't available in 1972 when Bob Irsay acquired the Colts. He would have been a beloved owner. He had a knack for doing things right. To his credit, he embraced the history of the Baltimore Colts and invited the old Colts to be sideline guests. For the beginning of 1994 season, the team was named the Baltimore CFL Colts until the NFL filed a court junction to prohibit use of the name. That didn't stop the fans from shouting "C-O-L-T-S" when the team was introduced before kickoff.

Baltimore was always the right town for a football team. In the case of the Colts, Bob Irsay wasn't the right owner. At press conferences, he frequently appeared drunk and argued defiantly with the press in regard to moving the team. Yes, Baltimore needed a new football stadium, but holding the city hostage was not the way to earn trust in a blue-collar town.

After seeing Bob's petulant behavior at press conference, I always wondered how he made his millions in the heating and ventilation business. Fans, the press, and even the players viewed him as a bully. He ran roughshod over everybody and everything in the organization. Did he run his business the way he ran his football team? No one ever commented. One thing for certain, he always vented in heated exchanges with the local media about the state of the team. He never learned to keep his cool.

After his first season as owner, Irsay traded Johnny U to the San Diego Chargers and waived other Colts who had formed the nucleus of the team. How could he trade away the greatest Colt of all time? Baltimore without Johnny U was like Baltimore with no beer, Natty Boh, of course! With the Stallions demise, Baltimoreans also lost its taste for Molson, Canada's premier beer. Too bad for Baltimore beer drinkers because the beer went well with steamed crabs.

And speaking of steamed crabs, Baltimoreans felt no sympathy for Cleveland Browns fans, especially after the way they pissed and moaned when Art changed his home address. To their credit, the wailing and the gnashing of teeth worked a miracle. Cleveland got to keep the team name, the colors, and the history with the promise of a new team. All we got when the Colts moved was the advice from NFL commissioner Paul Tagliabue to build a museum instead of a football stadium. With that attitude, it's no wonder the names Tagliabue and Irsay quickly became euphemisms for a bowel movement among Baltimore fans.

My CFL career officially ended on November 12, 1995, when the Stallions played for the South Championship at Memorial Stadium. A week later, the Stallions played in the Grey Cup without the hometown chain gang. I watched the game on cable and ironically noticed that Baltimore's first and last official games in the CFL were against Calgary. Both times, Doug Flutie, the inspiration for my Hail Mary call to Jim Speros, was the quarterback.

Like the Stallions, I was now part of Baltimore's football heritage, but I didn't want to fade into the pages of history. With the arrival of the Ravens, I hoped there was a place for me in the NFL. I just had to wait for that call.

CHAPTER 13
PINBALL FOOTBALL

When my tenure with the American Football Association ended in 2000, I had an opening in my football calendar. As usual, I didn't have to wait long to fill the void. In my world of football officiating, the next great adventure was just a phone call away, or at least that was the scenario during my career. While I couldn't predict when a call would occur, I was guaranteed that it would follow the blue highways of professional football. In this case, professional football loosely translated as the game of football wherever and whenever it was played for money, no matter how much or how little.

In January 2000, I received the invitation to hit the road once again. "Lou, are you ready for some spring football." On the other end of the line was Frank Kosman. I had worked with Frank during a DIV II playoff game a few years prior. I knew that Frank lived in Philadelphia, so I immediately had visions of working college scrimmages and inter-squad games in the

Mid-Atlantic area, hopefully somewhere near my home. With any luck, it could be a major DIV I school such as Rutgers, Penn State, Maryland, Navy, or Virginia.

"Where and when?" I quickly replied.

"Richmond, Virginia, at the end of April."

"Scrimmages or inter-squad games?" I asked anxiously, thinking Richmond Spiders.

"No, no, not the Spiders but the Richmond Speed."

"What in the hell is the Richmond Speed?" I asked bewildered. I quickly had my answer. He was talking about indoor football, or pinball football as I called it.

◆ ◆ ◆

The AF2, short for Arenafootball2, was the brainchild of Jim Foster, founder of the Arena Football League (AFL) in 1986. Foster hoped to cash in on the success of the AFL by bringing arena football to mid-sized markets. The idea had been tried in the 1990s with moderate success. Ultimately, it proved there was a niche for the game if marketed properly. Now was the time for the riverboat gambler of arena football to play his hand. Only this time, he had an ace up his sleeve. In 1990, Foster was granted a US patent on arena football's distinctive rules and customized equipment, namely the end zone cross bar with rebound nets and the padded sideline barriers. Frank had been officiating AFL games since the late '80s and was now working phones in an administrative capacity. The bottom line was that the new league needed officials.

After getting the seal of approval from Mrs. Hammond, I called Frank and accepted his offer. After eight years of marriage, Kelly realized she was hitched to a football junkie and was glad to get rid of me for one more night of the week. With the games being played on Friday nights, I could leave Friday afternoon for Richmond and return home that night. That's what the travel plan looked like on paper. For anyone driving on I-95 south of Washington DC, there were no guarantees of arriving in a timely manner on any Friday. The stretch of interstate highway between Washington and Richmond was one of the worst traffic hot spots in the nation. If there was a downside to Frank's offer, this was it. Then again, the chance to officiate professional football outweighed the three-hour commute each way.

Two weeks after mailing my application to join the AF2, I received a letter welcoming me to the staff of the inaugural season. Players were to receive between $200 and $500 per game with a minimum $50 victory bonus; officials would receive $225 per game. This parity with the players told me two things. One, there wasn't a lot of money in the coffers, and two, they valued their officials. Of course, I knew the former was the bold truth. Either way, I liked this parity with the players and promptly decided this should be the pay scale for the NFL. Imagine that? No way owners in the NFL could.

In order to share the wealth, or lack of it, I called the league office and asked if they needed more officials. They weren't asking; they were begging. Since the league had not established a track record, qualified officials were not knocking down the door to join. I immediately recommended Chris Garth, son of my good friend Lance Garth. Chris had experience at DIV II and had recently moved from Massachusetts to Stafford, Virginia, for a teaching position. Only one hour from Richmond, it was the perfect scenario for Chris, and I liked having a crewmember that I could trust.

The following month, I attended an all-expense paid officials' training seminar in Jacksonville, Florida, which coincided with the annual league meeting. The three-day conference included the history of the league and the unique rules of indoor football according to the gospel of Jim Foster.

"Gentleman, welcome to the future of professional football. We're moving forward by moving backward. We're returning the game to the small towns that gave birth to professional football," the director of officiating joyfully proclaimed to the assembly of wide-eyed officials. Hell, I wasn't totally sold on the idea but the unbridled enthusiasm of everyone in the room and at the clinic was contagious.

That year there were fifteen teams in two conferences. The National Conference had Augusta Stallions, Norfolk Nighthawks, Jacksonville Tomcats, Carolina Rhinos, Richmond Speed, Charleston Swamp Foxes, Greensboro Prowlers, and Roanoke Steam. The American Conference included Alabama Steeldogs, Arkansas Twisters, Pensacola Barracudas, Tallahassee Thunder, Tennessee Valley Vipers, Tulsa Talons, and Quad City Steamwheelers who should have been more appropriately named Steamrollers.

The sixteen-game schedule ran from April through July. In August, the top four teams in each conference made the playoffs. The season culminated with the Arena Cup, the AF2 Super Bowl. With names like Tomcats, Rhinos, and Swamp Foxes, the league reminded me of minor league baseball. Those teams marketed whacky names and wackier mascots to the delight of the fans who flocked to the ballparks. AF2 successfully followed suit. The Speed mascot was Speedy. One of the team logos was a cheetah outstretched over a black asphalt road. I loved it and couldn't wait to see what the rest of the league had to offer.

◆ ◆ ◆

During the startup year, officials worked games in their local area and did not travel to other cities in the league. I already knew that I would be working home games at the Richmond Coliseum, home of Richmond's River Dogs hockey team.

Emphasis at the clinic was on the field and the rules. The arena football field, the size of a hockey rink, was a padded surface 85 feet wide and 50 yards long with eight-yard end zones. Goalposts were nine-feet wide with a crossbar height of 15 feet (NFL goalposts are 18 1/2 wide with the crossbar at 10 feet). The goal side rebound nets were 30 feet wide by 32 feet high. The bottom of the nets was eight feet above the ground. Sideline barriers (dasher boards in ice hockey) were 48 inches high and made of high-density foam rubber.

The team consisted of eight players on the field, a twenty-man active roster, and a four-man inactive roster. Players went both ways on offense and defense except for the kicker, the quarterback, the offensive specialist (the kick returner on defense), and two defensive specialists.

Kickoffs were from the goal line. Punting was illegal. On fourth down, a team could go for a first down, touchdown, or field goal. The receiving team could field any kickoff or missed field goal that rebounded off the nets. Any untouched kickoff that was out of bounds was placed at the 20-yard line or the point where it exited the field, whichever was more advantageous to the receiving team. In other words, you didn't want to kick the ball out of bounds. Any pass that hit the nets was inbounds. The ball could be caught off the net and advanced.

On an unsuccessful field goal attempt or kickoff, the ball remained in play unless it was out of bounds or the player recovering the ball was down by contact or scored. On kicking plays, except for extra-point attempts, either team could gain possession of the ball and advance it. The rule was similar to blocked kicks in outdoor football.

The arena game was all about scoring, and scoring was all about passing. To maximize offensive output, rules were implemented to handcuff defenses. All defenses were required to play a 3-2 Monster Formation that consisted of three defensive linemen, two linebackers, two cornerbacks, and one safety. Linebackers could not blitz and were required to stay in boxes (perimeter areas) behind the line of scrimmage. Defensive linemen were prevented from using certain shedding techniques to penetrate the offensive line.

The season home opener on April 28, 2000, pitted the Speed against the Augusta Stallions as a near sellout crowd of 10,631 got its first taste of indoor football. From what I saw, the fans got their money's worth. As I looked around the arena, I just hoped people brought their earplugs. The pregame player introductions were deafening. The dazzling light show, and special effects were worthy of the World Wrestling Federation.

"It's go time," the team's rallying cry and loud rock music continually blasted from the speakers. The cheerleaders performed at a non-stop frantic pace. Who knows, maybe, they were hoping to be scouted by the NFL. If there weren't NFL cheerleader scouts in the stands, I was more than willing to fill out an after-action report. They would have graded out at A+. They didn't stop cheering until the coliseum had emptied. They probably burned more calories than the players. Everything was loud and up close, and that included the coaches who were allowed on the field. At times, it seemed as if we were playing on a billiards table.

Richmond scored the game's first touchdown. Unfortunately, that was their only highlight. Augusta scored 37 unanswered points en route to a 44-13 victory. After the game, fans were invited on the field to mingle with the players, take pictures, and collect autographs. Who knows, maybe someday one of the players would be a Super Bowl hero and an autographed card would fetch a king's ransom on eBay. All they had to do was remember Kurt Warner, the poster child for indoor football. Kurt went from bagging groceries to arena football. From there, it was an unbelievable ride to the NFL where he won Super Bowl XXXIV and the MVP award. After his career, the two-time NFL MVP was inducted into the Arena Football Hall of Fame and the NFL Hall of Fame.

Back in our locker room, the crew filled out postgame reports and discussed the game. It seemed like there was an inordinate amount of field conferences regarding penalties. That was expected. With the disparity in rules with the outdoor game, we wholeheartedly agreed that we wanted to get it right. We started slowly and finished with a flourish. By the fourth quarter, the crew was comfortable with the pace, the plays, and the penalties. I could see it in their eyes and hear it in their voices.

♦ ♦ ♦

On the drive home, I was pleased with our performance. Like the fans and players, we were learning the ropes. The players had daytime jobs and could only practice in the evenings, so play selection and execution needed some fine-tuning. That problem would be solved with time. However, there wasn't a lot of spare time anywhere in the league. I can remember officiating one pregame scrimmage as coaches and players familiarized themselves with the game. That event took place outdoors on a high school field that had been cut down to arena specifications.

The bottom line was that fans seemed to have a good time. Heck, I had a good time and was looking forward to the next home game. I couldn't believe that after one game, I was sold on arena football. I really liked the meet-and-greet with the players after the game. That was a great way to sell the game and build a dedicated fan base. I fondly remember those days when my dad and I would drive to the Colts summer practice facility at Western Maryland College. After practice, the players would mill around the field and mingle with the fans. It was like a family reunion.

Replaying the night's game in my mind, I laughed out loud at our most obvious gaffe, a moment worthy of any blooper reel. From the outset, it was obvious to the crew that our referee was not used to wearing a microphone when announcing fouls. While we were all learning on the fly with self-effacing grins, we didn't know just how comical a common play could be.

Early in the third quarter, I threw a flag for holding on number 52 of the defense. Nothing funny there until it was announced to the fans.

"Holding number 52 offense. Fifteen-yard penalty from the line of scrimmage," referee Bob Picher declared confidently.

After Bob's microphone was off, I leaned over to him.

"Bob, it was holding against the defense."

Bob stepped forward and turned on the microphone. "Correction. Holding number 55 on the defense."

As the Stallions head coach was screaming that he didn't have a number 55 on the team, I once again leaned over to Bob. "Bob, it was number 52, not number 55."

Unaware that his microphone was still hot, he vented his frustration. "Ah, Lou, fuck it. I'm done wearing this stupid thing."

That Monday, a memo was distributed by the league office reminding referees to familiarize themselves with the proper use of the field microphone and the proper language for announcing fouls. The crew laughed about that call for the rest of the season. By that time, even Bob thought it was funny. He had become an AF2 legend.

For the rest of the ride home, I couldn't get the Kurt Warner story out of my head. I had this silly notion that if it happened to Kurt, it could happen to anybody, even an AF2 official. Dreams died hard in professional football, no matter what level.

That notion and Kurt's rags-to-riches story was reinforced a month later when the Speed signed Shayne Graham to a two-game contract as he prepped for an NFL tryout. The Virginian who played at Virginia Tech was the Big East Conference Special Teams Player of the Year in 1999. He was the kind of beloved local hero who could win the hearts of the fans and help fill the arena. During his career, he was 68-of-93 (73.1 percent) in field goals and set a Big East record with 97 consecutive successful extra points. He couldn't miss, or could he?

In his debut against the Arkansas Twisters on May 26, I watched him warm up as I inspected the field. Pregame field inspection was paramount just as with the outdoors version. The checklist included carpet seams, padding on the dasher boards, tautness of end zone nets, and the plumb of the goalposts. If anything was loose or peeling, out came the glue guns.

Without a doubt, Shayne had an NFL leg. His powerful kicks sailed from one end to the arena to the other. I thought he could probably make a field goal from the parking lot. But as the game progressed, his kicking skills regressed. In a 60-21 loss, he missed two field goals from 36 and 44 yards, and two of three extra points. After the game, he told reporters that arena football was a big adjustment regarding the timing of the kicker as he moved to the ball after the snap. I could have told him that indoors affected everybody's timing one way or another.

While his arena career lasted only one game, Graham went on to have a sixteen-year career in the NFL that saw him kick for fifteen different teams. That was nearly half of the teams in the league. In 2005, he was First Team All-Pro and selected for the Pro Bowl. With the Cincinnati Bengals, he even had his own bobblehead. If that's not success, I don't know what is.

In the end, the AF2 had its own poster child in Shayne and every arena player had hope. As for me, I always loved those gritty and gutsy success stories from the outhouse to penthouse. In Shayne, I had another inspirational role model for my officiating career.

That weekend I read an article in a Richmond newspaper about the game. Harry Feuerstein, the Speed owner, was disappointed that fans didn't see real arena football because of his team's lack of scoring. Harry and the fans didn't have to wait long. That same week the Pensacola Barracudas outscored the Tennessee Valley Vipers 66-59 in overtime while the Jacksonville Tomcats slipped by the Carolina Rhinos 59-56. During week nine, the Quad Cities Steamwheelers (oops, I meant Steamrollers) scored 103 points against the Greensboro Prowlers. As for the Speed, they lost the next home game to the Charleston Swamp Foxes 51-44. I hoped Harry liked those numbers. In most cases, the final scores resembled college basketball games.

The perfect souvenir for any arena football fan.
Easy to fumble into the stands.

CHAPTER 14
A FAN CLUB

What I really loved about arena football in that first year was the fans. They were a hardcore group of about 6,000 to 8,000 fanatics who loved the team, the players, and the city. They were boisterous and fun but never rude or unruly. I don't know if it was the Southern hospitality of the capital of the South, but it made attending a game a true family experience. Even when berating an official for a perceived bad call, there seemed to be a soft edge as if to say, "Hey, ref, don't take us seriously. We're just having some fun."

Fans clubs had their favorite players, and one group had a particular favorite official, namely me. During the third game of the season, I noticed a father and son with front row seats who cheered for everything, even calls from the officials. During a TV timeout, the father reached out and tapped me on the shoulder. "Ref, you need a drink? Looks like things are heating up out there," he asked excitedly, leaning over the dasher board.

"Yeah, a gin and tonic," I joked as sweat poured down my face. Under the indoor lights, the plastic field radiated heat like an oven.

"Nah, I'm serious. Water, a Coke, name your poison," he asked sincerely. When he said poison, the red flag shot straight up the pole. I could see the headline now: *Football Ref Poisoned by Irate Fan*. The tabloids would have a field day with the story. The TV ratings for arena football would probably soar. There would probably be a book and movie deal for the father and son, and maybe a statue of me in front of the coliseum.

"Yeah, make it a cold Coke," I responded graciously.

I politely declined the offer of a hot dog to go along with the beverage, citing that I had to maintain the appearance of neutrality. No doubt, there would have been a league memo on Monday about officials accepting gratuities from the fans if I had accepted the offer.

At the next TV timeout, I was waved over to the sideline and handed an ice-cold Coke. I took a small sip to see if it tasted funny, then took a big gulp before handing it back. "Thanks. That hit the spot. Appreciate it. You guys are going to get my vote for fans of the year," I joked.

"No problem, Lou. Glad to be of service," the man replied with a wide grin. This was a fan's fan, a man who read every line in the game program, even the names of the officials. I didn't know if I was supposed to encourage that type of behavior by fans, but it resulted in a two-person Lou Hammond fan club.

◆ ◆ ◆

As the season progressed and the sodas and snacks kept appearing, I wondered how I could repay the continued kindness of my fan club. *What does every football fan want more than anything in the world?* I wondered. The answer was right in front of me. *A football, of course!* And it couldn't be just any football. It had to be an official Spaulding AF2 football. Light tan in color with black stitches, a blue diagonal strip running lengthwise, and the unique AF2 logo, it was by far the coolest looking football in any league. It was a ball that would look good on anybody's bookcase. The problem was how to transfer it from the field to a fan in the stands.

By the fifth home game of the season, I had solved the problem. Late in the fourth quarter, one of the officials tossed me a football that was being exchanged on the field. I artfully juggled the ball as if it was a hot potato. Making the toss look like a bounce, the ball careened out of my hands and a nanosecond later inexplicably landed into the hands of my youngest fan club member. W. C. Fields would have been proud. The fans in that section of the arena applauded wildly. The rest of the crowd was oblivious to the apparent blooper by an official. My fan club gave me a thumbs-up.

For the remainder of the season, there was always a cold Coke waiting for me during a TV timeout. "Anything for my pal, Lou," the father would announce to the delight of the fans next to him. He was enjoying this connection to the game, and I wasn't going to burst his bubble. Before the last game of the season, he presented me with a box of home-baked cookies. Thank goodness he didn't know it was my birthday.

As for the AF2 footballs, they filled the air like butterflies during the game. Any balls that entered the stands were the property of the fans. You can imagine the pandemonium every time a ball left the playing field. The melee always reminded me of my teenage days with the teenage soccer fanatics at Radecke Park. These impassioned players, who lived and breathed soccer, were obsessed with the game and the idea of playing pick-up games with a professional soccer ball. With the price of a top-line ball out of reach, they devised a haphazard plan to get one.

That opportunity presented itself at the home games of the Baltimore Bays, Baltimore's professional soccer team from 1967 to 1969. Games were played in the cavernous Memorial Stadium, home of the Colts and Orioles. With an average of six to 8,000 fans per game, there was ample room to roam from section to section and follow the game, or rather the ball in flight.

One fan would strategically position himself in the lower stands and wait. When an errant kick entered the stands, he would quickly grab the ball and toss it toward one of the exits where another fan would catch it and sprint for the exit with security guards and police in hot pursuit. Although the ploy rarely worked, if ever, the chase provided slapstick relief that reminded fans of the Keystone Cops from the silent film era. Unlike the AF2, the league did not have money to spend on souvenirs for fans. Balls entering the stands were to be returned to the field of play.

Fans weren't the only ones who craved the Holy Grail of the AF2. For the sake of the game, my crew once again perfected the art of finding something before it was lost. Each game we found a way for a member of the crew to receive a game ball. With nearly two-dozen footballs stowed along the sidelines for each game, it was inevitable that one or two would find its way into the trash bag in the officials' locker room. To generate goodwill among fans and promote the popularity of AF2 officials, we would give the balls to fans as door prizes at special events or donate them to charities for auctions. I'm sure to this day some lucky recipient is still wondering about some of the autographs on the balls. *Lou, who?* Just another Pied Piper from the AF2!

The first season concluded with a total attendance of over 868,000 fans, an average of 7,200 per game. Some teams like those in the playoffs averaged over 10,000 fans. With regional

TV contracts and support from local business, the league was treading water financially. Deemed a success by owners, the league returned for a second season with thirteen additional franchises. That seemed like good news for fans, players, and officials, but I had my doubts. I had seen it before with minor league football teams. After only one season, the Mean Green Fever was running amuck among arena owners who were waiting in the wings to sing the money anthem. For the AF2, it was the beginning of the end. The greed of the owners didn't allow the game to take root. Instead, they watered down the product with catastrophic results as predicted.

♦ ♦ ♦

In my second season, our crew remained the same. However, with the expansion, we now hit the road for cities other than Richmond. In addition to our game fee, we now received travel expenses that covered a night's stay at a Holiday Inn. While the locations had changed, the faces and places remained the same. We were playing football in venues that housed minor league hockey teams. No matter what the building looked like on the outside, inside they all looked the same. With each game, the field, or rug, appeared to be shrinking. I started feeling claustrophobic every time I left the locker room. Spring was no time for indoor football or indoors anything. Spring was time to stop and smell the roses. As a result, my mind would start to wander before the game. Perhaps, I should have been outside enjoying the spring weather and officiating baseball or softball. If not that, then the garden always needed work.

On the flipside, playing indoors had its pros and cons. While you didn't have to worry about the weather, you still had to worry. Two of my memorable moments in arena football had nothing to do with the action on the field but the action above it.

The first occurred in Albany in 2001 when a long-distance field-goal attempt struck the chandelier scoreboard hanging over the center of the field. The ball ricochetted into the stands with a loud *bang* like someone throwing a basketball against the side of a house with aluminum siding. All eyes looked to the heavens as the colored lights on the scoreboard blinked wildly.

The scoreboard buzzed and vibrated like an alien spaceship ready to land. The crowd held its collective breath in deadly silence, not sure what was going to happen. Was the scoreboard going to suddenly break away from its moorings and drop to the field like a bomb?

"Let's clear the field. I don't like the looks of this," Bob the referee said nervously as the crew huddled off to the side. We nodded in agreement and quickly ushered players to the sidelines. Once the field was cleared, we hustled to the sideline and stood behind the dasher board, ready to hit the ground in case the scoreboard fell. Still looking to the scoreboard, we watched in wonderment as a cloud of gray dust gently floated to the carpet.

"Bob, do you think it's toxic? I asked worriedly.

"Could be. Who knows what's been piling up there for the last ten years? Maybe radioactive pigeon shit," he joked before conferring with coliseum officials and the head coaches.

Walking toward me, I saw him stifling a laugh. "They said the scoreboard was fine. It's just this shit on the field that needs to be removed. Can I call the game because of a dust storm?" he chuckled.

Seconds later, several maintenance crews with industrial-size vacuum cleaners ran on the field and began the cleanup. Fifteen minutes later, the bright green luster of plastic grass returned and play resumed. For the rest of the game, I intermittently gazed up at the to make sure it wasn't swaying or drooping.

The second incident occurred at the Richmond Coliseum in 2002 during a promotion night. Rebounding from their dismal performance in 2000, the Speed reached the Arena Cup in 2001. Although they lost to the Quad Cities Steamwheelers in a 55-51 shootout on the last play of the game, there were enough highlights from the season to produce a highlight reel. To the marketing people, the idea probably sounded like pure genius. In reality, it was a disaster waiting to happen. Obviously, no one in marketing had heard of Disco Demolition Night. To learn from the past, all sports marketing personnel needed a course in sport marketing history.

In between games of a doubleheader between the Detroit Tigers and the hometown Chicago White Sox on July 12, 1979, a Chicago DJ blew up a box of disco records collected from the fans. After the explosion, the sellout crowd (who wouldn't want to blow up disco records) stormed the field, started fires in the outfield, and destroyed everything in its path like a tornado. However, the fuse for the time bomb was actually lit during the late innings of the first game when impatient fans began tossing records onto the field. Vinyl records filled the air like Frisbees. Only these Frisbees were hard plastic disks that could kill or maim.

Midway through the third quarter of the Speed game, I called an offensive foul on a Speed player that squashed a scoring drive in a hotly contested game. Seconds after the referee announced the foul, a barrage of silver plastic disks sliced through the air and rained down on the field.

While the players had helmets and pads for protection, the crew had only striped uniforms that must have looked like a bull's-eye. We sprinted to the sideline benches as the PA announcer warned fans about inappropriate and illegal behavior that could result in fines and arrests. Believe it or not, that did the trick. The incident was over within minutes. I wouldn't have been surprised if the scolded fans had walked down the field to retrieve their souvenirs. Instead, an animated cadre of maintenance people with trash bags speedily removed the debris from the field. In the locker room after the game, the referee had only one announcement; "Lou, next time you make that kind of call, wait for seat cushion night." We roared with laughter.

◆ ◆ ◆

My last season with the AF2 in 2003 was almost the last year of my career, maybe even my life. I noticed the crowds growing smaller with each game and wondered how long the Speed franchise would remain solvent. Regardless of the team's woes, players and officials were professionals who always gave it their best effort. Winning was everything. There was no time to worry about the team's ledgers. We always focused on the game.

For officials, being in the right place at the right time on the field was our article of faith. In arena football, the right place was the center of the field. When the ball was snapped, we instinctively moved to the center to cover our area of responsibility. With five officials and sixteen players on a field the size of a hockey rink, there wasn't a lot of room to maneuver. This was contrary to our outdoor training where we focused on our keys and trailed plays from our original positions on the field.

During the next to last home game, I got caught in the crosshairs and gunned down. The play was a quick pitch to my side of the field where I was straddling the line of scrimmage. As soon as the ball was snapped, I knew I was in trouble. My reflexive first stutter step to the center field placed me on a collision course with the ball carrier. I stopped my momentum with the next step, but it was too late. In the corners of my eye, I saw tacklers converging on the ball carrier in slow motion as if in a dream.

"Oh, shit, I'm in trouble," I mumbled.

"Look out, Lou," I heard someone yell. I thought I heard the crowd gasp before everything went black. I had been slammed into boards like a hockey player by two tacklers and the ball carrier. I was buried under seven hundred pounds of human flesh in helmets and pads.

I was only out cold for a few seconds, but it felt like hours. When I finally opened my eyes, the team physician for the Speed was kneeling over me with a penlight in hand. After a cursory exam to make sure that I was still alive (how many fingers do you see and follow the light with your eyes), the crew helped me to my feet. I staggered off the field to a standing ovation. In the locker room, the doctor checked my vitals and recommended that I sit out the rest of the game. With my heart still racing, I wholeheartedly agreed. I felt like a human pinball.

The ride home to Baltimore was long and hard. I should have spent the night in a hotel room with a hot tub, but the creature comforts of home beckoned. I thought that since I was now sporting the home team's color of black and blue colors over my lower body, I should be made an honorary team member.

That one play showed that forty and fifty-year-old officials are no physical match for professional football players. Arena players were often the size of those in the NFL and just as powerful. I knew that I had been lucky. Officials get bowled over, tackled, and run over by players all the time. They just never make the highlight reels. As in my case, officials usually end up with some lumps, bruises, sprains, and sore muscles. However, there have been incidents resulting in concussions, broken bones, torn ligaments, and in rare cases life-threatening internal injuries.

◆ ◆ ◆

When the Speed franchise folded after the 2003 season due to financial woes, I folded with them. At this point in my career, the novelty had worn off and the travel was starting to wear me down. Helping Kelly with the garden in the spring seemed like the perfect elixir to rejuvenate an old official. I continued to follow arena football and kept in touch with my fellow officials. Eventually, the novelty of indoor football also wore off for fans. After expanding to thirty teams in 2007, the league disbanded due to financial reasons in 2010. I was not surprised. In minor league sports, the Green Reaper always wins. Take heed of greed should have been the mantra for those ill-fated franchises.

Touchdown Tree at Ursinus College.
Landscape reminded me of Radecke Park.

CHAPTER 15
COLLEGE ENTRANCE EXAMS

"Where are you headed, Lou?" Ron Klages asked in a fatherly, hushed tone as we walked off the field after a Friday afternoon high school game.

"Home. Got another game tomorrow," I replied casually, certainly not catching his drift. Finally, after five years, I was assigned private school games that were played on Saturday afternoons. Most of these schools were the top teams in the Baltimore metropolitan area. To be assigned these games was a sign that my high school career was peaking. That was the good news. The bad news was I didn't know where my officiating career was headed. Perhaps, Ron sensed that in the fall of 1979.

"Nah, I mean where are you headed in your career? Have you thought about moving up?" he asked candidly.

"To be honest, Ron, that's all that I've been thinking about this season."

"You're in luck, my friend. The ECAC is looking for officials. I've talked to some people, and they think that you'd be a good fit."

"Let me think it over this weekend, and I'll get back to you," I replied now hesitantly. Who was I kidding? Certainly, it wasn't Ron or me. There really wasn't much to ponder regarding my informal invitation to join the collegiate ranks. I made my decision before I opened the car door. If Ron thought I could succeed at the college level, then it was time to make the move.

Ron had the football pedigree that garnered respect from everyone associated with the game. On November 26, 1959, he scored the only two touchdowns as Poly toppled City in the annual Thanksgiving Day game 12-0. Played before a crowd of 25,000 at Memorial Stadium, the game decided Baltimore's public-school championship.

Highly recruited, Ron stayed close to home and accepted a football scholarship to the University of Maryland. His backfield partner Ed Stuckrath headed to Penn State on a football scholarship. City's coach for the annual showdown that year was native Baltimorean George Young who later found fame as the general manager for the New York Giants. That was the caliber of Baltimore high school football in the late '50s and early '60s.

While Ron's college career didn't capture the glory of his high school days, he became one of the most successful officials to ever wear stripes. Over a thirty-five-year career, he officiated numerous Top Ten showdowns in the Big Ten and ACC, nine bowl games, and five Army-Navy contests. When Ron talked football, people listened. When he talked football with me, I acted. That Sunday afternoon, I called Ron and told him that I was ready for the challenge.

"Lou, good move, but remember it's more of a process than a procedure. Give it time," he cautioned after he provided me contact information for the ECAC (Eastern College Athletic Association) and the ACC (Atlantic Coast Conference). Ron's words couldn't have been more prophetic. Having finished my sandlot career, I was still officiating semipro, flag, and high school football. I knew about the waiting game while progressing through the ranks. Despite the frustration at various times, I always persevered with the patience of a saint. Persevere was all I could do.

That week, I filled out the required paperwork. For the ACC, the process was handled internally with their coordinator of football officiating. His office was responsible for the recruitment, selection, and training of officials. With the ECAC, the process was layered. Before I could officiate in the conference, I had to become a member of the EAIFO (Eastern Association of Intercollegiate Football Officials).

The EAIFO was a consortium of football officials who served eight regional chapters in DIV I, II, and III. They provided crews for independents and conferences throughout the Northeast and Mid-Atlantic regions. Claiming to have the highest number of former officials in the NFL, they immediately garnered my attention. That statement, fact or fiction, was a great selling point. I didn't hesitate to complete the forms.

I had five years of officiating experience and twenty-five varsity games that were the minimal requirement. With Ron's contacts, two letters of recommendation from current or former EAIFO officials wouldn't be a problem. I filled out a statement of interest that included my football resume, a headshot, and a check for $25 (application fee). A few weeks later I received notice from both organizations that I had been accepted as a member. All I had to do now was attend monthly meetings and annual clinics and wait.

While I didn't sit by my phone day and night waiting for calls, I stubbed many toes whenever it rang. Due to my high anxiety of missing that life-changing phone call, I invested in an answering machine. Although primitive by today's standards (basically a tape recorder connected to a rotary phone), it was a lifeline that saved my career.

◆ ◆ ◆

A year after being accepted for membership, I received calls from the ACC to work junior varsity (JV) games. Even though the NCAA granted freshman eligibility in football and basketball in 1972, a number of DIV I schools fielded JV teams. With nearly a hundred players on a roster, sometimes six-deep at each position, not all players dressed for regular season games. Sanctioned JV games provided a chance for players to perform under game conditions. It was good practice, or dress rehearsal as I referred to it, for players and officials. Even with only a few students and scouts in the stands, there was an understated intensity on the field. Walk-ons vied for scholarships; scholarship players vied for the travel squad. For everybody, the dream was suiting up for a varsity game.

One of my most rewarding experiences while waiting for the call from the ACC or ECAA was officiating sprint football games. The game lived up to its billing as "football the way it should be played." Players with Division I skills in DIV III bodies is how I described the game to the uninitiated.

The Eastern 150-Pound Football League, today the Collegiate Sprint Football League, was founded in the 1930s to allow undersized football players the chance to compete at the intercollegiate level. The league originally included Cornell, Lafayette, Penn, Princeton, Rutgers, Villanova, and Yale. Army and Navy, who have won twenty combined championships since 1998, joined the league in the mid-1950s. Over the years, the weight limit was increased to today's limit of 178 pounds for all players to include linemen.

Sprint was renamed Lightweight in 1998 as a marketing tool to attract more teams. They should have renamed it Lightning because that's exactly what it was. With an emphasis on technique and execution, the game was fast and furious. With no overpowering physical presence, players relied on quickness, speed, and agility as if they were on roller skates. Every player was capable of manning any position on the field.

In 1982, I officiated the annual Army-Navy sprint game at Annapolis. Although there were only a few hundred fans in the cavernous Navy-Marine Corps Stadium, the teams played with an intensity that rivaled the varsity showdown.

Gamesmanship and sportsmanship were the hallmarks of both teams. With every player a bona fide scholar-athlete who opted for a service academy, I couldn't help but feel a sense of patriotic pride when the national anthem was played before the game. I looked up and down the sidelines and thought about the sacrifice these men might be asked to make someday. There were no winners or losers on the field that day, only heroes.

After every sprint game, I left the field thinking that maybe all college divisions should have height and weight requirements. I wondered if fans wanted to see football played by the finest athletes where athleticism trumped specialization. That would be the only way tackle football could become a true international sport and possibly an Olympic event. If that day ever came, sprint football, not flag football as envisioned by the NFL, would be the working model.

◆ ◆ ◆

After what seemed like an eternity, I received the call in the fall of 1979 from Tom Beck, head of the local college official's association. "Lou, can you step up today? Bill Ryan's daughter had an automobile accident last night. We're a man short for today's game at Ursinus," he asked with a sense of urgency. Tom would fill in for Bill as the referee, and I would take Tom's place as the line judge. Ursinus College was northeast of Philadelphia, just south of Princeton University.

"When and where do we meet up?" I replied without hesitation. My game bag was already packed and waiting.

"Brownie's at ten," he replied. "I'll fill you in on the details while we're on the road."

Brownie's Tavern, just off the beltway and not far from my home, was becoming a pivotal place in my career. Only a few months earlier, I had my publishing party there for the flag football rulebook. Now it would be launching my college career. Due to its location, the tavern was a poplar place for officials to meet before and after the game. My Marine Corps friends quickly reminded me that it was a good omen. After all, the Corps had been founded in 1775 at Tun Tavern in Philadelphia. I couldn't argue with their logic.

During the two-hour drive, the crew discussed college rules and the differences between high school and college football. As we neared the college, Tom had one last bit of advice for me. "Don't forget, there's a lot of tradition at these Little Ivy schools, especially the playing of the national anthem before the game. You need to be in position thirty minutes before kickoff." He then told me where to stand, what direction to face, and how to stand with my hat over my heart.

After dressing in a room that was slightly larger than the closet in the coach's office, the crew proceeded to the field for our pregame field inspection.

"What about the tree in the end zone? I asked incredulously, staring at this humungous tree in the corner of the end zone about twenty feet from the goalposts.

"No problems with that. It's not in the field of play, but it is part of the school's tradition," someone responded. Touchdown Tree was a sycamore estimated to be between two hundred and two hundred and fifty years old. The secluded spot was reportedly the site of romantic interludes, fraternity/sorority initiations, beer parties, and other non-academic pursuits. I couldn't help but notice that the word *tradition* was once again mentioned. But curiously, the stands were mostly empty.

"Where are the fans?" I asked hesitantly. For a moment, I thought the game was an initiation ritual into the officials' association, much like fraternity hijinks.

"They'll be marching in behind the band," Tom quipped. *Another college tradition*, I thought sarcastically.

"Hey, Tom, it's thirty minutes before kickoff. Shouldn't we be in position," I asked nervously.

"Don't worry. We're good," Tom replied.

Ten minutes before kickoff, the teams were on the field, but there were no bands or fans. I looked around the field and never felt more depressed or lonelier. For all intent and purposes, I might as well have been standing on planet Uranus instead of Ursinus College.

"Let's do the coin toss. The band and the fans must be hung up at the gate," Tom announced hurriedly.

"What gate! There's no gate, only the field and the tree," I muttered, wondering what the hell was happening.

"Okay, guys, let's take our positions and wait for the band," Tom cheerfully declared after the coin toss. Standing near the sideline, I heard some commotion behind the home team bench. Looking over my shoulder, I saw four students dressed in jeans and T-shirts standing in the front row of seats. They were holding musical instruments. The band had arrived.

"Please rise for the playing of our national anthem," the announcer intoned as about fifty people rose to their feet. As the band played, the crew looked at me with shit-eating grins. I stared back grimly with pursued lips, ready to burst out laughing at any second. They got the rookie. I fell for the prank hook, line, and sinker.

Back at Brownie's, the crew stopped for a couple of beers and rehashed the game. It had been a low scoring affair that featured two underwhelming offenses. "Christ, I bet before the season is over there'll be more scoring under the sycamore tree than on the field," I joked to the delight of the crew.

"Lou, welcome to the world of Division III football," they cheered in unison as they raised their glasses in a toast to my successful debut. I drove home still on the adrenaline high from officiating my first college game. I could have cared less about the numbers of points, fans, and band members. I had taken another major step in my career, but I couldn't help but wonder if Radecke Park had a Touchdown Tree.

CHAPTER 16
FINDING A HOME

With a sense of relief, I finally had my foot in the door as a college official. I picked up a couple more games that year and the following year I had six assignments for DIV II and III teams in the Maryland and southern Pennsylvania region. Now that I was firmly established with the ECAC, I was faced with another career dilemma. Do I cast my lot with the ECAC or wait on the ACC?

I felt like a football recruit in a tug-of-war over what school to attend. With the ACC and the ECAC, it was the question of whether to partner with the DIV I-A, later known as the Football Bowl Subdivision, or the DIV I-AA, later known as the Football Championship Subdivision. Both affiliations offered quality football with highly skilled players.

However, DIV I-A had the bigger budgets and the brighter lights of major bowl games. It made me question my reasons for becoming an official. Was it love of the game or love of the money?

Although it was obvious that I was not being heavily courted by the ACC, I was still doing a handful of JV games. In my mind, I was still on the radar, even if it was just a faded blip. Having grown up with University of Maryland football when they were an ACC member, I secretly harbored the dream of big-time DIV I football like many athletes.

While the ECAC offered the opportunity to advance to DIV I games, the ACC was already established as a powerhouse with major bowl games and national championships. However, there was no guarantee that I would ever get to officiate a DIV I varsity game. And if I did make it on the field in the ACC, there was no guarantee how long I would stay.

After consulting with some of my sandlot and high school mentors who highlighted the pros and cons of each conference, I decided to remain with the ECAC and drop my ACC affiliation. I made my defining career decision and never looked back. Did I want to be the big fish in a small pond or a small fish in a big pond? I opted to swim in the ECAC pond where there was more opportunity to advance.

◆ ◆ ◆

Rooted in football legend, the ECAC proved to be the perfect fit. James Lynah, an engineer by trade who later became the first athletic director at Cornell, founded the athletic consortium in 1938. Lynah's claim to football fame was that he was one of two players to have played for both John Heisman (Clemson) and Pop Warner (Cornell) during his college years. For football trivia buffs, the other player was Joe "Big Chief" Guyon, a member of the Ojibwa tribe (Chippewa).

In 1912, James played alongside Jim Thorpe at the Carlisle Indian Industrial School that was coached by Warner. He later starred for Heisman at Georgia Tech and led them to a national championship in 1917.

Eventually, the ECAC developed into the nation's largest conference with over three hundred members at all three NCAA divisions. The umbrella organization stretched from Maine to North Carolina and sponsored leagues, championships, bowl games, tournaments, club sports, and competitions that did not fall under domain of the NCAA. That was a big pond.

My decision paid quick dividends. Within a few years, I had a full slate of DIV II and III games as part of a regular crew. I was now unofficially tenured as a head linesman. The DIV II games were with Pennsylvania State Athletic Conference and the DIV III games with the Middle Atlantic Conference (MAC). Since I was being reimbursed for travel expenses in lieu of per diem (translated no lodging funds), I did most of my work with the MAC because its members were closer to home.

On game day, I could leave my house early in the morning and arrive at the stadium with plenty of time to spare. The drive was always a relaxing excursion through the bucolic countryside of Maryland and Pennsylvania. There was no more enjoyable way to spend a Saturday morning, especially in the fall when autumn colors bathed the landscape in an orange glow.

Over the years, I fell in love with the MAC because I fell in love with their campuses. The conference consisted of small, private liberal arts colleges usually nestled in verdant valleys and surrounded by low mountains. With their tree-lined streets and vine-covered brick buildings with white columns, they resembled their larger counterparts in the Ivy League.

If Norman Rockwell painted college campuses, he would have painted the MAC. The schools reminded me of fictitious Faber College from the movie *Animal House*. (The campus used in the movie was actually the University of Oregon in Eugene.)

Of all the college campuses at any level, my favorite was Gettysburg College. For an American history buff and football historian such as myself, it was a collegiate paradise. While the architecture was a complementary blend of old and new brick buildings that reflected an Ivy League campus, its history mesmerized me. The place oozed history, specifically the Civil War. The campus was part of the battlefield on the first day of the Battle of Gettysburg. While waiting for the opening kickoff, it wasn't hard to envision Johnny Reb and Billy Yank chasing and charging each other across the football field. Residential development around the outlying battlefields that surrounded the school had been curtailed. The panorama of corn and wheat fields resembled the landscape from July 1863. In truth, the school was a time machine. If that wasn't enough to get your blood flowing, the campus was one of the haunted in America. Whenever I worked at Gettysburg, I spent hours walking and driving along the battlefields. While I never saw any ghostly apparitions, I met a lot of people who were ghost hunting.

After my first year of officiating football at MAC campuses, I finally understood the antics of a handful of neighborhood friends, the Gardenville Guys as I often referred to them. While my unofficial college major was officiating, their unofficial field of study was college road trips. Were any of them matriculated? Hell, no! They were high school graduates who were attending local community colleges or out working their first job.

At least once a month, two or three unofficial students would grab a few six-packs of beer and head down to the University of Maryland in College Park to visit fellow Gardenville Guys who were official students. Actually, visit was a misnomer. They went to party, and party they did. They became such prolific and frequent hell-raisers in the dorms that residents actually thought they lived there. If the university had a major in debauchery, they would have been honor students.

Even without the parties, they admitted to a dark academic secret. They were trapped in a primordial pull to these institutes of higher learning that were out of their reach financially and academically. At times during their campus visits, they even attended classes to scope out the co-eds and hopefully score a date with the quintessential hippie chick of their dreams. In retrospect, they probably attended more classes in college than they did in high school.

Without a doubt, they were the first generation of non-degree, non-traditional students. They didn't have professors, but they had school pride, often returning from their road trips with University of Maryland T-shirts and hats that featured a terrapin, the school's mascot. Gardenville finally had its own version of Notre Dame's subway alumni. I was just glad that no one from Gardenville attended college in the MAC.

This happy-go-lucky band of pseudo intellectuals was greatly aided by high draft numbers. They knew that they would not be heading to the University of South Vietnam to conduct field studies in a green uniform. The only way they were going to see combat would be if the Viet Cong stormed the beach at Ocean City, Maryland. I had no doubt that without a moment's hesitation they would answer the call to arms. Upon their last breath, they would defend the ocean resort where hordes of debauched and depraved adolescents gathered to celebrate summer.

But who was I to judge these vagabond academics? Like them, I was a college wanderlust. In the fall, I always felt that invisible, geomagnetic pull to these idyllic campuses. Maybe, it was something genetically imprinted in all recent high school graduates, including me. At MAC campuses, I often daydreamed about being a student. With my long hair and bushy mustache, I envisioned walking across campus with a frisbee in hand instead of a football. Give me a tweed jacket and I could easily pass as a professor.

However, instead of college, I opted to pursue careers in business and football. Feeling the pressure to bolster that resume, I eventually succumbed to the call of higher education. To further my career with BGE and the ECAC, I enrolled in evening classes at Towson State College, later Towson University. After ten years, I received a degree in business management. With many football officials totting resumes that had college football playing experience and a college degree, I needed to stay competitive. However, there was a price to pay. Taking evening courses during the week and officiating football games during the weekends took its toll on my social life. There wasn't a lot of time to drink beer and chase women with the Gardenville Guys. That was a good thing because if I did, I would have been left in the dust. These guys partied and dressed like rock stars and lived to tell about it. People stood in awe about their exploits. Not aspiring to become a rock legend in my 30s, I indulged in the pursuit of wine, women, and song on a lesser level.

Keeping my cool with Towson Head Coach Gordy Combs over a disputed call.

CHAPTER 17
TO THE HEAD OF THE CLASS

Eventually, I reached a point where I needed bigger college campuses, a place where athletics were more emphasized. In my mind, I was ready for DIV I. My dance card was growing stale with DIV II and III games. While many officials were content at those levels, I was young and restless. Anxious to dance in a bigger and brighter spotlight, I wondered if that moment would ever come.

I finally got the call to attend the ball on Friday afternoon, September 19, 1986. "Al is removing you from your game tomorrow at Western Maryland," Sally Benson stated tersely. Sally was the secretary of the ECAC and wife of Al Benson, supervisor of officials. A million thoughts, all of them bad, ran through my mind. What did I do to get pulled off my game? Did I screw up last week? The technical adviser had no negative comments after the game, but that didn't mean anything. With film review and comments from advisers and coaches, maybe somebody saw something that had been previously overlooked. That was second nature in this business. My palms were sweaty and my throat dry.

Before I could respond, Sally chimed in. "Lou, tomorrow you're going to Bucknell. Congratulations," she stated cheerfully. Due to a death in the family earlier that day, the head linesman had to cancel. After thanking Sally, I immediately called my dad.

"I got the call just a few minutes ago. William and Mary at Bucknell tomorrow. Do you want to go to Lewisburg with me? I asked excitedly.

"What time do we leave?" he replied eagerly.

"What about work?" I asked anxiously, knowing that he had been working Saturdays for the past six months.

"Lou, they can get along without me for one day. We're wiring houses not nuclear reactors," he snickered. That was all I needed to boost my confidence. Later, Al Hynes, referee for the game who later became supervisor of officials for the NFL, called to review the game-day routine and agenda.

My bag was already packed for tomorrow's game at Western Maryland, so all I had to do was wait for morning. Tossing and turning in bed throughout the night, I managed to get a couple hours of restless sleep while replaying every scenario that I had witnessed since my first game at Radecke Park.

My dad and I drove up to Lewisburg, PA, early Saturday morning to meet the crew for breakfast. I was more than willing to meet the crew at the stadium, but my father was adamant about having a working man's breakfast, namely eggs, bacon, hashed browns, and toast. While my nervous stomach couldn't handle a cup of coffee and a doughnut, my father, who ate breakfast every day, insisted it was the most important meal of the day. "A full stomach gets you a full day's work," he joked much to my chagrin.

Surprisingly, the only football discussed on the trip was the stadium where I would make my DIV I debut. Sometime after my phone call, my father had done his homework. He eagerly rattled off the facts. Christy Mathewson-Memorial Stadium, originally named Memorial Stadium, was built in 1924 to honor Bucknellians who served the nation in times of war. The tag Christy Mathewson was later added to honor the alumnus who was a standout fullback/drop kicker and baseball player. After a stellar pitching career with the New York Giants, Christy was one of the five original members of the Baseball Hall of Fame. Baseball my dad knew; his knowledge of Bucknell football was a mystery. Either way, I thought that making my debut at Memorial Stadium was a good omen. After all I had worked the big-time high school rivalries at Baltimore's Memorial Stadium. Maybe, my dad was thinking along the same lines.

For part of the ride, my father reminisced about his time in the Navy during World War II. Mention the Navy and he could talk for hours. I heard the stories previously, but it helped to pass the time. We also talked briefly about my Little League baseball days at Radecke Park. The tryouts were on the same field where I started my football officiating career. He also told me how proud he was of my career and college degree.

As we progressed through the moments of my life, I knew the big hit was coming. "When are you ever going to settle down and get married?" he asked nonchalantly. "You know you not getting any younger." Before I could respond with some kind of rationale answer, we pulled up to the hotel to have breakfast with the crew. *Hey, that's what dads are for,* was all I could think.

The crew was most welcoming. They introduced me around the table and immediately put me at ease about my DIV I debut. I guess my dad was right about breakfast. I not only left with a full stomach but a head full of confidence.

The game itself was uneventful. Bucknell lost to William and Mary 30-13. After the first possession, my nerves had settled. I had no trouble adjusting my game to the next level and felt good about my performance. College football was simply football. That was my only DIV I game that year. All I could do now was go home and once again play the waiting game.

I proved that good things happen to those who wait and persevere. The following year, I was promoted to a full-time DIV I crew that comprised Newt Whittaker, referee; Mike Semcheski, umpire; Lance Garth, field judge; Larry Sciancalepore, back judge; and Bobby Pickett, head linesman. Although I was the head linesman during my DIV II and III days, I moved to line judge to fill a vacancy at that level. I had no problem adjusting. I would do whatever it took to advance.

Our first game of the season was the University of Richmond Spiders versus the University of New Hampshire Wildcats on September 5, 1987. Since I had never been to New England, I decided once again to mix business with pleasure. I took off from work that week and then drove the scenic route. The blue highway syndrome I picked up in the MAC was a tough habit to break.

◆◆◆

My first stop was Mystic, Connecticut, where I visited the Sea Port Museum, Mystic Aquarium, and Mystic River Park. Rewarding myself, I stayed at a B&B for a few days and acquainted myself with New England seafood delights, such as clams, quahogs, oysters, cod fish and, of course, chowder. If it wasn't for those damn Red Sox, I could easily fall in love with New England.

Meandering up the coastline on country roads off the interstate, I finally arrived in Durham, New Hampshire, on Friday morning. Once again, I stopped at another B&B and spent the night reviewing the rulebook and my position mechanics. Now that I was a full-time member of a crew, I wanted to make a favorable impression. The next morning I woke up thinking that in a few hours I would be heading into the biggest game of my career. Taking my father's advice, I made sure that I had a solid breakfast before meeting with the crew.

The crew arrived at Wildcat Stadium at 10 a.m. for a 1 p.m. kickoff. As I parked my car and headed to the dressing room, the excitement in the air was palpable. Three hours before the game and fans were already tailgating in the parking lot. It was the Labor Day weekend, and New Englanders were wasting no time in celebrating the holiday and the return of college football.

I hurried to the dressing room and stopped dead in my tracks when I opened the door. Our dressing room was the locker room used by the men's swimming team. It reeked of musty swimsuits and chlorine that made you feel as if you just climbed out of the pool. Welcome big-time college football!

After introducing myself to the crew, I began emptying my game bag, carefully extracting each item and laying it on a bench as if it was a sacred vestment. "Son of a bitch. I can't believe this," I mumbled, sweat forming on my brow. I had packed everything but my game socks. *Now what in the hell was I going to do*, I wondered as I frantically turned my game bag inside out and upside down.

"What's wrong, brother? Lance Garth quipped, seeing my panicked look.

"I forgot my socks. How in the hell did I forget my socks?" I shrieked. Within the blink of an eye, I was pelted with five pairs of socks.

"Take your pick, Lou. Just make sure you wash'em before you return'em," Lance howled with laughter. A rookie mistake and a lesson learned the hard way. Shoes and socks seemed to be my nemesis. From that day forward, I always packed two of everything. Before leaving the locker room, I double-checked my pockets to insure I had my whistle, game card, penalty flag, and beanbag. As security escorted us through the crowd, I heard boos from the fans. We hadn't even taken the field and the fans already hated us. The accompanying catcalls sent shivers down my spine, and I loved every minute of it.

The game progressed smoothly for the crew until the end of the third quarter when the Wildcats quarterback threw a pass to his wide receiver on my side of the field. The ball glanced off the receiver's hands and into the waiting hands of a Richmond defensive back who ran ninety-five yards for a touchdown. The Richmond players were ecstatic, racing up and down the sidelines to celebrate as the frenzied home crowd fell silent. A close game had been broken open.

Seconds later, the crowd roared when they realized that a penalty had been called against Richmond. A Richmond linebacker committed a holding penalty on another receiver away from the ball. Two flags were thrown on the play for holding, one by me and one by Lance, the field judge.

As the crew hustled back to the original line of scrimmage to assess the foul, the Richmond sideline went ballistics to the delight of the fans. With the crowd drowning out the bitching and complaining I couldn't hear all of the compliments about my officiating skills. After Lance and I explained our call to the referee, I returned to my position along the Richmond sideline. The next fifteen minutes were the longest minutes of my life as I stoically endured an endless barrage of insults and expletives from the Richmond fans seated behind the Richmond bench.

Richmond players and coaches quickly calmed down and focused on the game as I did. With no instant replay available to be flashed on the scoreboard, I wasn't sure that I blew the call. I was taught to call'em as I see'em and that's what I did.

Richmond prevailed 14-7 in a tightly contested match. Even though they were victorious, the Spiders were still angry. It just so happened that Lance and I called back the longest interception for a touchdown in Richmond school history on what ultimately proved to be a phantom penalty.

The next day, Al Benson sent me and Lance a clip of the game film for our review. Even though it had no direct impact on the game, it was important to make the right call. That was our job. On Monday, Al called me to inquire about the play and the holding call after receiving a call from Richmond's athletic director. When he asked what I saw, I knew that he did not agree with the call. "What did you see" in football lingo translated to a blown call. After reviewing the film, I agreed with him and admitted that I booted the call. For a rookie official, it was a hand-wringing experience. Fortunately, Lance and I did not call back a game-winning touchdown. Although he has never admitted it, I'm inclined to believe that Lance threw his flag to cover my ass. How could there not be a penalty if two flags were thrown for the same play?

After the game, the crew went to Bobby Pickett's mobile home to enjoy some adult beverages and a cookout. While the play was not discussed, I couldn't help but think that my career was in jeopardy. Feeling sorry for myself, I remembered that Johnny U's first pass in the NFL against the Chicago Bears on October 21, 1956, was intercepted and ran back for a touchdown.

WWJD? (What would Johnny do?) Of course, the confident rookie would saunter onto the field and throw a touchdown pass to win the game. Not quite. He fumbled the ball on the next two possessions that resulted in Bear touchdowns. In the end, he managed to turn a 27-21 deficit into a 58-27 route by the Bears. There was hope for me after all. That's why I'd always be a Baltimore Colt at heart. I always seemed to be in the select company of my childhood heroes.

"Lou, where are you staying tonight? Bob inquired casually.

"A local motel down the road," I replied.

"Nah, that won't work. That's where the Richmond fans are staying for the night. You'll be tarred and feathered," he joked. "You're spending the night with us at the campground." Who was I to argue? I may have missed a call on the field, but I was cordially embraced by my crew. I would have slept on the ground if asked because I wanted to be part of the team.

"Lou, what are your plans for the rest of the holiday weekend?" Lance's wife, Kathy, asked politely.

"I would like to see more of the coastline. I had plans to visit New Bedford and see some of the whaling history," I replied.

"This is your lucky day. Lance and I live there, and we want you, no we insist, you stay with us," Kathy declared with a smile.

I ended up staying three nights with the Garth family. Over the following days, they took me to the New Bedford whaling museum, the fishing harbor, lobster restaurants, and many other tourist sites that highlighted the town's maritime history. I was single at the time and had nothing but time on my hands.

That was the beginning of a lifelong friendship that I owed to my officiating career. We became family, and Lance would be a member of my wedding party. My wife, Kelly, my daughter, Kathleen, and I attended the weddings of their two sons, Chris and Geoff. Over the years, we'd gather at Christmas time to enjoy each other's company and catch up on family news.

Lance was an assistant district attorney and later became a district court judge. Kathy was as a schoolteacher and later served as the local school board union president. They always had great stories to tell. All I had were stories about problems at Baltimore's gas and electric provider from inside an office. Too bad I wasn't outside as a lineman climbing poles and battling the weather. That would have sounded more heroic.

♦ ♦ ♦

Later in the season, I unpretentiously picked up the nickname Sweet Lou while traveling to a game. On a Friday afternoon, I boarded a plane at BWI en route to Bangor for a game at the University of Maine. Their opponent that week was none other than the New Hampshire Wildcats. After a tough week at work all I wanted to do was relax and catch a nap during the two and a half hour flight. I usually selected a window seat so I could stretch out a bit and look out the window, but today was different. The only vacant seat was a middle seat next to me.

The murmuring of passengers and the banging of luggage were signs that I was in trouble. With dread, I nervously watched a hunched over woman stumble and fumble down the aisle with her carry-on luggage. As expected, she found the last seat on the plane that happened to be next to me. Being the gentleman that I was, I quickly forgot about my nap and began a pleasant conversation with an attractive and personable young lady for the rest of the flight.

"Lou, what brings you to Bangor this time of the year. You don't look like a moose hunter," she joked.

"Not moose but zebras," I chuckled, displaying some of that magical Hammond wit. "I'm a football official working tomorrow's game at the University of Maine."

"Then this could be my lucky day because I'm looking for tickets to the game for me and my sister," she replied.

I didn't know if I was being fleeced or conned, but I told her that I had two tickets (a crew perk) to the game that I wasn't using. She was more than welcome to have them.

"What can I do to repay you?" she said excitedly. Before I could respond she had the answer. "How about a ride to the hotel and dinner with me and my sister?"

"It's a deal," I said with a gentle handshake. Dinner with a pretty lady was an offer that I couldn't refuse.

When the plane landed in Bangor, we were the last passengers to exit. After retrieving my luggage from the overhead bin, she insisted on carrying my game bag. I agreed and away we went. My unnoticed getaway like a thief in the night was quickly foiled. Waiting for me at the arrival gate was my crew. As soon as Bobby Pickett saw who was carrying my game bag, he yelled, "Here's come Sweet Lou." On cue the rest of the crew joined in the chorus. "Hey Sweet Lou, over here sweetie," they clamored.

I regretfully and politely declined the offer from my hostess and left with my crew. Forget about the details on what could have been the greatest night in the history of a football official, a legend had been born out of circumstance. The nickname has remained to this day. The next morning at breakfast, the crew was waiting at the table with beguiling grins. "Sweet Lou, did you bang her or Bangor?" they razzed in unison. I could only applaud their humor and imagine what could have been.

◆ ◆ ◆

Within a few years of my first DIV I game, I was working a full schedule of games in the Ivy League, Patriot League, and Yankee Conference as a head linesman. The Yankee Conference whose charter members included state universities in the New England region merged with the Atlantic 10 Conference in 1996. In 2007, the Colonial Athletic Association (CAA) absorbed football schools from the Atlantic 10. In most cases, realignment translated to financial survival, an enduring feature of both collegiate and professional football.

Fans needed a map of the East Coast and a compass to find where their favorite team would be playing. Despite the nomadic tribes in the football wilderness, there was one constant. A topnotch pool of football officials provided stability and credibility to any nascent conference. We were America's finest, ready and willing to serve and protect the game of football. We viewed ourselves as the good guys in black with the exception of one white hat (the referee) who stood for law and order between the white lines, or so we thought.

However, there was a problem that needed immediate attention. Simply put, all officials are not created equal. As with every sport at any level, there's a mix of good and marginal talent on the field. While marginal talent did not translate to no-talent, it meant that an individual had reached their potential. That's one of the immutable laws of sport. So it was with football officials.

There were rumors circulating among the locker rooms that the CAA was not happy with the level of officiating. To them, putting a better product on the field included both athletes and officials. They were not alone in their opinion. The cry for change started with the athletic directors. Officials, myself included, felt slighted and betrayed, but we were simply employees of the conference.

In 2007, the Patriot League and Ivy League broke away from the ECAC and joined the CAA to form an alliance known as CIP, an alliance of the CAA, Ivy, and Patriot Leagues. In the best interests of better football, CIP would maintain their own cadre of officials.

Of course, this was nothing unusual in the world of football. A decade later, the pursuit of excellence continued. In 2018, the CIP joined an alliance under the administration of the ACC that also included the AAC and the Big South Conference.

While the ACC's supervisor of football officials would head the alliance, each conference would be autonomous. Each conference supervisor of football officials would be responsible for weekly evaluations of their officials and serve as the point of contact between the conference and its head coaches.

The selling point for the lesser conferences was expanded training, development, recruitment, retention, and evaluation for officials. The long-term goal of the alliance was to increase proficiency and consistency among veteran officials across the officiating landscape and facilitate entry of younger officials into the profession. If I didn't know better, I could have sworn that John Carrigan had written the mission statement. It was that good.

Of course, being associated with a superpower such as the ACC would also aid schools in recruiting players. The sales pitch would be along the lines that we have the best product that includes players, coaches, facilities, and now you, Mr. Official.

With the formation of the CIP, my career was at another crossroad. As much as I enjoyed my association with ECAC, I believed that CIP had some valid points about the officiating. Once again, it was time to make my move and quickly. Not wanting to be lost in a backlog, I immediately filled out my application. A few weeks later, I was notified that I had been accepted as an official in the CIP. It was the same game, same uniform, just a different boss. I had no problem adjusting.

The crew eager to make Ivy League history.
The beginning of my longest day.

CHAPTER 18
THE GAME – HARVARD VS. YALE

Throughout my DIV I career, I officiated many CAA games late in the season that were literally sleepwalkers. Usually, they were teams with losing records, counting down to the end of the season. There were some notable exceptions such as the Harvard-Yale classic. This was another reward game toward the end of my career. It was the CIP's way of saying thanks for a job well done and don't forget to tell us when you're ready to step aside in the near future. There's somebody waiting in the wings.

Every official has a football wish list that begins with the question: If you could have your dream game, what would that be? For an NFL official, it most likely would be the Super Bowl. For a college referee, it might be the Army-Navy game or the national championship.

For me, there was only one game, and that was known simply as *The Game*—the rivalry between the Harvard Crimson and Yale Bulldogs. During my collegiate career, I had the opportunity to work some Ivy League games but only a few involving Harvard or Yale. That just whetted my appetite. Over the years, I campaigned, cajoled, and connived to work The Game. Finally in 2005, I got my wish.

◆ ◆ ◆

Dating back to 1875, the game has been traditionally the last game of the year for both schools. Since Ivy League schools do not participate in post-season games, the game often is played for the Ivy League title, which only intensifies and magnifies the contest.

To understand the rivalry, read the book or watch the documentary *Harvard Beats Yale 29-29*. You don't have to be a football fan to enjoy the story about the legendary 1968 matchup. For the first time since 1909, both teams entered the game undefeated. Yale, led by quarterback Brian Dowling, who was the role model for the comic strip Doonesbury's "B.D.," was riding a sixteen-game win streak. Across the field for the Crimson was All-Ivy League guard Tommy Lee Jones, who later found fame and fortune on the silver screen.

In a miraculous comeback, Harvard scored sixteen points, two touchdowns and two two-point conversions, in the last forty-two seconds to tie the game. At the time, there were no tiebreakers in college football. The next day Harvard's newspaper *The Crimson* immortalized the game with the headline, *Harvard Beats Yale 29-29*.

How do you top a game like that? Twenty-seven years later, Harvard and Yale almost did it with the first overtime game in one hundred twenty-two meetings and the first triple overtime in the history of the Ivy League. The game had all the thrills of the 1968 contest with fumbles, interceptions, and missed field goals. Only this time, I was on the field to witness another unbelievable chapter in football history. The date was November 19, 2005.

The crew's day started with a hotel breakfast at 7:30 a.m. As usual, my breakfast routine included waffles, bacon, sausage, coffee, and something sweet for Sweet Lou. Around 9:30 a.m., we arrived at the school where we were met by the security staff in front of the field house. Since there were no locker room facilities at the stadium for players, coaches, or officials, we had to dress at the field house and make a five-minute walk to the stadium. Keeping with their tradition, Yale players would enter the stadium in a tradition known as the *Bulldog Walk*. They would be accompanied by the *avant garde* (What else do you call a band that's been disciplined and banned for political satire?) Yale Precision Marching Band playing the fight song "Bulldog, Down the Field."

After dropping off our bags, we headed to the stadium in our dress clothes. The sun was shining, and the temperature was already in the upper thirties. It promised to be a great day for a football game. Either way it was going to be fun. Kickoff was 12:30 p.m.

On our way to the field, we checked out the ESPN production trailers and chatted with some of the fans who were starting to tailgate. Within minutes, we had politely declined several rounds on the house. It seemed like every preppie in New England was walking around with a beer in hand. What else would you expect from a school that claims to have originated the sport of tailgating in the early 1900s?

As we drew closer to the stadium, an ESPN crew that included big-time broadcasters Erin Andrews and Charley Steiner were busily setting up for the day's broadcast. People milled outside the roped area to watch the stars at work. Already there was a buzz in the air, and we were still a couple hours from kickoff.

Inside the stadium, we walked and inspected the field for any unusual signs of foolery such as suggestive slogans painted in the grass or on the goalposts. Over the years, the rabid student bodies were notorious for creating some of the all-time sports pranks. The previous year, two-dozen Yalies, disguised as the non-existent Harvard Pep Squad, had distributed crimson-and-white placards to Harvard fans for a card stunt. When the fans raised the placards on cue, they spelled out, *We Suck*.

With everything in order, we returned to the locker room for our pregame conference. Practical jokes, pranks, and hijinks that could disrupt the game were discussed. As long as the disruptions stayed off the field, we didn't care. After that, we put on our *costumes,* as one official used to call our uniforms, and nervously waited. We double-checked the backs of our jerseys to ensure we weren't going to be victims of a prankster. Once we left the locker room, we would not return until after the game. Halftime would be spent in the tunnel underneath the stands.

Side judge Chris Garth, and back judge Bryan Thomas were the first to leave the locker room for babysitting duties one hour before the game. The head linesman and I would relieve them forty minutes prior to the game. The rest of the crew, referee Jack Winter, umpire John Shigo, and field judge Jack O'Keefe, would meet on the field twenty minutes prior to kickoff.

As the Yale Bowl started to fill with fans, Jack Winter met with the television technician to check his microphone. Bryan and Chris located the game clock and play clock operators in the open air press box for final instructions. John checked the players' equipment while they went through their pregame warm-ups. Greg instructed the chain gang on their duties and responsibilities. Jack O'Keefe and I instructed the ball boys about providing a replacement ball when the game ball went out of bounds.

Three minutes prior to the game, the captain from each team (yes, only one from each team) met the referee and umpire for the coin toss. Finally, we were ready to play football. Another event on my football bucket list could be scratched off. Standing on the field and gazing up at the crowd, I felt a cold chill run down my spine. For some unexplained reason, the goose bumps on my arms told me today's game would be one to be remembered. Looking at the sky, I noticed the clouds swirling in surrealistic patterns. An omen that cosmic forces were aligning for a supernatural event? I wasn't sure about metaphysics, but I was positive that history would be made. I just hoped it wasn't because of something the officiating crew did or didn't do.

And what a game it was! The last game of the season for both teams would give die-hard fans something to talk about during those cold New England winters for decades to come. After underdog Yale built up a surprising 21-3 lead in the third quarter, Harvard rallied to force overtime with two fourth-quarter scores that included an interception returned for a touchdown and a 22-yard touchdown pass with 2:43 remaining in the game. The two-point conversion tied the game 24-24. One thing I noticed midway through the third quarter was an increase in noise and the decrease in the number of empty seats. The crowd of over 53,000 had swelled considerably.

"Where did all the noise suddenly come from?" I asked one of the chain gang.

"The parking lot," he replied with a sly grin.

"What's happening in the park lot? I asked incredulously.

"Nothing now because they shut down tailgating after halftime. The party has moved to the bowl," he quipped. I had to love those Yalies. They went to a tailgate party and a football game broke out. Lucky for them, it was a classic.

Yale managed to turn the ball over in each overtime period, but also managed to stop Harvard twice before the winning score. Yale fumbled on the opening play of the first overtime, and Harvard took possession. After three running plays, a 37-yard field-goal attempt sailed wide right.

In the second overtime, Yale stopped Harvard with an interception. Taking possession once again, Yale moved within range of a short field goal when a wide receiver fumbled the ball while fighting for extra yards after making a first down. It was Harvard's turn once again, but they threw an interception.

During the commercial timeout between the change of possession, referee Jack the waved me over.

"Lou, what do you notice?" he asked apprehensively.

"It's getting dark," I replied casually.

"What else do you notice?" he asked warily.

"There's no lights," I chuckled.

"That's not funny. What in the hell are we going to do if it goes to more overtime? If I call the game a tie, there'll be a riot."

"Relax. I've seen this situation before. Someone will score before we have to break out the flashlights. Let nature take its course," I added confidently. I didn't have time to tell my story, but I knew darkness would provide a winner. On second thought, we could easily go down in football history for inciting the biggest riot in college football. We were definitely flirting with banishment from New England forever.

On the first play of the third overtime period, Yale's quarterback was chased out of the pocket and flipped a pass that was intercepted by the Harvard nose tackle near the sideline almost directly in front of me. Despite the tired feet, I was sure that I could shadow a defensive lineman if he sprinted to the end zone. No need to worry, he was tackled immediately. It was now Harvard's turn to break the tie. Five plays later, Crimson running back Michael Berg scampered into the end zone for a 30-24 victory.

With the sun setting on the Yale Bowl, Harvard fans stormed the field in celebration. There was also a horde of Yalies stumbling and staggering across the field, probably celebrating the end of the game so they could resume tailgating. Then again, maybe both schools were deliriously happy the game didn't end in a tie. I know that I was. As for the crew, we just wanted to get out alive. With our security escort, we threaded our way to the locker room while knocking away hands trying to grab a souvenir, such as a whistle, a hat, a badge, or anything that wasn't secured.

Back in the safety of the locker room, we plopped down on our stools in jubilant exhaustion. We had literally been running at full throttle since the kickoff. Sweat was still beading on our faces when the technical adviser walked in and gave us a two thumbs-up. The game took nearly four hours and included nine turnovers. Starting in the fourth quarter, victory for either team seemed to hinge on every snap. The level of intensity was more than I had ever experienced. I was mentally and physically drained.

Before heading to the showers, we just looked at each other with a wry grin of satisfaction and a nod, too tired to talk. My band of brothers belonged to the history of The Game. This was the first triple overtime in the history of the rivalry that dated back to 1875. We felt honored to have been part of it.

After a hot shower, it was off to have a well-deserved and hard-earned taste. Jack Winter called supervisor Jimmy Mac to report that all went well. Jimmy, who stayed in his office the last week of the season to field calls from coaches and league officials, had watched the game on TV. He liked what he saw. That was all that needed to be said.

That evening we dined in downtown New Haven with the clock operators and technical adviser. While eating, we talked about the game and how we would have ended it because of darkness.

"Lou, what did you mean by let nature take its course?" Jack asked anxiously.

"Darkness will challenge but never triumph," I replied with a knowing smile like an ancient mystic. My cryptic response had everybody's attention. It was story time.

◆ ◆ ◆

Long ago on a gray, overcast Thursday afternoon in early November, I worked a public school JV game. Due to a late start, which pushed the kickoff to four, coaches agreed to play two twenty-minute halves instead of the normal four twelve-minute quarters. Midway through the second half (the normal third quarter) with the game tied, evening gently fell over the field. With no lights and everything covered in coal dust from the nearby train tracks, the ball and the chalk lines were fading from view.

The referee didn't want to call the game, so he improvised. Both teams would be given one more possession to break the tie. The visitors, who had possession at midfield, ran four plays without a first down. On cue, the home team offense ran onto the field with stifled laughter. I should have known something was up. After a quick, playful huddle, they lined up and ran a sweep to my side of the field. As the ball carrier was being wrestled to the ground, a roar came from the home team sideline on the opposite side of the field. A barely visible player with the ball over his head was sprinting to the end zone. No other player was within twenty yards. The back judge chased the play and signaled a touchdown. Game over and time to head for our cars.

To this day, I don't know what happened. I thought I clearly saw the ball in the arms of the running back who was heading toward me, but I never checked to see exactly what he was carrying. It could have been a loaf of bread. Was it a legal play or was there some illegal deception? Were there two footballs on the field for a trick play? Was there a twelfth man on the field, or did a player on the home team sideline just pick up a football and start running for the end zone? I'll never know but can only imagine what would have happened if it was Harvard and Yale.

"Hell of a story, Lou, a real classic," Jack chuckled along with the others. "But I was thinking about having the tailgaters park their cars around the edge of the field and turn on their lights."

"That would have never worked," I shrieked madly. "Just about every Yale alumnus would have been arrested for driving under the influence."

We laughed until dessert was finished and kept grinning as we headed out the door.

CHAPTER 19
INSTANT REPLAYS

Mention instant replay and hardcore football fans immediately recollect Jerry Kramer's book *Instant Replay,* his diary of the 1967 Green Bay Packers under coach Vince Lombardi. While it wasn't on any high school summer reading lists in 1968, the book found a permanent home in my bedroom bookcase. With some trepidation, I squeezed my copy next to my collection of Johnny Unitas biographies and Baltimore Colt anthologies. Knowing the history of the teams, these were highly combustible materials. Any second I expected the books to ignite in an angry inferno of white-hot flames. These books had to be stored properly.

As a result of my eclectic reading habit, I certainly couldn't bring any friends to my room. If they saw my Packer contraband, they would have reported me to the local chapter of the Colts Corral, a regional network of fan clubs that supported the team. They would send some henchmen to my house for a taste of frontier justice. Kicking and screaming, I would be unceremoniously dragged to Radecke Park for a trial. The judge and jury would be none other than Hurst "Loudy" Loudenslager, the Colts number-one fan, maybe, the top fan of any sports team in the world. Needless to say, my chances for acquittal would be non-existent. "Guilty as charged, Mr. Hammond," Loudy would firmly declare with an evil grin. "For your crime against the city of Baltimore, you shall forever be banished from the Land of Pleasant Living."

In Baltimore you can't talk about football without mentioning Loudy. In over forty years, he missed only one home game due to a heart attack. His club basement was a shrine to his team, filled with ephemera and memorabilia that included game-worn jerseys, helmets, cleats, and even splinters of goalposts. Over the years, he sent thousands of birthday and Christmas cards to players, coaches, and staff. When his hand got tired from signing cards, he baked birthday cakes for the players.

Whenever the team arrived or departed from Friendship Airport, he would run onto the tarmac with his record player and a hundred-foot extension cord to play the Colts fight song. He was buried wearing a Colts sweater and gym shorts from his days as a training camp equipment manager. His pallbearers were Colt alumni that included Johnny U, Art Donovan, and Lenny Moore. In many ways, he was a typical Colts fan. Every kid in my neighborhood wished they knew Loudy, or someone like him. When reporters talked about his collection, we would salivate. All we had were card collections, bottle caps, bobbleheads, logo knit hats, game programs, a replica jersey or T-shirt, and, if lucky, a white football with replica signatures.

However, our most remembered items were the Coca Cola bottle caps. They got the neighborhood kids out of the house on the weekends. In a stroke of marketing genius, Coke put black-and-white headshots of your hometown gridiron heroes under the cap. To young football fans with no money to buy a Coke (they were a dime at the time), they were treated like gold doubloons. To mount your collection, a local bottling plant provided saver sheets. Completed sheets could be redeemed for bobbleheads, pennants, and facsimile autographed footballs. There was no such thing as too many caps. They could be traded or pitched.

On Saturday mornings, my good friend Butch Hensel and I would walk along Belair Road to businesses, mostly grocery stores and gas stations, which had outside soda machines. In those days, soda machines had a built-in opener. When you opened a bottle, the cap automatically dropped into a bin inside the front panel. Using a magnet tied to the end of a string, we methodically fished out the caps with surgical skill. The key was to drop the magnet straight down to avoid sticking it to the sides of the chute. On a good day, we could bag a hundred or more caps. We were revered like gods for our hunting skills.

◆ ◆ ◆

Thinking back to Jerry Kramer and his book, he was not my first encounter with instant replay. On December 7, 1963, I witnessed the unveiling of instant replay in America during the Army-Navy game. That year family members gathered in the living room for the yearly ritual with somber smiles.

Two weeks earlier, President Kennedy had been assassinated in Dallas, Texas. Two days later, Jack Ruby gunned down the alleged assassin Lee Harvey Oswald on live TV. It took the networks nine minutes to replay the videotape. Although I was too young at the time to comprehend the ramifications of these events, I knew that I was witnessing history in the making. The future of America belonged to television.

If you lived in Maryland, the Army-Navy game was church. Every family with young children, especially young males, made a summer pilgrimage to visit the Naval Academy in Annapolis, only thirty miles south of Baltimore. Likewise, it was a rite of passage for male members to gather around the TV and watch the game. With families having veterans who served in the military during WWII and Korea, everybody had a rooting interest. Patriotism was proudly on display in 1963. For preteen fans such as myself, we were ready to storm the gates at one of the academies to be part of the pageantry. Five years later, we were running in the opposite direction as nightly news delivered the Vietnam War to our living rooms.

In the fourth quarter of the 1963 game, legendary announcer Lindsey Nelson described the action on a replay of an Army's touchdown. "This is not live. Ladies and gentleman, Army did not score again," he bellowed excitedly as the play was rebroadcast within a few seconds of the actual event. I was one of those fans rubbing his eyes in disbelief, thinking that Army had miraculously scored again. After the game, I wondered, *What will be the next step in technology?*

◆◆◆

Replay, as not instant, was nothing new in football. In the past, the major networks provided taped replays for the benefit of viewers. However, due to the time involved in preparing the tapes, highlights were usually shown only at halftime or postgame. Frustrated by the long periods of inaction between plays, Tony Verna, CBS director for football telecasts, was determined to speed up the process. He envisioned an instance that would allow the television audience to experience the game through his eyes. However, bringing fans into the director's booth wasn't easy.

During the game, Verna and his production team struggled with their equipment. The twelve-hundred-pound Ampex tape/

replay machine with a plethora of fragile vacuum tubes had been jostled on the trip from New York. With temperamental tubes, the broadcast crew couldn't predict how long the machine could operate.

The bean counters at CBS didn't help either. Pinching pennies to save $300 dollars for a new reel tape, Verna was given a used reel with an *I Love Lucy* episode and several soap commercials. Early in the game, Verna discovered the old footage was bleeding through the football images. Finally after thirty unsuccessful attempts, Verna captured the Stichweh touchdown, and the rest was TV and football history.

With no pregame promotion, the seminal instant replay went largely unnoticed. The game tape was eventually reused for another event, and the moment was lost to history. I always wondered what other unintended events were on the instant replay reel. Instead of Lucy taking the field, maybe it was Lindsey Nelson in a cameo with Lucy and Desi at the Tropicana. No doubt, the viewing public would have paid to watch it.

From the beginning, the marriage of instant replay and football was bittersweet. For better or worse, it kept us glued to our seats and provided plenty of grist for Monday morning quarterbacks. For Colts fans, the love-hate relationship with replay started on December 28, 1958, and I was there. No, not at Yankee Stadium but in front of the family TV for the Greatest Game Ever Played.

With 2:50 left in the game, the Giants, leading 17-14, had the ball at their own 40-yard line. On third and three, halfback Frank Gifford took the handoff for a sweep to the right side where defensive end Gino "The Giant" Marchetti was anchored. I swear the collision of tacklers and blockers shook our TV set. Gifford went down in a cloud of dust along with Gino. Frank got up; Gino didn't. He had broken his ankle on the play and was carried off to the sideline where he watched the rest of regulation play on a stretcher. After the field was cleared and order restored, the ball was spotted inches short of the first down. The apoplectic Giants had to punt.

Family members heaped mountains of praise upon the officials for their visual acuity and the intestinal fortitude to make the call. "They got it right. These guys are the best in the business," someone barked jubilantly. The game crew would always find a free round of drinks in Baltimore. *What a noble profession*, I thought. I easily pictured myself standing on the field next to my gridiron heroes dressed in black and white. My family would be proud.

The Colts took over at their own 14-yard line. Inventing the two-minute drill, Johnny U engineered one of the most famous drives in football history. A 20-yard field goal by Steve Myhra with seven seconds tied the game and sent it to the first overtime game in NFL playoff history. The Giants won the coin toss and elected to receive. After a three-and-out series, John sauntered back onto the field for what would be the greatest drive in football history. John was hot, and I swore I saw his right hand smoking, or maybe it was just the snow on our black and white TV.

John cemented his legend by herding the Colts eighty yards in thirteen plays. The drive culminated when Alan "The Horse" Ameche bulldozed his way into the end zone on a one-yard run for the 23-17 victory. The game was over but not the controversy over Gifford's third down run.

With no instant replay, only a replay of the game film was available to settle the disputed play. Until his dying day, Frank Gifford claimed that he made the first down. He believed that in the chaos after Gino's injury, referee Ron Gibbs picked up the ball and placed it inches short where he finally landed or bounced forward after being tackled. Who was right, Frank the player or Ron the official?

Sportswriter Peter Richmond fueled the controversy in 2008. In his book *The Glory Game*, he reported that after Gibbs' death, his son sent a letter to Frank updating the call. Reportedly, a few days before his death, Ron told his son that maybe Frank was right about the first down. The deathbed confession reignited the dispute. It now was time to end all the hearsay and dissect the game tape scientifically.

In the ESPN documentary *The Greatest Game Ever Played*, Gifford's landing spot was reconstructed by a forensic mapper as if it was an accident scene. The computerized lines and grids concluded that Gifford fell nine inches short of the first down line. Sorry, Frank, but science doesn't lie.

Cynical fans would say, "What's that prove?" It proves that officials more often than not make the right call at the right time. Official calls, right or wrong, are part of the game. There's simply no time for a forensic mapper to review every replay or challenge on the field. To ease a troubled mind after your team loses a close one due to an official's call, simply follow the adage: "Believe nothing of what you hear and only half of what you see." At least, that's what the official would say. The bottom line is that replays from one or two angles are not always accurate. You need composite camera shots.

The flipside of instant replay, or the lack of it in officiating, occurred seven years later on December 26, 1965, in Green Bay, Wisconsin. Once again, the play involved my beloved Colts. That year the Packers and the Colts finished in a tie for first place in the Western Division. To determine who would play Cleveland in the championship game, the teams met in a playoff. The previous year, Cleveland routed us in the championship game 27-0. We wanted nothing more than to return the favor at Memorial Stadium.

Late in the fourth quarter with 1:58 left in the game and Baltimore leading 10-7, Don Chandler attempted a 22-yard field goal to tie the game and send it to overtime. After kicking the ball, Chandler looked up and immediately threw his head back and to the side in disgust, believing he had missed. Colt players who had turned around to watch the kick waved it off with their arms. As they began to celebrate, field judge Jim Tunney, positioned behind the end line underneath the goalpost, raised both arms to signal that the kick was good. The Colts were involved in another historic overtime game. Only this time, Chandler won it for the Packers with a 25-yard field goal that split the uprights.

Once again, I witnessed the game at home with my family in front of the TV, only this time we had a color set. When Chandler's tying field goal left his foot, we craned our necks and held our collective breath. "Wide right. He missed it. He missed it," we shouted joyously as the wobbler veered away from the goalpost. A few seconds later, our joy turned into sorrow. "Son of a bitch if we didn't get robbed by the officials," someone snorted in a sullen voice that pierced the silence. We just nodded in agreement.

At dinner, the adults repeatedly commented on the worthlessness of the officiating crew with rather salty language that would make a sailor blush. I just kept my mouth shut and replayed the kick over and over again in my mind. *How could the officials have missed such an obvious miss,* I wondered. Likewise, I was amazed at how my family's opinion of football officials had changed in seven years.

The consensus was that we had been duped by a group of charlatans masquerading as honest men. Truth, justice, and the American way, espoused by my favorite comic book hero Superman, had been stolen from the citizens of Baltimore. Football officials were now lower than lawyers and politicians. After hearing about the vices of NFL officials, I put any thoughts about becoming an official on hold.

Was Chandler's game tying field goal good? The end zone angle provided by NFL Films showed the ball above and outside the right upright. Tunney, the only official under the goalpost, simply didn't have the proper angle. No doubt, the kick looked good from where he was standing. He had the proper position in accordance with the mechanics at the time.

His call proved that you not only needed the proper position but also the right number of people to properly cover the game. "I think I got it right. But every time I'd run into Don Shula, Tom Matte, and John Unitas, even years later, they'd always tell me I was wrong." Tunney said later in life.

The next spring, NFL owners voted to extend the height of the uprights from ten to twenty feet above the crossbar and station two officials in the back of the end zone on extra-point and field-goal attempts, one behind each upright. To Baltimore fans, that answered the question about Chandler's field goal.

Despite the disappointment, I managed to find two heroes in the aftermath of the tragedy, one obvious and the other ambiguous. The obvious was Colts running back Tom Matte. With Unitas and his backup Gary Cuozzo out for the season, coach Don Shula turned to Matte.

The former signal caller at Ohio State for Woody Hayes had never lined up as a quarterback in the NFL. It didn't matter; there were no other options. Matte still knew how to play quarterback, even if he didn't like to pass the ball because he claimed his hands were too small.

To simplify the offense, Shula outfitted Matte with a plastic wristband. Underneath the plastic cover was a handwritten card, carefully printed by Matte's wife, Judy, with all of the plays. Tom was the cutting edge of innovation.

Today quarterbacks around the country at every level use a play wristband. Has the game become that complicated or have quarterbacks become that incompetent in play calling? I'll leave that answer to the fans. As for me, I just can't imagine Johnny U in the huddle or at the line of scrimmage checking his wristband.

Matte's glory days with the Colts were only half the story. After retiring in 1973, the Ohio native remained in Baltimore as a successful businessman. After the Colts snuck out of town, he became an outspoken and untiring advocate in bringing back professional football.

He paved the way for the USFL Philadelphia Stars to move to Baltimore in 1985. In 1994, he was instrumental in obtaining a CFL franchise as a 10 percent owner. For both the Stars and CFL Stallions, he also worked radio broadcasts. When the Browns moved to Baltimore in 1996, he became a goodwill ambassador for Art Modell while working the radio broadcasts with Scott Garceau for nearly a decade.

At heart, Tom was a true blue-collar Baltimorean, a role model for young fans like me. After the 1965 season, every pick-up football game in Baltimore had a Tom Matte. Overnight, number 41 had become synonymous with number 19. Later in life, one of my most enjoyable experiences was befriending Tom when he was the color commentator for the annual Calvert Hall vs. Loyola Turkey Bowl games.

◆ ◆ ◆

My ambiguous hero, plucked from the wreckage of the 1965 season, was not placed on my pedestal until I started my officiating career. During his career in the NFL from 1960 to 1990, Jim Tunney worked a record twenty-nine post-season assignments that included ten championship games and three Super Bowls.

Nicknamed the "Dean of NFL Referees" he was the first official to be named to the All-Madden Team in 1990 and won the Gold Whistle from the National Association of Sports Officials in 1992. He worked some of the most memorable games in NFL history including The Ice Bowl in 1967, The Kick (Tom Dempsey) in 1970, The Catch in 1982, The Snowball Game in 1985, The Fumble (Ernst Byner) in 1988, and the Fog Bowl in 1988. Perhaps, his nickname should have been The Weatherman.

Jim started officiating while in high school and after retiring from the NFL became an observer of the field officials. While officiating, he was easily recognized for his classy trademark move. For touchdowns and field goals, he threw his arms with clenched fists above his head, then simultaneously opened both fists and stretched his fingers to the sky. I liked it. Following his style, I always ensured my hand signals and movements were clear and crisp. Instead of Sweet Lou, I could have been called Cool Hand Lou or Slow Hand Lou. They all had a nice ring.

In retirement, Jim wrote a couple of sports books and became a motivational speaker focusing on leadership skills and team building. Looking back on my career, I'm proud to realize that we had a number of things in common other than black and white stripes.

CHAPTER 20
ROLL THE TAPE

Not surprisingly, instant replay was an instant hit with the fans. Football is fast and furious. Blink an eye and you might miss the play of the day or the year. Thanks to technology fans now saw the "big" plays at full speed and slow motion over and over again. Another dimension had been added. Now the beauty of the game could be fully appreciated as a true art form. On the flipside, instant replay had a dark side.

The unbelievable one-handed, diving catch that defied gravity was no longer viewed for its aesthetics. Football fans didn't necessarily want to watch the Bolshoi Ballet in pads and helmets. They wanted to know if the receiver had one or both feet in bounds, and, more importantly, did the official make the right call.

Overnight, technology had poisoned the relationship between aesthetics and athletics. Instead of black and white stripes, the officials now had black and white bull's-eyes on their backs. Instant replay had morphed into instant replay review (IRR). It was time for officials to start wearing Kevlar jerseys.

Retired field officials are not put out to pasture, they're put out to the press box. Following my stint as a game-day technical adviser and grader, I extended my career as an instant replay official.

In 2016, the Colonial Athletic Conference (CAA) initiated IRR for all home games. Instant replay officials (IRO) and Replay Communicators (RC) were needed to operate the equipment. Jimmy Mac asked me if I would be interested in working with instant replay. Although I enjoyed working with field officials as a technical adviser, I was ready for a new challenge. It was time to journey down another road and learn new skills.

At our annual summer football clinic that year, the new replay recruits trained for two days on equipment by DVSport. We used custom-designed software that was installed on desktop computers. The wheel, or mouse, was used to view different camera angles, slow down the speed of play, and capture key components of the play. Playoff bowl games from the previous season were reviewed and dissected. It was intensive hands-on training that would mimic the experience in the press box. As a follow-up, we attended a two-day spring clinic in Chicago to learn the replay rules. Yes, there are separate rules for instant replay. Not all plays are eligible for review.

Two years after the CAA instituted instant replay, the Ivy and Patriot Leagues followed suit with different companies. Now all three leagues serviced by the CIP officials' association were on the same page. Not only did it offer more job opportunities for officials, but it resulted in a consistent and transparent replay process. The Ivy League opted for DVSport and the Patriot League went with WingWrap. Prices varied depending on the number and type of cameras, and the personnel to man, maintain, and monitor those cameras. Custom packages were available to fit any budget. In the end, cost became a deciding factor for most schools.

My first time in the instant replay booth was at Elon University in North Carolina. The IRO was the supervisor of replay officials from the CIP, and I was assigned as the RC. My primary duties were to always keep my eyes on the field and ensure the replay technician (RT) entered the correct information into the computer regarding down, distance, location of the ball on the field, penalties, and the number of players on the field. After my training clinic in Chicago, I was confident that I could do the job. However, with the boss man in the booth looking over my shoulder, I was nervous.

Late in the first quarter I sprang into action. "We should look at this one. This is really close," I stated calmly to the IRO. The question was whether the play was a touchdown or ball down short of the end zone. The IRO immediately buzzed the field officials, who had individual pagers, to stop the game. That was the first step in the review process.

I then informed the RT that we needed a camera shot down the goal line and an end zone camera shot so we could see the ball in relation to the goal line. After the referee stopped the game, he walked to the designated sideline where the sideline assistant, who also had a pager, handed him a radio headset to speak with the IRO. The IRO reviewed both camera shots and confirmed the touchdown. The referee quickly returned to the field where he could be seen by fans, coaches, broadcasters, and press box officials. "The ruling on the field of a touchdown was confirmed," he declared confidently.

The second stoppage of the day involved a pass play. Was the receiver in or out of bounds on a long pass down the sideline opposite the press box? "The side judge ruled a catch, but he was looking at the down judge for help," I informed the RO. The two officials conferred on the play and ruled a catch.

"We got smoke," I warned the IRO immediately after the ruling. *Smoke* is the term used in the replay booth when coaches and players verbally disagree with the call on the field.

The field crew was buzzed, and the game stopped for a closer look. "The previous play is under review," the referee announced to the crowd. By that time, I had already requested a camera shot down the sideline from the end zone and the program feed that showed a close-up of the receiver's feet in relation to the sideline. The IRO zoomed in on the shot from the end zone camera, which clearly showed the receiver in contact with the sideline when the ball was caught. The IRO relayed his decision to the referee via the headset. "After a further review, the receiver did not complete the catch in bounds. The result of the play is an incomplete pass. It will be fourth down," the referee declared.

Our third review of the game came in the fourth quarter on a pass play over the middle of the field. Did the receiver catch the ball then fumble it or was it an incomplete pass? The receiver had his back to the back judge who couldn't see the ball once it was caught. The two deep-wing officials, who had better angles on the play, conferred and ruled the pass incomplete. The IRO took a quick look at the play and determined the pass was incomplete. I immediately called down to the field officials via the official-to-official radio and informed them the call was correct.

Immediate is the buzzword in the replay booth. To keep the game flowing, replay officials must make instantaneous decisions during the review process. Although every play is reviewed, there's no need to stop the game to review every call. However, if the game is a blow out, we utilize *competitive effect*. That's when we keep the game moving because a replay review will have no bearing on the outcome of the game. For the entire game, we had stopped the game only three times for reviews. While in the booth, I kept reminding myself that I was no longer on the field. On the field, I was responsible for covering my designated area of responsibility. Now I was responsible for the entire field.

In the replay booth, we relied on the video feeds from the TV producer for a televised game or the on-site video production crew if the game was not televised. What appeared to the fans to be a seamless process had glitches. Many times the video feeds from the TV production truck were lost for a number of reasons, such as the camera became unplugged from the field to the truck, the camera person was not operating the camera correctly, the battery in the camera lost its charge, or the satellite signal was lost. All those feeds were essential if we were to do our job efficiently. Without the proper camera angles, video review (AKA instant replay) was virtually worthless.

The IRR team arrived at the replay booth two and a half hours before game time. At this point, our job was to check the equipment and ensure our camera feeds were functioning. At one hundred minutes before kickoff, commonly called the one-hundred-minute meeting, game management conducted a pregame conference with medical and security staff, clock operators, replay staff, and the TV producer. We discussed the evacuation of the field if there is an emergency or weather situation, the weather forecast for the game, pending lighting, the location of medical staff and equipment, the length and number of media timeouts (TV and radio) in the quarters, the exact start time of the game, location and number of cameras, possible problems with field conditions, location and number of replay sideline assistants, and anything else that could affect the flow of the game.

The first home game of the season was when new equipment and cameras were tested. In college football, there are no preseason games like the NFL, so the season opener is the first time the IRR system goes live. It's a time when anything could happen.

During the first game of the 2019 season at Stony Brook University, *anything,* happened. "Lou, we have no feeds from anybody. We're dead in the water," the frustrated RT announced over the air fifteen minutes before kickoff.

"Our computers are down on this end. Is there anything we can do?" I asked nervously.

"Yeah, just sit back, enjoy the game, and pray for a miracle," he replied half-jokingly.

Calls were placed to the local TV production crew, DVSport support personnel, the game-day operations center for the CAA, and anybody else who we thought could help. If the replay system is down, all we could do was watch the game on the field.

With fifteen minutes to go before kickoff, technicians were feverously checking, rechecking, and troubleshooting the systems. Taking the advice of the RT, I leaned back in my chair and folded my hands behind my head. *This is going to be an easy payday,* I thought. *The toughest thing might be deciding what to eat.*

"What the hell is that?" I shouted excitedly as I pointed to the ceiling. Above my head, a lone cable was dangling in the air. The baffled technicians came running over to investigate. They quickly scrambled around the booth and found another unconnected cable. The problem was easily solved. Our computer cable had not been connected to the mainframe. Minutes before kickoff, we were up and running ready for the first replay of the game. So much for sitting back and enjoying the game!

During a game at the College of William and Mary, there was a question as to whether a punt was touched by the receiving team and recovered by the kicking team. A timeout on the field was called. It was time for a replay review. Only we didn't have one; someone else did.

When the television broadcast went to a commercial break, so did our video feed. Viewers at home were watching our replays from the on-field cameras while we watched TV commercials. Somewhere and somehow in cyberspace, the transmission signals crossed paths. For two and a half minutes, we had no video access to the replay system.

From the press box, I could see the confusion in the faces of the referee and coaches as they conferred. It was late in the fourth quarter of a three-point game and the possession call could easily decide the outcome of the game. In the booth, we were stalling for every second we could get. Just as I was throwing my hands in the air in frustration, someone shouted, "We're online." Like magic, our replay screens reappeared. That was the good news. The bad news was that it took me another two minutes to review the play. Everyone in the stadium and on the field was now looking at the replay booth and wondering what happened. So did we. I hastily made a decision, and the referee made the call.

"Upon further review, the ruling on the field stands," the referee calmly announced as if the delay was routine. I leaned back in my chair and wiped the sweat from my brow. We dodged a cyber bullet.

As expected, the supervisor of replay called me at home on Sunday evening. "Lou, I need to hear it from you. What happened and why did it take so long?" After I explained our predicament to the best of my ability in layman's terms, he had one bit of advice. "Next time something like that happens, just let the play stand from the beginning."

◆ ◆ ◆

When did the IRR originate? While college football claimed the first use of instant replay, it didn't advance the cause of instant replay for officiating. Instead, conferences waited for the NFL to develop a viable process that could be adapted to their budgets.

The NFL began tinkering with the concept in 1976 during a Monday night game between the Dallas Cowboys and the Buffalo Bills. Art McNally, director of officiating, charted the game with a stopwatch and a video camera to time the process. Two years later, seven nationally televised preseason games were tested. The results were lackluster due to the lack of camera angles from a lack of cameras and lengthy delays in reviewing the play. The technology was deemed not viable.

In 1985, the review system was again tested during the preseason with more favorable results. Finally, the anachronistic owners were forced to confront and embrace technology. However, the love affair between computers and the owners was short-lived.

After the 1991 season, the owners ended the experiment, claiming the number of reviews and reversals didn't directly impact the outcome of the game. The owners saved a few bucks, but it was just a matter of time before technology returned. Good or bad, football fans enjoyed the review system.

In 1996, replay was again tested during preseason. This time referees had the authority to review plays on the field inside a booth and later under the hood. Finally in 1999, owners approved a new and improved system. Instant replay was here to stay with continued modifications to keep the game from slowing to a crawl.

The NFL finally realized that sports fans are IT junkies hooked on computer chips. They want to be electronically connected and craved instant gratification through instant replay. Instant replay was the new drug that kept fans in front of their TV sets. If you missed the play because you had to grab a beer or use the bathroom, no worries. You can catch the play on instant replay.

The tweaking process was never ending. In 2014, senior officiating staff members inside Art McNally's GameDay Central (AMGC) in New York began consulting directly with the referee during reviews to ensure consistency and timeliness. While the referee worked the challenge on the field, replay officials in the stadium and at AMGC studied the best available angles from the broadcast feed. The best replay shots were ready for review in seconds.

Before the 2017 season, the NFL's competition committee implemented two additional changes. Final decisions on all replay reviews would come from designated senior members of the officiating department at AMGC and referees would view all replay video on wired, hand-held Microsoft Surface tablets. Technology was marching on. To their credit, the NFL was carrying the banner.

In college, IRR first appeared in 2005 at the DIV I-A level. However, unlike the NFL, head coaches were not required to challenge rulings on the field. Requests for reviews were initiated by the RO in the booth who reviewed every play. If he spotted something that warranted scrutiny, he buzzed officials on the field about a booth review. If there was no clear evidence to overturn a call, then the original call stood. Keeping in step with the NFL, the ACC in 2016 employed a centralized replay center for all conference home games. Centralized replay officials would communicate with field referees and stadium replay officials.

The rules regarding IRR vary between the NFL and college. In the NFL, coaches must challenge an on-field call for a replay review outside of two minutes in the second and fourth quarters. Inside two minutes, the replay booth initiates the replays.

In college, all plays are reviewed from the replay booth. A coach has one challenge per game if he feels the replay official is mistaken. The plays that can be reviewed are the same in the NFL and college.

While the role of the IRO varies from league to league and from sport to sport, there is one elemental difference in football; the instant replay process operates under the fundamental assumption that the ruling on the field is correct. The replay official may reverse a ruling if and only if the video evidence convinces him beyond all doubt that the ruling was incorrect.

The lingo used by officials is often another confusing issue for fans. If the call is confirmed, officials saw definitive proof that the call was correct. If the call stands, they did not see definitive proof it was incorrect. The wording is not simply a matter of semantics. If the process sounds rather complicated, it's due to the nature of the game. In football, there's a time element with game and play clocks. While there are timeouts on the field, the clock is always running in the replay booth to decide within a prescribed time. Like the officials on the field, replay officials are evaluated on their performance. If that's not enough to think about, you also have twenty-two players colliding with each other and the potential for twenty-two calls by the officials on each play.

Other sports quickly copied the IRR, most notably college basketball. Like football, it also uses a game clock and a shot clock (similar to football's play clock). Was the shot taken before the expiration of the shot clock? Was it a two or three-point shot? Instant replay answered correctly every time. Yet, there's still controversy.

Sports that don't have game clocks have an easier time with IRR. In tennis, Hawk-Eye technology makes the game almost error-free. Players can challenge line calls up to three times per set. When they do, the tech upholds or overturns the call within seconds as clear visuals are broadcast to the audience.

In Major League Baseball (MLB), the Mitel system is used for managerial challenges and normally reviewable plays, such a home runs, fair/foul balls, tag plays, trapped balls, missed bases, and spectator interference. Beginning in the seventh inning, umpires can also initiate reviews of questionable calls from the field. The system sends video footage of every camera angle to a replay command center in New York staffed by former umpires. Their decision is relayed to the field where the umpire with a headset and microphone makes the announcement to the fans. Once again, indisputable video evidence is the law of the land.

MLB also uses replay systems such as Pitchf/x which records pitch location within .5 inches. If that's not enough burden on the umpires, there's the zone evaluation system that uses postgame algorithms to evaluate umpire performance. In World Cup Soccer, a replay system called Video Assistant Referee instantly determines whether the whole of the ball has crossed the goal line to score a goal. That information is transmitted to the referee within one second to avoid any unnecessary stoppages or delays.

Where does it end? It doesn't. The sky is the limit for adapting computer technology to sports. In the minor leagues, baseball is already experimenting with a computer home plate umpire. In 2022, the USFL (United States Football League) experimented with a sky judge official. The sky judge, an additional official in the replay booth, is used for the sole purpose of reviewing on-field decisions.

New technology also introduced Lazser Down, chain crew equipment that uses wideband radio waves to precisely measure the spotting of the ball. In the USFL, they complemented that technology by adding a ball judge to the officiating crew. Wearing a red hat, his sole duty was to quickly spot the ball at the end of the play. The goal was to have the ball spotted within five or seven seconds. And to think that not too long ago, I had to use spectators as human yardsticks.

Now is the time for the fans to stretch their imaginations. Is the future now? You decide. Could the infallible machine finally replace the finite and fallible man. It's been done in the cartoon world. I always tell fans who fantasize about the future to watch *The Jetsons*, the futuristic cartoon sitcom from the early '60s. In the episode "Jetson's Nite Out," George Jetson sneaks out with his boss to attend a football game. In the plexiglass domed stadium, there's flat screen TVs, videophones, ticket scanners. On the field, the game is played by robots that are controlled by coaches in an upper press box. The show was a weekly ritual in the Hammond house, along with *The Flintstones*.

Peeking into that future, computers and cameras could replace entire officiating crews. Computer implants could track and record every move by an athlete. Imagine a playing field with no flesh and blood officials. Who would the fans blame for a call against the home team? You can't argue with cameras and computer chips, although I'm sure fans would find a way. Humans play games for the entertainment of humans. Remove the human element and you have a video game. Imagine Madden NFL 24 replacing the NFL with George Jetson as the new commissioner. I can't, and won't.

Either way you view the argument about sports technology, technology creates jobs, especially for officials. And from where I stand, that's a good thing. Take a look at the USFL. With every technological advance, they add an official. Instead of subtraction by addition, it's addition by subtraction.

In 1987, when I started in DIV I college football, there were six officials. Now there are eight with the addition of a center judge in the offensive backfield and a side judge in the defensive backfield. Who knows, someday there could be an official for every player on the field. It could get a little crowded in the end zones. Regardless of the controversies surrounding IR and IRR, it kept me in the game after I left the field. For that, I'm most thankful. Roll the tape, one more time! I see smoke.

From a bumblebee to a zebra and back.
Working the sideline as the penalty reporter.

CHAPTER 21
THE CHAIN GANG

Once again, a phone call led to my next football adventure. Only this time I was making the call, and this time the call was to the NFL. Hey, if they weren't going to call me, I was going to call them. In early spring of 1996, I received a phone call from Larry Yocum asking for a favor. Larry, the longtime chain crew supervisor for the University of Maryland Terrapins, had hired me to work the chains, or rather the guns, in the CFL. I owed him a favor, and more.

"Sweet Lou, I'm interested in supervising the chain crew for the Ravens. Could you call someone at the league office and put in a good word for me?" Larry asked.

"Let me see what I can do, and I'll get back to you." I replied. Even though chain crews were employed by the home team, the NFL vetted the personnel for the crews. A good word from the right person could make the difference. In this case, I was lucky enough to go right to the top. Al Hynes had recently been appointed supervisor of officials for the NFL. I had worked with Al early in my college career. Over the years, he had been a friend and mentor. I didn't know what he could do for Larry, but at least I knew that he would take my call.

Three weeks later, Larry called me with an update.

"Lou, I got the job. I need to fill out my crew. Are you interested?" he asked giddily.

"Whatever you need, buddy. Just tell me when and where," I replied eagerly. Regardless of the pay and working conditions, a chance to be a step away from the playing field was too good to pass up. Larry even echoed my own words, "Don't forget, Sweet Lou. It's the best seat in the house, but you have to stand." No truer words were ever spoken. Football karma was working its magic.

Once again Larry and I were lucky to be in the right place at the right time. Many chain crews, or *chain gangs* as they are popularly called, had become family affairs with positions handed down from generation to generation. Since the chain crew from Cleveland was not moving to Baltimore, we were starting a family from scratch. There were a number of slots to be filled. With Larry's connections, we had a good labor pool.

How many slots were filled? Quite a few would be an accurate answer. Most fans don't realize how many people are working along the sidelines. The average fan at home or in the stands usually sees the chain crew only when they run out on the field or when they're panned on the sideline by a TV camera. Before 2020, crews usually had eight members with an alternate for emergencies. The chain crew does occasionally get bulldozed on a play, and people get hurt. You won't see the replay on TV or the scoreboard because it doesn't make for good copy.

On one side of the field positioned a yard behind the sideline, there's the primary crew consisting of two rodmen who hold the sticks connected with a ten-yard chain, a box man who holds the pole that marks the line of scrimmage and displays the current down, and a clip man who clips the chain at the five-yard increment closest to the front end of the chain. Before going hi-tech with a clip on the chain, a low-tech screwdriver was stuck in the ground to mark the spot.

For field measurements, the chain is stretched from the clip to the front stick. Likewise, if the sticks are moved or knocked down to prevent a collision with a player, the clip is used to reset the sticks in the correct spot.

Also, on the same sideline, there's the penalty-card reporter who details every penalty on a clipboard and the down-and-distance person who tracks ball position for each play. Not crowded enough? At one time there was the X stick that marked the start of every drive. Standing away from sidelines, he held a white stick (pole) with an X at the top. That stick marked the beginning of each possession and only moved when the ball changed hands. This marker was used primarily by the media to denote the start of the drive by the offense.

Across the field, there are only two members of the chain crew. The auxiliary box person holds a marker and is positioned directly across from the primary down marker. This is used mainly by the quarterback to see the line of scrimmage when he rolls out of the pocket. The box man only moves after the primary rod man has been repositioned. The other person is the alternate box marker who holds a down marker across from the main box man. Again, that marker is moved only after the primary line-to-gain marker has been repositioned. This marker is used by the offense for obtaining a first down. Both stick holders mimic their counterparts on the opposite side of the field. In truth, they are both relatively easy jobs that allow you to watch the game.

What's the sound of the men working on the chain gang? It ain't Sam Cooke singing "Hoh Ah, Hoh Ah." Think of Paul

Newman in the cult classic film Cool Hand Luke. It's more like the shuffling of feet and the light chinking of chains or poles. The crew is under the direction of the head linesman or down judge and does not make any decisions regarding down or spotting the ball. The main function of the chain crew is for players and coaches to see the line of scrimmage, the down number, and the line-to-gain. They move the chains only at the command of the head linesman and normally speak only when spoken to.

If the chain crew gets confused on the down or the line-to-gain, they can query the down judge or line judge. They do not have the authority to rule on downs or spots. Today they can also assist the field crew with information. Only recently, the league authorized chain crews to approach field officials in the case of egregious errors (those that would cause a riot), such as the correct down.

The main rules for the chain crews were not to root for any team and get the hell out of the way when the play is moving toward where you're standing. Drag or drop'em! That mantra came about after Bubba Smith, stellar defensive star for the Baltimore Colts (why does it always have to be a Colt), suffered a freakish knee injury in 1972 that nearly ended his career.

During a preseason game against the Pittsburgh Steelers, while blocking along the sideline after an interception, his six-eight, 265-pound frame became entangled in the rods yard and chain. At that time, the chain crew would stake the sticks upright in the ground and retreat. That procedure was changed after the 1972 season. Too late for Bubba who suffered multiple ligament tears around the kneecap, missed the rest of the season, and lost a step after his comeback.

◆ ◆ ◆

With two preseason games under our belts, the chain crew was chomping at the bit for the season opener. On a gorgeous, sun-drenched Sunday afternoon, the newly christened Ravens led by quarterback Vinny Testaverde beat the Oakland Raiders 19-14 in front of a sellout crowd of 64,124 giddy fans. The number 19 proved lucky once again. Before the kickoff, none other than Johnny U walked onto the field to deliver the game ball to the referee. The good times had returned to Memorial Stadium after a seventeen-year absence. The city of Baltimore had been vindicated thanks to the courage of Art Modell.

For me, it was an emotional homecoming, déjà vu all over again. Before the game, the crew changed in one of the utility locker rooms, the old dungeon, that I used during my high school and CFL days. On the field, I felt as I did for the Stallions first home game, only this time it was the NFL. Watching the pageantry unfold, I looked around the stadium with tears welling. The Old Gray Lady of 33rd Street held a lot of memories for me over the course of my life, probably more than most fans. Some of the best days of my life were spent in the stands and on the field. My only regret was that I never got the chance to play on the field.

I started my chain crew career as the clip man, certainly one of the physically demanding jobs on the crew. This involved a lot of standing and bending in contrast to standing and holding a pole. Pay and perks varied around the league, however we made about $50 per game with no add-ons, such as free tickets and meals.

The chain crew arrived at the stadium about an hour and a half before the game with game bags in hand. We wore sanctioned uniforms that included blue hats, white shirts, uniform pants (same as field crew), and colored vests. Except for the box man who wore a maroon vest, the rest of the crew had vests with black and yellow vertical stripes. I had been transformed from a zebra to a bumblebee. After changing into our uniforms, we assisted Larry with inspecting equipment to include the spares sets of chains on the sidelines.

Today measuring sticks have flexible aluminum eight-foot poles with padded triangular banners, topped with fluorescent bull's-eyes. The chain links are finished in a smooth orange rubberized coating. I don't know if the new technology would have lessened Bubba's injury, but softer has to be better in a collision. Over the years, the down marker has also evolved. The flip-over signpost has been replaced by the Dial-A-Down, a high-impact plastic marker with foam protection.

Before taking the field, the head linesman, now the down judge, stopped by our locker room for last-minute instructions to make sure everyone was on the same page regarding personnel and procedures. He'd usually want to know who was clipping the chain, who was spotting the yard line for field goal attempts, and who was working the penalty cards. In the early days, each head linesman clipped the chain in different locations. Some wanted it in the middle of the line, others at the front or back of the line. Nowadays, the down judge wants the back of the line clipped. Being a head lineman, I was more than familiar with the process.

Since this was the first year for the crew, we needed to ensure that all lines of communication were open. The last thing in the world we wanted was a screw up on the field by either crew. Fans don't see it, but there are instances where equipment breaks or officials are confused regarding a spot or down. No one better than me knows that mistakes can easily happen in the heat of battle. At times, the clip fell off the chain and I had to spot by eye. Another time the chain broke or snapped as the stick men ran onto the field. I immediately grabbed the two ends in my hand and held them tight until the measurement was over. No one in the stands or in front of a TV was the wiser.

At halftime, we switched sides on the field with the auxiliary crew. Now we had a chance to hear the other team bitch about the officiating. Coaches would often tell the officials, "We're glad you're on our side of the field. The other guys are terrible."

Teamwork is paramount between officials and the chain gang. I frequently kept my eye on the officiating crew for the sanity of the officials and sanctity of the game. You never knew what situation might arise.

"Sweet Lou, I left my penalty flag in the locker room. Can you get it for me?" the linesman asked anxiously with a worried look before the kickoff of a Ravens game in 1998. I had no problem doing a favor for a friend. I had known Tom since we worked college games. I quickly ran back to the locker room during the national anthem and found the flag in his game bag. I also noticed that he forgot his down indicator. I raced back to the field and handed him the tools of his trade.

"Hey Tom, I brought out my penalty flag as well. Just in case I see something you may have missed, I'll throw it over your shoulder," I kidded. He laughed and went on to have a great game. Nerves can get to anybody. I'll always remember when I forgot my socks.

A year or so later, Tom was back in Baltimore to work a Monday night game. Late in the second quarter, he threw a flag against the Ravens for too many men on the field goal team. The kick was good, but the defense accepted the penalty. The Ravens missed the next kick. Tom started to question himself. Usually there are two or three flags on the field for too many men on the field. At the commercial break, he walked over to me. "Sweet Lou, did you count twelve men on the field?" he asked.

"Hell, no. I can't count that high. That's why you're getting paid the big bucks," I bellowed playfully. Tom just smiled and laughed. Back on the field, no one challenged the call, so he must have been right.

In another game, I got involved to prevent an embarrassing error by a friend. With less than two minutes in the game, there was a penalty called on the other side of the field. After the officials conferred, it was determined there was no foul on the play, and the clock would start on the ready play signal. The referee signaled the clock would start on the snap.

I quickly told the linesman the clock should start on the ready for play. That meant it was a restart of the clock at twenty-five seconds instead of forty seconds for administrative stops. He agreed and told the referee, who disagreed. This gave the Ravens an opportunity to kick a field goal and send the game into overtime. The Ravens won. Unfortunately, the referee was suspended for any post-season games. Just another day at the office.

CHAPTER 22
SIDELINES AND SNACK LINES

My claim to fame with the chain crew came during my third season. Although Larry made sure everybody was properly and professionally dressed for the field, there was something missing in our appearance. That something was shoes. One day on the field, I noticed the chain crew was wearing different brands of black shoes. We were in uniform but not uniform, and that had me thinking. After checking with Larry, I called my contact with Spot-bilt.

"Ed, I have a proposition for you that could benefit both of us," I explained as I outlined my plan of free shoes for free publicity.

"Let me check with my boss. From where I sit that sounds doable, but I can't promise anything. Money's tight" he replied.

I didn't think my business proposal was well received but I was wrong. Two days later, Ed called for sizes. A week later I received eight pairs of Spot-bilt coach's shoes with black leather uppers and rippled soles. The next home game was Christmas morning. The crew was giddy over the gifts. We always looked sharp; now we looked sharper. I noticed that everybody had an extra bounce in his step walking onto the field. No one seemed to notice or care about the upgrade in our uniforms. The field crew, players, and coaches were already wearing free shoes courtesy of an NFL sponsor.

I really didn't pay much attention until a few weeks later. After a disheartening last-second loss, an inconsolable Raven was seen sitting on his helmet as the chain crew walked off the field. The picture made the front sports page in several newspapers and later appeared in a national sports magazine. In the foreground was the player with his head in his hands, and in the background were the shoes moving away from the camera. On the heel tabs were the words *Spot-bilt* in highly visible white letters against a black background. I emailed Ed one of the pictures.

An elated Ed called me at home later that week and asked me how many pairs of shoes I needed. "Lou, many thanks here. We're not Nike or Adidas. That kind of advertising would cost tens of thousands of dollars that we don't have. Does anyone need a different size or second pair? Just let me know and I'll send you more."

Unfortunately, Ed wasn't the only one taking notice. At the end of the season, a memo from the Ravens director of operations informed the crew that at no cost we would be supplied officially sanctioned shoes in compliance with NFL endorsement contracts. I don't know if the shoes make the man as they say in advertising, but they certainly made the chain gang. Somehow, I'm genetically imprinted about footwear and its appearance. Grandpa Hammond would be proud.

Two years later, my job on the crew got even better. I was now the penalty-card reporter. Armed with the penalty card and a clipboard, I recorded any and all information regarding the penalty to include what official called the penalty, player number, time of penalty, type of penalty, and whether the penalty was accepted or declined. Most importantly, I was free to roam the sidelines. And that's where the fun began. I could mix indiscreetly with players, coaches, medical staff, and front-office people and eavesdrop on their conversations like the invisible man. It was the ultimate wish of any football fan.

The best time to roam the field was during the pregame warm-ups. In this relaxed, calm before the storm atmosphere, owners and front-office people strolled the field to socialize like campaigning politicians. As long as you were on the field, you were in the social club and free to chat with anyone. The Modells of the Ravens and the Rooneys of the Pittsburgh Steelers were two of my favorites. They always took time to stop and say hello. It didn't matter if you were a ball boy or benchwarmer.

Easily recognizable in two-piece business suits, they made you feel like you were part of the NFL family. Over the years, I noticed they always seemed to remember names, especially my name. There was no "Lou, who?" I guess that's what made them successful businessmen who parlayed their personal bankrolls into mountains of NFL money.

When Art Modell moved his team to Baltimore, there were no complaints from fans about the new owner. Art was one of the finest gentlemen to ever own a football team. Art and his son David always worked the pregame field like game show hosts. After the owner of the defunct Baltimore Colts played the city for a fool and left town under the cover of darkness, we knew that we were truly blessed to have the Modell family in Baltimore. In addition to football related events, they became major philanthropists for various charities and cultural institutions around the city.

Despite all of the money that he made for the owners with TV contract negotiations, I still can't fathom why Art isn't in the HOF. Could it be because he moved his team to Baltimore under the watch of Commissioner Tagliabue? I'll let the talk shows handle that issue.

◆ ◆ ◆

While the crew was popular with owners and front-office personnel, we were even more popular with players. Our good standing hinged on keeping our pockets stuffed with goodies. What started out as a few snack items for the crew quickly expanded once the word reached the players. We became walking vending machines. Roasted peanuts, pretzels, and M&Ms were some of the favorite items.

In the second half of a preseason game, Scott Mitchell, quarterback of the Ravens, finished his workday and was hungry.

"What are you holding?" he asked.

"What would you like" I replied.

"How about a hot dog?" he joked.

"I'm not a cafeteria. You know a player got fined last week for eating a hot dog during the game," I chuckled. John Madden, former coach turned color analyst, had caught the player on the sideline and launched into a hilarious tirade using his Telestrator, a hi-tech Etch A Sketch that could be imposed over videos and pictures. The player was fined ten grand by the league.

"Maybe, that's not a good idea. What else you got?"

"How about a bag of M&M's?" I countered. Like a kid in a candy store, he ripped open the bag and began eating. "Don't tell anybody where you got'em," I cautioned. Scott gave me a high five and went on about his business. Of course, everybody along the sideline knew where he got the goods.

If you fed the players, then you had to feed the distinguished alumni who stood along the sideline. Larry, our crew chief, always had an ample supply of root beer barrels (the hard candy) for Johnny U.

No matter how much social goodwill we generated, dispensing snacks goodies to the Ravens players had boundaries. No matter how much we enjoyed the camaraderie, we had to remember we were not fans, at least not when on the field. Cross that line and you're waived with no questions asked.

During my years with the crew, I remember only one time when Larry had to fire someone. The individual had a penchant for seeking autographs while on the field in uniform. Needless to say, there was a long list of qualified applicants for the opening. Every year the Ravens front office forwarded hundreds of letters to Larry from fans wanting a job. One fan even offered to pay him.

Fans had their favorite players, and so did the crew. My most memorable Raven, probably because he was the most entertaining, was Tony Siragusa. Known as The Goose, the mammoth defensive tackle (6'3", 340 pounds) was a larger-than-life character who spoke freely about the current state of the Ravens during the game. In 2000, he found the lackluster performance of the offense to be particularly troubling. During a three-game stretch in October that included home games against the first-place Titans and Steelers, the offense averaged five points per game. The Ravens lost all three games.

At the two home games, Tony's ire caught my attention as he frequently paced the sidelines in the vicinity of the chain crew when the offense was on the field. In the 9-6 loss to the Steelers, he was as vocal as any fan in the stands. "Vanilla, that's all we got. Every game, every play, just plain vanilla," he sputtered repeatedly.

"Goose, what are you talking about? Vanilla what?" I asked one time when he was standing next to me. I knew he wasn't talking about ice cream.

"The offense, the fucking offense. It's run right, run left, and run up the middle. We need to mix it up. Some new flavors," he bugled. Goose was right about the anemic offense. It consisted of a bruising ground attack behind Jamal Lewis and Priest Holmes. Instead of vanilla, it should have been rocky road.

After replacing Tony Banks with Trent Dilfer, the offense started to click, averaging thirty points a game through the month of November. When the Ravens routed the Dallas Cowboys 27-0 at home behind two long TD passes from Dilfer, Goose was singing a new tune.

"Still vanilla, Goose?" I asked casually as he came within range during the fourth quarter.

"A chocolate sundae with sprinkles, whipped cream, and a cherry," he whooped merrily, prancing along the sidelines, and backslapping everybody insight.

Goose always knew when the camera was on and the microphone hot. One game in the middle of the 2000 season, I overheard him talking to Bill Testerman, a Ravens trainer, during warm-ups.

"Bill, I'm clogged. Too many chicken wings last night," he moaned in obvious discomfort with his stomach hanging over his unbuckled football pants.

"Goose, it's a little late to tell me that. How about a laxative to ease the pain and hopefully clean you out a little?" Bill offered with a grim expression.

"Yeah, that might work," Goose responded halfheartedly. "And one more thing, if I'm flat on my back in the middle of the field, don't roll me over," he added with a sly grin.

After meeting Artie Donovan numerous times, I thought no one could possibly follow in his footsteps. I was dead wrong and glad about it. Goose was an Italian-American version of the beloved Irishman and a worthy heir to his football legacy in Baltimore. After his playing days, he worked as a game analyst for Fox Sports and dabbled in show business that featured a guest appearance on *The Sopranos*. The gentle soul passed away in his sleep at the age of fifty-five.

Another favorite of mine on the sidelines was Kelly Gregg, a defensive lineman from Oklahoma. Small as defensive tackles go in the NFL at six feet tall and 310 pounds, he was tough as nails. The soft-spoken country boy, nicknamed Buddy Lee after the mascot for Lee Jeans, always answered "yes, sir" and "no, sir." Win or lose, he was always available for fans after the game to chat and sign autographs. He was Artie's country counterpart.

In 2000, the Ravens qualified for the playoffs as a wild card. On New Year's Eve, they played a first-round game against the Denver Broncos at PSINet Stadium. In front of a sellout crowd of nearly 70,000, the Ravens record breaking defense, one of the best ever in the NFL, manhandled the Broncos in a 21-3 victory. The Bronco offensive crossed midfield only once while Jamal Lewis ran for 130 yards on thirty carries for the Ravens. I had a ringside seat as the penalty report man.

With the temperatures in the low twenties and a windchill factor of five degrees, I was thankful there were only six penalties during the game. Late in the fourth quarter, there were two consecutive penalties on a punt that had been replayed due to a penalty. I had work to work quickly, but first I had to find my pen. I had moved it to an inner pocket to keep the ink from freezing.

Removing the glove from my writing hand and shaking like a leaf from the cold, I managed to hastily scratch the information on the penalty card. Miraculously, the pen worked for a few seconds before freezing up. It was a good thing that I wasn't being graded for penmanship because I was probably the only one in the stadium who could decipher my handwriting.

Over the years, I had officiated a lot of cold games, such as the infamous frozen whistle bowl, but never experienced a numbing cold like this. Despite layers of thermal clothing that had me looking like a defensive lineman, I couldn't get warm much less stay warm. Perhaps, what I really needed was a thermal pen.

The cold didn't seem to affect the Ravens. It's funny how the weather never bothers the winners. For the rest of the playoffs, I was back home enjoying the march to the Super Bowl from the comfort of my lounge chair with an adult beverage or two. My only concern at this time was the date for the chain crew's annual end of season culinary fete. Nothing says family in Maryland more than a crab feast.

That playoff game was one of many highlights during my time on the chain gang. I had personally witnessed the return of the NFL to Baltimore, the last NFL game at Memorial Stadium, and the first NFL game at PSINet Stadium. With the Ravens resounding 34-7 victory over the New York Giants at Super Bowl XXXV on January 28, 2001, I was already looking forward to the upcoming season. I didn't know how things could get any better for the Ravens or me.

How do you tune up before the game?
You get the latest copy of the mechanics manual.

CHAPTER 23
THE CALL

In August of 2001, the NFL and the NFL Referees Association (NFLRA) were at an impasse on contract negotiations for the coming season. Rumors of a lockout or work stoppage filled the airwaves on talk radio. What would happen if an agreement could not be reached? Football fans around the country were worried, and I was worried about my job with the chain crew.

On Wednesday, August 22, 2001, my wife, Kelly, and I arrived home after dining out to find a message on the answering machine. Kelly hit the replay button. "Lou, Larry Upson, supervisor of officials for the NFL. Give me a call ASAP."

"What do you think he wants? Certainly doesn't sound like it has anything to do with the chain gang," Kelly said.

"There's only one thing he could possibly want with me. Shoes," I chortled, remembering my deal with Spot-bilt that stirred up the Nike hornet's nest. In my heart, I knew why he called, but I didn't want to get my hopes up too high. Being a football official, I was following closely the contract dispute between the owners and officials. As always, the issue was money. The bottom line was that officials wanted salary increases that were deemed exorbitant by the owners. Negotiations had been on-going since March without any hint of an agreement.

After Kelly left the room, I replayed the message a couple of times. I had spoken with Larry years ago, but I wasn't sure that I remembered the sound of his voice. It was possibly a prank call.

I remembered a Turkey Bowl between Calvert Hall and Loyola that I had refereed. The back judge called a questionable pass interference late in the game that quashed a scoring drive. Somehow a couple of fans got my home number and called to indignantly protest the call. "Hey, guys, you got the wrong number. I didn't make the call. I'm just the messenger," I responded angrily with a few expletives of my own.

After the third replay of the phone call, I was sure that it was Larry. I immediately dialed the return number.

"The NFL needs officials. Are you interested?" Larry asked immediately. "There's no movement on the contract. Starting with the last preseason game, there will be a lockout."

"Larry, count me in. Just give me a time and place. My game bag is already packed," I kidded as my heart raced. I couldn't believe what I had just heard. This was a dream come true. Ever since I started officiating at Radecke Park, all I ever wanted to do was officiate an NFL game. I didn't care about working a major college game like Notre Dame or Alabama. I wanted to work one NFL game. That would be the crowning achievement of my career. However, I quickly realized there was a likely chance the regular officials could sign a new contract tomorrow. I just hoped and prayed that I'd get my one game.

For the next twenty minutes, my body was numb as I listened to Larry recite the details. The game fee for the assignment was $2,000 with $395 per diem. I would receive a minimum of $4,000 regardless of whether I worked a game or not. As Larry was talking money, I was thinking about my good fortune. "Larry, I'll pay you two grand to work an NFL game. There's no price tag on a dream," I felt like shouting into the phone.

With the money issue out of the way, it was time to start work. The situation with replacement referees was being fast tracked with NFL owners who were trying to keep one step ahead of the officials. Larry informed me that I had to attend a mandatory clinic in either Atlanta or Chicago and that my contract would be in the mail tomorrow. He then asked me for my various uniform sizes. "Lou, one final thing. Don't discuss this conversation with anyone. The lockout hasn't been released to the press," he cautioned.

After hanging up the phone, I walked into the family room where Kelly was watching TV. "Honey, are you okay? You look like a deer in the headlights," she asked worriedly.

"I'm going to the NFL. I'm going to The Show," I whooped as if I couldn't believe the words that were coming from my mouth.

After I calmed down, we sat on the couch, and I rehashed my conversation with Larry. Seconds later, I felt a chill run up and down my spine. A dark shadow had suddenly shrouded my soul. My smile slowly turned into a frown. I stared at the floor, wringing my hands. "Jesus, I don't know. Maybe it's not the right decision. I could be running headfirst into a shit storm," I murmured ruefully, aware that NFL officials would retaliate against replacements.

"You already made your decision, and it's the right decision. This is the chance of a lifetime. There won't be another," Kelly confided gently. She was right. I was fifty years old with more experience than most NFL officials.

Time wasn't running out; it was time to be a doer not a dreamer. I thought about one of my friends who had recently been rejected for an upper-level position with the federal government. "Best qualified but not selected" was the reason. I could never understand the logic behind that statement, but I could certainly feel the pain. I had been there many times. This time I just wanted to be selected, and I was.

That night I went to bed around midnight, confident that I had made the right decision. With adrenaline still coursing through my veins, I tossed, turned, and stared at the ceiling for what seemed like hours. I finally went downstairs and fell asleep in front of the television. Thank God for reruns of TV Westerns.

In the morning, Kelly resumed her pep talk much to my delight. I needed all the bolstering I could get for the challenge in the coming weeks. That night the Ravens were scheduled to play the Carolina Panthers in a preseason game, but I wasn't sure that I should work. I was still with the chain gang.

Once again, Kelly set me straight. "If you don't work tonight, the guys on the crew might get suspicious. If you go, you might get more info about what's going on. You always said the place had eyes and ears. Go!" she barked. I could see the wheels spinning in her head. "Be you. Be Sweet Lou," she blurted playfully.

I laughed madly. That was the funniest thing I heard in the last couple of days, but it put the situation in perspective. Once again, she was right. I just had to keep my eyes and ears open. The contact impasse would be on everybody's lips. The replacement battle was going to be a heavyweight fight and I needed a good corner man. In this case, I had a great corner woman. *Be you. Be Sweet Lou,* I mused. That would make a great bumper sticker. Now you can see why I fell in love with this woman.

◆ ◆ ◆

I arrived at the game an hour before kickoff instead of the normal two hours. I wanted to avoid any unnecessary conversation with the guys. I was glad that I did. Earlier that day the NFL announced that it was hiring 120 replacement officials from the ranks of college, arena, and NFL Europe. The cat was out of the bag. Everybody in the dressing room was talking about who would be invited. I kept quiet and casually shrugged off any questions directed at me.

About a half an hour before kickoff, the head linesman for the game entered the room to review our game duties. "This will be my last game for a while. The fuckin' scabs will be here next week," he snarled angrily, flashing his two Super Bowl rings. Some of the guys tried to make small talk, but he was not in the mood to speak to any potential scabs. To ease the tension, I offered safekeeping for the rings. That seemed to put everyone at ease. If you couldn't trust Sweet Lou, who could you trust? Little did he know that he was collaborating with the enemy. I was already feeling the first drops of vitriol from the shit storm. I needed a sanctioned NFL umbrella.

Before heading to the field, I chatted with the chain crew supervisor Larry Yocum. "Sweet Lou, I just heard from the back judge that the NFL is recruiting high school officials. Seems that major college officiating supervisors will not assign games to any official that works in the NFL as a replacement."

"Haven't heard that yet. As a matter of fact, I haven't heard too much at all," I replied offhandedly, not wanting to chance a slip-up. I knew for a fact that officials were being recruited from college conferences across the country.

However, there was a grain of truth to the rumor. Before working NFL games, officials would be required to fulfill their obligations to conference schedules. Larry was a close friend, and it was tough not to reveal the biggest opportunity in my life. But I had to keep in mind that it was also the biggest secret in my life. Sadly, the gossip and innuendo had already started. Next would be the angry finger pointing.

My contract did not arrive on Thursday as promised. I found nothing but junk mail in my mailbox. As far as I was concerned, anything not from the NFL was junk. *What the hell is going on here? Is the postal service back to using horses?* I fumed impatiently. I had some friends, Gardenville Guys, of questionable reliability who had worked as letter carriers in the past. I pictured my letter at the bottom of a dumpster behind a shopping mall or stacked in a basement with 50,000 pieces of mail. Or just maybe, the enemy, agents of the NFLRA, had stolen my mail.

Following my explicit instructions, my daughter, Kathleen, called me on Friday morning and said that I had received an envelope from the NFL. I raced home at noon and opened the packet. Enclosed were the contract and other forms that needed to be completed immediately. I quickly read the forms (the fine print could wait for later), signed them, faxed a copy to the NFL, and then stopped by the post office to mail the originals. For all I knew, I could have been signing my soul to the devil. Who cared, as long as they played football in hell, I'd have a job.

Back home after work, I sat in my lounge chair and meticulously read the fine print. I didn't have to surrender my soul, but I did have to attend a clinic in Chicago on Wednesday, August 29. That evening I received a call from the NFL security office. The security representative had received a fax from the league office in New York and needed to schedule a meeting with me tomorrow. The league was not wasting any time in procuring replacement officials. The process was now on greased skids.

The next day at work I picked up copies of *USA Today* and the *Baltimore Sun* to update the possible lockout of the NFL officials. The articles talked about replacement officials, the one-day seminar, and the NFL commissioner's (Paul Tagliabue) involvement in contract discussions. On my way home from work, I listened to a local sports talk show for updates. As expected, there was nothing in the way of useful information. The host, Nasty Nestor, talked about the dire consequences if the NFL used replacement officials. I turned off the show and listened to music instead. Talk is cheap. That's why there's the proliferation of talk shows. If Nestor only knew the other side of the story maybe he could have a sensible conversation with his audience. But ranting and raving attracted listeners and improved the ratings. That's the game of talk radio.

That Saturday morning, I met with the NFL security investigator at my house to begin my background check. I breathed a sigh of relief when I saw him walking up my driveway. We knew each other from M&T Bank Stadium. He was the NFL security rep who sat outside the locker rooms for the chain crew and officials.

In a relaxed and cordial atmosphere, we rigorously reviewed my employment application line by line. It covered a wide range of topics to include personal finances, criminal record, drug/alcohol usage, gambling, and references. Thank goodness he didn't ask about any neighborhood references while growing up. He also wanted a copy of my college diploma from Towson University. After about an hour, he left my house and headed to New Jersey to interview another applicant.

After our meeting, Jimmy Mac, still the supervisor of officials for the Atlantic 10 Conference, called with an urgent update. "Lou, Larry Upson has been in touch with me about you and possibly two other officials working as replacements. The conference's position is that you're independent contractors. As long as you honor your commitment to the conference, you're free to work anywhere." That was good news from a good friend. Before he hung up, Jimmy wished me well. "This is your chance. Have fun with it," he added cheerfully.

That evening, I browsed through my sports library and found the 1998 NFL rulebook. I wasn't cramming or brushing up. I just wanted to calm my nerves. Preachers read the Bible in time of need; football officials read the rulebook. The NFL was going to send a new set of rulebooks and a mechanics manual on Monday. Then I could start to cram.

◆ ◆ ◆

Over the next couple of days, there was no movement on the contract negotiations. No updates were coming from either side. The media and fans were clueless about what was happening behind closed doors. Everyone was anxiously waiting for an answer to the question of a lockout. They got it on Tuesday, August 28. Both sides had rejected counteroffers, and the NFL announced they had locked out the NFLRA. Games would proceed on schedule. I was scheduled to work the Ravens last preseason game on Friday night, but first there was the clinic.

On Monday, I spoke with Larry Upson about hotel arrangements for Tuesday night. He advised the site and location were confidential and an NFL rep would meet me at the arrival gate at O'Hare. "Look forward to meeting you, Lou," he added.

That afternoon, I received another packet from the league office that included a rulebook, three video training tapes, a clinic agenda, a television schedule, airline tickets, and hotel information. I immediately viewed the tapes and started cramming with the 2001 rulebook. There had been a number of significant changes since 1998.

Later in the day, I started receiving phone calls from irate NFL officials, some I knew and others I had never met.

Everyone strongly advised me not to work as a replacement. I was somewhat shocked. How did they know I was going to work on the field? Everything was supposed to be confidential. *Dammit, there must be a leak at NFL headquarters. No wonder there's all of this cloak-and-dagger nonsense*, I thought. One of the callers was a former minor league baseball umpire, now an NFL official, who worked as a replacement umpire during the 1979 strike in MLB.

"You crossed the picket line for your chance to be in The Show. What's so different about my situation?" I demanded.

"Lou, you're talking apples and orange here," he barked angrily and abruptly hung up. There was no way in hell he could honestly answer that question.

Wanting to avoid any verbal confrontations, I decided not to answer the telephone for the rest of the evening. That didn't stop what I considered job harassment. The next day, I received a letter from the president of the NFLRA asking me not work as a field official. I also received an email from a well-known NFL referee who warned, "Working as a scab will actually hurt and likely kill any chances you would have of ever getting into the NFL."

What chances? I knew that I had only one chance, and this was it. It could last one game or one season before the regular officials returned. There was no doubt in anyone's mind that one day they would return. The union was too strong. I should have sent the emailer flowers and candy with a thank you note.

At dinner that evening, my corner woman had balloons and a congratulations card at my seat. The meal was topped off with my favorite dessert—carrot cake. After dinner, we retired to the hot tub and enjoyed a relaxing dip and a bottle of champagne. Tomorrow, I was heading off to fulfill my destiny. I couldn't decide if the evening had been my last meal or the calm before the storm. No matter the outcome, tonight was a great way to mix pleasure with business.

CHAPTER 24
UNDERCOVER IN CHICAGO

The next morning Kelly drove me to the airport while I constantly checked the rearview mirror. I was expecting to be tailed by a hit man from the NFLRA. Along the way we chatted nervously about the clinic and listened to the radio. Just as we put the vehicle in park, we heard a news bulletin: "The NFL has locked out the NFLRA." Over the past weekend, there still had been no movement on contract negotiations. Both sides had rejected counteroffers. College officials would replace regular officials beginning this week. My palms suddenly got sweaty when I closed the car door. The games would proceed on schedule, and I was to work the Ravens last preseason home game against the New York Giants on Friday night. I was now officially in the cross hairs of the union and looking for the tiny red dot to appear on my shirt.

Upon arriving at the O'Hare terminal, I was met by a man with a hand-held sign that read in bold letters, *Hammond*. My greeter escorted me to the baggage claim, picked up my bag, and walked me to the limo in the waiting area. As he opened the rear passenger door, the driver quickly picked up my bags and placed them in the trunk. Looking around, I noticed people were staring and probably thinking, *Who in the hell is this guy? I don't recognize him from the movies, TV, or the tabloids.* For a second, I wondered hilariously what I would do if someone recognized me as one of the Oakridge Boys and asked me for my autograph.

On the road to downtown Chicago, the driver broke the ice with a few announcements. "Mr. Hammond, for security reasons the hotel location has been changed. When you arrive at the hotel, go to the front desk. There will be an envelope with your name. Inside that envelope, there will be instructions for the rest of the day. Enjoy your stay in Chicago," he stated calmly. *Is this the NFL or the CIA,* I wondered.

I expected him to turn around and say, "By the way, the name's Bond, James Bond." Unsettled by the cloak-and-dagger routine, I immediately looked around for the portable bar. If I ever needed a drink, now was the time. As luck would have it, there wasn't a limo bar, but I'm sure there would be one at the hotel wherever that was.

Arriving at the hotel, I noticed it was the same hotel mentioned in my packet. I said nothing to the driver but hurried inside to make sure I wasn't being tailed by the NFLRA. At the desk, I picked up my envelope. Inside was a room key and the room number to pick up by uniform and equipment. Following my written instructions, I proceeded to Room 505 at exactly 11:30 a.m. Outside the room, an NFL security person scrutinized my ID before opening the door. Inside the suite, workers were busy arranging piles of shirts, shoes, and socks. They checked the sizes that we had provided and handed us our uniforms. We couldn't leave until we had tried on the shirts and shoes to ensure a proper fit. A good first impression to the fans and media was imperative.

I got lucky with my shirt and selected number 59. Other replacements ended up with numbers 161, 169, and 189. That was too many numbers for me. It reminded me of minor leagues baseball players at spring training who had no chance of making the big club. "They should add two numbers and make it a zip code," someone joked aloud. That was the punch line of the day.

Giddy with the excitement of getting our NFL uniforms, we laughed. Then again, they could have given me number 10,000 and it wouldn't have mattered. Fans always see the stripes before they see the numbers. To our disappointment, the NFL logo caps weren't available. Instead we were given adjustable hats that looked like replacement hats for replacement officials; the last thing in the world I wanted to look like was a replacement. *Dress like a pro, play like a pro* was my mantra. I decided to use my sized college hat until the new hats arrived.

From Room 505, we were directed to Room 900 to meet with NFL security representatives. We were definitely moving up in the NFL hierarchy. From there, we headed for the meeting rooms on the upper level of the hotel. Outside, there were five security guards to usher us through the doors. Inside, a smiling Larry Upson welcomed and thanked us for attending.

The first speaker was Dick Maxwell, vice president of broadcasting. Dick talked about the green hat and orange glove person on the sideline for television and radio timeouts. He reviewed the duties and responsibilities of each person on the field and along the sidelines who were involved in the broadcast. We spent an hour discussing the number of time outs per quarter, the length of timeouts, communication signals with on-field officials, and locations on the sideline for each person.

After his presentation, Dick quickly left the room for a flight to another replacement meeting. There were clinics scheduled for Newark, San Francisco, and Atlanta. I chuckled about the first portion of the clinic. The emphasis on TV timeouts told everyone in the room about NFL priorities; maybe it was just coincidence.

Later at lunch, I had the opportunity to meet with officials from other college conferences. We came from everywhere: Big East, ACC, Big Ten, Mid-American Conferences, and the AFL. We shared stories about how we got the call from the league office, the harassment calls from the regular officials, and rumors about our assignments. Everyone agreed enthusiastically this was the once-in-a-lifetime chance to live the dream. No matter what happened on or off the field, we would weather the storm.

After lunch, we met with Larry Upson to review more administrative procedures. The first thing on the agenda was the announcement that we were going to be paid for four games, regardless if we worked them. That meant we would be paid $8,000 at a minimum. It left no doubt the NFL was serious about standing their ground in the contract dispute. Neely Dunn was introduced as the supervisor of officials for the back, field, and side judges. Upson also announced the crews that would be working on Friday and Saturdays. In addition, there would be alternate replacement officials to the regular replacements; all the bases were being covered.

My assignment was line judge for the Ravens game. At our afternoon break, I reminded Larry Upson that I worked on the Baltimore Ravens chain crew. "Lou, we don't have a problem with that. We trust the integrity of our officials. As a matter of fact, I'll be working the game to help train the replacement officials. Just relax and do the job we know you're capable of," he said assuredly.

Our late afternoon session continued after the break. More administrative procedures were discussed including media interviews. After the game, one pool reporter from the home team media would meet with the referee to get a statement on any controversial plays in the game. The reporter would share the answers with other interested media personnel. The referee would be provided with a recorder to record the conversation. Immediately after the game on the way to the airport, he would send the tape to the league office.

At around 3 p.m., Neely Dunn began his portion of the training. He discussed the seven-man on-field mechanics used by the NFL. After reviewing the coverages for each official, Neely then discussed player uniforms, specifically eye shields and foreign substances on the uniform and gloves.

Eye shields had to be clear or tinted in such a way that the team trainer or doctor could see the player's eyes. Before kickoff, two players from each team would have their uniforms inspected by the officials to look for foreign substances. The main culprits were petroleum jelly to make the jersey slippery and tacky substances (Stickum and other pine tar derivatives) on gloves to help the receivers make a catch. Banned in 1981, they were still being covertly used by those who needed an advantage and took delight in gaming the system.

The Stickum comment struck my funny bone. I almost burst out laughing when I remembered wide receiver Fred Biletnikoff of the Oakland Raiders. Back in the late '60s and '70s, he had so much pine tar on his uniform that he looked like he had been dipped in shit.

For the rest of the session, we reviewed videos, videos, and more videos, studying the most common fouls, such as pass interference, holding, and personal fouls on both defense and offense. We watched three videos and were given four more to be watched at home during the coming week.

At 6 p.m., with our brains fried and our stomachs growling, Larry made the announcement we had been awaiting impatiently. "Guys, dinner's getting cold, but don't eat too much. We have more work this evening." As we headed to the banquet room, a few officials returned to their rooms to grab their suitcases. They had college games to work tomorrow.

After dinner, we met to discuss the importance of good sportsmanship on the part of players and coaches. The emphasis was to reduce trash talking, disrespecting opponents, showing up your opponent, and other breaches of football etiquette. Again, a video was shown of players committing these ungracious fouls. It made sense for an image-savvy organization to curb this childish look-at-me behavior. Trash talking had infested every sport at every level. Professional athletes were supposed to be role models. Did they not get the memo, or didn't they know how to read it? Finally at 8:30 p.m., we were dismissed.

I returned to my room ready to relax for the evening. Watching television, especially a sports show, was not in my plans. I had seen enough football videos to last a lifetime. Instead, I called Kelly and replayed my day. "Lou, you had some phone calls that you should listen to. Nothing to worry about," she added before we hung up. I knew that it was more warm greetings from the officials.

Lying in bed, I couldn't unwind. Those videos kept replaying in my head in an endless loop. I tried to review my notes and read the handouts, but my eyes were too buggy and brain too foggy. That could wait for the plane back to Baltimore. To clear my mind, I focused on one thought: *Sweet Lou is going to realize his dream of working in the NFL.*

Despite the happy thoughts, there was an evil intruder beckoning in the shadows of my mind. *This is too good to be true*, I thought. Something bad was bound to happen, an earthquake in Baltimore, a death in the family, or a plane crash. Sleep was difficult because I suddenly realized that dreams could easily turn into nightmares, and in two days I could be living one.

◆ ◆ ◆

The next morning the limo bus took a group of replacements back to the airport. Half of us were flying to Baltimore for the Ravens game while the rest were flying to Philadelphia for the Eagles game on Saturday. Arriving at BWI, I grabbed my luggage and headed to Embassy Suites with the crew for tomorrow's game. Even though I was only twenty minutes from home, NFL rules required me to spend the evening at the hotel with the crew.

After checking in, I headed home to take a shower, change clothes, and repack my bag for my college game at James Madison University (JMU) on Saturday. Like the NFL, the college crew was required to be in the city of the home team the night before the game. I planned to leave for Harrisonburg right after the Ravens game.

Before returning to the hotel, I met with Kelly and Kathleen for dinner. They were going to attend the game, so we discussed parking and travel plans to the stadium. After dinner, I gave the girls a big hug and a kiss and drove back to the hotel in a driving rainstorm. *Dark clouds are gathering,* was all I could think in a moment of doom and gloom.

At the hotel, I met my roommate and fellow crew member. Buddy Gingas was from Louisiana and worked games in the Southeast Conference. We talked a bit about our different backgrounds in officiating before studying the rulebook in preparation for tomorrow's game. At 9:30 p.m., there was a knock at the door. "Room service," someone called out from the other side of the door. With all the security from yesterday, I did not want to open the door. Thanks to the NFL, I was quickly becoming paranoid. "Buddy, your dinner's here," I said.

"Already ate, partner," he drawled.

"I think you have the wrong room. No one here ordered room service," I called out with my eye next to peephole.

"No, sir, I'm sure I have the right room. I'll just set the tray down and leave."

I slowly opened the door and quickly peeked down the hallway to make sure I wasn't being ambushed. Next to the door on a folding tray stand was a silver platter with a slice of carrot cake and a card from my two sweeties wishing me a great game tomorrow. I shook my head with an easy smile. Love conquers all. Buddy didn't mind sharing a second dessert.

Around 10:30 p.m., I hit the rack and stared at the ceiling for what seemed like an eternity. In twelve hours, I would be on my field of dreams. Lost in thought and worrying about how I would perform, I heard a voice from the shadows. Forget paranoid, now I was becoming schizophrenic. I recognized it immediately; Queen singing the first verse of "Bohemian Rhapsody" over and over again, asking whether this is real life or fantasy?

It's truly amazing how a troubled mind worked. That verse perfectly described my predicament. I started to softly sing along with the music in my head until I realized that I might wake Buddy. Somehow, I finally fell asleep thinking maybe this was all a dream. "Lou, this is not the time to get metaphysical," I muttered under my breath. *Dreams do come true,* I reminded myself.

A dream come true. On the field as part of an NFL crew.

CHAPTER 25
WELCOME TO THE NFL

I opened my eyes and stared into the darkness as daylight slowly flooded the room. It was 6 a.m. During the night, Queen had stopped singing in my head and I somehow had managed to get a few hours of sound sleep. Friday, August 31, or more appropriately my Christmas in July, had finally arrived. I already knew what I was getting for the early holiday, and it wasn't an autographed football or Colts jersey for this child at heart. Under my tree this year was a real NFL game, and I couldn't wait to open and play with it. I scrambled out of bed, stepped to the window, and peeled back the curtain.

Below me, the city was already hustling and bustling. As I gazed upon the scene lost in thought, a sudden rapture filled my heart and awakened my soul. It was the spirit of football past, present, and future. I felt like Ebenezer Scrooge on Christmas morning. From out of nowhere, the words from *A Christmas Carol* came to mind, replacing last night's Queen concert. In my mind, I was dancing madly around the room and shouting,

"I am as light as a feather, I am as happy as an angel, I am as merry as a schoolboy. I am as giddy as a drunken man. A merry Christmas to everybody!" No matter what happened today on the field, this day, this game was truly a gift that would keep giving forever.

A sudden nudge on my arm broke my reverie. While I was absentmindedly celebrating my holiday, Buddy crawled out of bed and stood by my side. Together in silence, we shared the same thought, *Our day of glory had finally arrived, and we were here to fulfill our destiny.*

◆ ◆ ◆

At 7:30, we met the rest of the crew for breakfast at the hotel restaurant. We nervously joked about the game to ease our anxiety. Somebody mentioned the Philadelphia crew did not get to their hotel until 2:30 a.m. "Christ, that's just about the time I fell asleep," I joked as everybody laughed. We had all been in the same boat, or should I say bed, with our emotions.

After breakfast, we met with Larry Upson in the hotel conference room to start the pregame routine. Larry ran down the day's itinerary with times and places as if we were going into battle. He told us what to expect once we get to the stadium and what will be expected of us once we're on the field. At 9 a.m. sharp, we promptly boarded the bus with game bags in hand for our ten-minute ride to PSINet Stadium.

Kickoff was scheduled for 12:07 p.m. Although it was only mid-morning, the heat and humidity were slowly building like a pressure cooker. Temperatures were expected to be in the mid-80s by game time, a typical summer day in Baltimore. Not too bad for working outside; not too good for playing a football game outside. I was acclimated to this type of weather. If the rest of the crew wasn't, they could have a long afternoon.

Our fellow passengers included Rex Stuart, replay official; Mike Wimmer, video operator; the game-day observer; and the NFL security team. The presence of the observer was a subtle reminder that the eyes of the NFL were upon us. He was in contact with the league office and ready to report any problems or concerns that might develop.

Approaching the stadium, I peered out the window and grinned at the spectacle unfolding before me. Lines were already forming at the entrance gates while parking lots overflowed with tailgaters. Football fans were taking the day off to lengthen the holiday weekend. Make no mistake, it was game day in Baltimore. This was no ordinary preseason game in the minds of Ravens fans. This was a rematch of the Super Bowl.

As we pulled into the stadium, two uniformed Baltimore police officers boarded the bus and guided the driver through two checkpoints to the service area underneath the stadium. As we disembarked, a security rep guided us to our locker room. I knew the way blindfolded. I was home in more ways than one.

After dropping off my bag, I headed to the television production truck with a security person to meet with the producer. One of the most important tasks, if not the most important task, was to confirm the exact time of day because the game had to start exactly on time as dictated by the TV producers. Time was money, and wasted seconds could end up costing thousands of dollars somewhere along the broadcast.

To aid with keeping the official time of day and game time, line judges received a game watch. At that time, the NFL used a Sportline 125, a lightweight, uncomplicated, easy to read (large numbers) timing device designed for sporting events that probably cost less than a hundred dollars. To make it the official watch, the faux leather case and the watchband sported the NFL logo.

Back in the crew locker room, everyone was busily getting dressed in silence. We were nervous rookies making our NFL debut. Umpire Paul Frerking took a locker next to side judge, Howard Curry. I had a locker next to the head linesman. Everybody was self-consciously looking at their watches as if we were counting down for a rocket launch. Our biggest fear was that at the last minute an NFL lackey would burst through the doors, followed by a phalanx of regular officials, and announce the lockout was over.

With the pregame clock ticking and little time to waste, referee Ernie Briggs hurriedly conducted a pregame conference to review our pregame duties. Normally that conference is conducted the day before the game at the hotel. Today the locker room was unusually crowded because there were alternate replacement officials assigned to work the game. Everywhere you turned there was a guy in a striped shirt.

"Gentlemen, relax and enjoy the day. The league has all the confidence in your abilities," Larry Upson reminded us cheerfully before he left the locker room. That was the extent of his pep talk but that was all we needed to calm our nerves. From the shadows, someone breathed in a raspy voice, "*Carpe diem.* Seize the days, boys." Had Robin William snuck into the locker room? It was the same message as Larry's but with more dramatic flair. I loved it.

Above the din, there was a steady stream of people coming in and out of the locker room. Game and play clock operators, television commercial coordinators, ball boys, and audio personnel for the referee's microphone were among the minions getting last minute instructions. There was literally an army of support personnel for every player on the field.

Baltimore native and football icon George Young, now the vice president of league operations stopped in the locker room to wish us well. Seconds later, Kevin Byrne, Ravens public relations director, introduced himself and escorted me and field judge Bob Powell to a meeting with Ravens Head Coach Brian Billick. After finishing a radio interview, the coach invited us into his office and introduced himself. He shook my hand and paused pensively. "You look familiar. Have we met before?" he asked cordially.

"Coach, you see me here every Sunday. I'm with the chain crew," I replied amiably.

Brian quickly provided us with the captains for today's game and info on today's quarterbacks and kickers, such as right or left-handed and right or left footed. He also gave us the name of the "get-back coach." While not really a coach, this person had a crucial function for field management. For field officials, he was the go-to guy if players were creeping or drifting out of the team area into and down the sideline. In return, we gave Brian the exact time and the scheduled kickoff time.

"Hey guys, thanks for stopping by and have a great time," he offered warmly as we left. Coach Billick made a favorable impression. I just hoped he was that cordial during and after the game.

From Billick's office, we headed to the Ravens locker room to meet Jeff Friday, strength and conditioning coach. We informed him what time we would collect the captains for the coin toss. In return, he gave us the location of the tunnel where the players would be introduced. Returning to our locker room, we shared our information with the crew. The side judge, who had visited with Head Coach Jim Fossil of the New York Giants and his staff, reciprocated.

Before heading out to the field, I stopped by the chain crew locker room to see the guys. As I stepped into the room, everyone stared at me slack-jawed in disbelief. I had a shirt with a number. I was part of the on-field crew. "Brother Lou, you made the varsity," someone shouted comically amid a round of applause.

"Hey, guys, this game's for you. I couldn't have made it without your support," I replied amid the hugs and handshakes. They were beaming with pride that someone from their ranks had been selected.

"Just don't fuck it up 'cause you've already been replaced by a replacement," someone joked. The room broke out in laughter. I knew my chain crew had my back today.

Larry Yocum, chain gang supervisor, was the only person who knew that I had been hired as a replacement. I told him a few days before I flew to Chicago for the clinic so he could find my replacement. I recommended my close friend and fellow official Jack Winter for the job. It worked out perfectly because immediately after the game, Jack and I were driving to JMU for Saturday's game.

"Stay hungry out there today, boys" I quipped before heading out to the field.

"Ain't we always," somebody shot back. At halftime and after the game, the chain crew was lucky to get a soda and hot dog—a cold dog at that after someone stole the microwave. Meanwhile, the on-field field crew feasted on a catered buffet platter that included roast beef, roast turkey, corned beef, cheeses, salads, and the sometimes Maryland crab cakes. Hell, I'd work for free for that kind of meal.

An hour before kickoff, the crew headed to the field for a pregame field inspection. Again, two city police officers and NFL security personnel accompanied us. Hallelujah! We were finally standing on *terra firma* for an NFL game. The sun never shone brighter nor felt warmer. I was feeling that state of rapture from earlier this morning. I wasn't walking on the field; I was floating over it.

My pregame duties were to ensure the clocks were functioning properly, the field was marked properly, and the auxiliary chain crew was briefed. While walking around the field, I occasionally glanced into the stands to see if someone I knew recognized me. I noticed some fans leaning over the rail and shaking a sign in front of their faces with the number 59 in bold letters. That number belonged to rookie long snapper Joe Maese. It was nice to see he already had a fan club.

As I moved closer, the sign suddenly dropped. "Lou, Lou, we love you," two female fans shouted as if they were teenyboppers at a Beatles concert. The joke was on me, and I broke out in laughter. My fan club was Kelly and Kathleen. As they leaned over the rail to chat, Kelly told me that she secretly switched seats with some friends to be closer to the field. I knew they were coming to the game, but I didn't know where they were sitting.

Those seats turned out to be the best in the house. A week after my debut, a BGE coworker attending the game sent me a picture. As fate would have it, I was on the field along the sideline and behind me in the stands was my fan club. The photographer had no idea that my wife and daughter were the women in the picture.

Nine minutes before the game, I led the Ravens from their locker room to the tunnel for their introductions. With this being the last preseason game and final cuts looming over the weekend, there were a lot of nervous and excited players squeezed in the portal. In the shadows, all I heard was shouting, clapping, and the sharp crack of banging shoulder pads that sounded like gunfire. When the last offensive player was introduced, the rest of the squad stampeded onto the field like a herd of wild stallions. Hearing the roar of the crowd was a shot of pure adrenaline to the heart. I slowly jogged to midfield behind the last player and tried not to smile too much. How could I not?

A few minutes before kickoff, I stood with the crew near the 50-yard line as the Marching Ravens band played the national anthem. In my mind, someone hit the pause button. Time had stopped, and I was instantly transported back in time. PSINet Stadium had magically become Memorial Stadium in the early 1960s. Amid the sights and sounds of 60,000 raucous fans, I was standing at attention with my father. The mellifluous sound of the Colts Marching Band echoed in my mind as they high stepped and strutted across the field.

While the Marching Ravens played, I swore that I felt the hand of my father on my shoulder. When the band finished, I peered at the Ravens sideline. The gathering of old Colts, to include Johnny U, Lenny Moore, Art Donovan, Jim Parker, and Raymond Berry, exchanged handshakes and easy smiles. I smiled also, wondering if they had just stepped out of the same time machine. Yes, only seconds ago, I believed that I saw them standing along the sidelines at Memorial Stadium with the same smiles on much younger faces ready to take the field.

◆ ◆ ◆

After the coin toss, I moved to my position and waited for the kickoff. With goose bumps on my arms, I watched anxiously as the field judge got the all-clear signal from the green hat, part of the TV broadcast field crew, and then handed the ball to Ravens kicker Matt Stover. Self-consciously I looked down at my highly polished shoes to make sure that I wasn't wearing baseball cleats and standing in Radecke Park. This was no barren, brown, dirt field beneath my feet. Today I was standing in a sea of high-tech natural grass that looked like a fairway at Augusta National Golf Club.

As the kicker stepped into the ball, I took a deep breath and exhaled thirty-two years of football memories. The resounding thud of a foot striking a leather ball broke my reverie. As if shot out of canon, the ball arced end over end toward the end zone. The game had begun; the dream was real. I was officially an official in the National Football League.

As the teams lined up for the first play from scrimmage, my football instincts automatically kicked in. Hard to believe, but it was just another football game. My eyes focused on the deep return man on my side of the field and the blockers that were moving in front of him. When the ball sailed out of the end zone, I gave the timeout and signaled the touchback.

With 4:24 remaining in the first quarter, I had the first foul of the game. It was an easy call with number 55 of the Ravens, Jamie Sharper, jumping offsides. In the second quarter at 10:16, I had the first touchdown call, a run up the middle by Ravens running back Terry Allen. Later, I had a swing pass to my sideline. I called the pass complete and a fumble by the receiver. From the sideline, I heard Larry Upson yelling. "Incomplete, incomplete, incomplete." I immediately gave the incomplete signal. There was no challenge by either coach, so no replay was needed. To my knowledge this was the only mistake that I made all game. Thanks to Larry, it was quickly corrected.

The second quarter ended, and the crew headed into the locker room for half time. In the NFL, half time is twelve minutes, compared to twenty minutes in college. This doesn't seem like much of a disparity, but in the NFL it's a big deal. Here every aspect of the game on and off the field is managed as if minutes were hours. I had just enough time to grab a soda before I had to retrieve the Ravens from their locker room. We arrived on the field as scheduled. However, the Giants were two minutes late, and the television people were complaining.

To the relief of the TV moguls and the broadcast booths, the third quarter kicked off on time. I still had the same view but from a different location. During the second half, the wing officials switched sides of the field. I was now on the same side of the field as Kelly and Kathleen. I gave the girls a quick glance and got a thumbs-up and a loud cheer. Who knows if they cheered loud and long enough, they might start a new football tradition of cheering for the officials. *If my fan club in Richmond could see me today, they would be beaming with pride,* I mused.

Back on the field, there was a long run to my side, and I ran forty yards to get the spot. There was another run to the goal line, and I was in position to make the call. As the ball broke the goal line, I methodically threw my arms in the air like a seasoned pro. Touchdown Ravens! The stadium erupted in thunderous cheers. Was that for the Ravens or me? I know who my fan club had in mind. Either way, Jim Tunney would have been proud.

The quarter ended all too quickly, and I found myself standing on the sideline, now a spectator. My alternate had taken over. On the first play of the fourth quarter, there was a false start by the Ravens quarterback. The official ruled the Giants defense was offsides. Jim Fossil, the Giants head coach, was apoplectic and called the referee to the sideline for an explanation. I was glad that I wasn't in the game at that time. Meandering behind the Ravens bench, I slowly made my way over to the sideline where the rest of the crew was standing.

David Modell, president of the Ravens, approached me and thanked me for working today and working on the chain crew. "Lou, what do you see as the major difference between college and professional?" he asked sincerely.

"For a fan, it's the talent level. Everybody in the NFL is the cream of the college crop. For me as an official, it's mainly two things," I replied. I first explained about having two feet in bounds in the NFL for a completed catch versus one foot in college. I then talked about how hash marks in the NFL were closer together and in line with the goalposts, where in college the hash marks were four yards wider. He nodded his head politely, thanked me once again, shook my hand, and moved back to the Ravens bench. He struck me as a businessman who was a great fan of the game but not an *X's* and *O's* kind of guy. No matter, he made me feel like I was part of the Ravens and NFL family. In his heart, he just wanted to be one of the guys. He was a good fit for Baltimore. I liked him immediately.

The game ended too quickly as if in a dream, and the officials headed back to the locker room. The announced crowd of 66,197 fans was ecstatic. With starters for both teams playing most of the first half, the Ravens thrashed the Giants 38-7. In many aspects, the game resembled the Ravens 34-7 Super Bowl win over the Giants in January with one major difference; Elvis Grbac replaced Trent Dilfer who was ignominiously released. I wasn't enamored with the move. Trent had just won the Super Bowl. He was a blue-collar gamer.

Back in the locker room, we breathed a collective sigh of relief. We had weathered our first battle with flying colors. Wellington Myra, Hall of Fame owner of the Giants and Hall of Fame gentleman, stopped by and thanked us for a job well done. Team management or coaches were not normally allowed in the officials' locker room. However, this was an exception to the rule, or more appropriately, an exception for one of the most benevolent rulers in the NFL.

Larry Upson made his rounds, personally thanking each official and presenting each of us with a game ball. I expected him to announce that the regular officials had agreed to the contract and our services were no longer required. To my relief, that was not the case.

As the locker room slowly cleared, the crew filled their game reports and headed to the showers before heading home. There had been ten penalties called during the game. Overall, I was pleased with my performance and that of the crew. I couldn't wait to read what the reporters were saying and writing about the game. Outside the stadium, I met briefly with Kelly and Kathleen before heading to Jack's car for the ride to JMU.

"Lou, I have some advice from the chain crew. Stay hungry," Jack chuckled as we headed out of the parking lot. They had enjoyed the premium lunch platter that I had provided out of my own pocket.

◆ ◆ ◆

When I returned home on Sunday morning, Kelly had the reviews about the replacement officials waiting for my perusal.

One of the best quotes came from Giants owner Wellington Mara: "I went into their dressing room after the game and thanked them. I thought they did a good job handling the transition."

"Some of the guys were saying the refs were a little lenient on the holding, but I don't think it was enough to make a difference in the game," said Ravens center Mike Flynn. "Believe it or not, we get away with a lot of holding anyway. There was a lot of pressure on them, and I think they did a good job. No one was really complaining," he added. Believe it or not, Mike spoke the truth about holding calls.

One beat writer reported that having never worked together as a crew, the replacements exhibited fine teamwork and turned in a laudable performance. On a key third-down pass play in the first quarter, an official credited Ravens receiver Shannon Sharpe with a catch. Two other officials rushed to the scene and correctly changed the call to an incompletion.

"I think they did an excellent job. They administered the game very well," said Ravens coach Brian Billick. "That's a tough situation to come into," he added. Believe it or not, Brian spoke the truth about our current plight.

Hopefully, I would have another chance to relive the dream. No matter what happened over the weekend with the lockout negotiations, I proved that I belonged on the field with the best in the game. Life doesn't get any better than that.

Bengals versus Patriots : In a close game, a pensive rookie official checks the game clock late in the fourth quarter.

CHAPTER 26
OFFICIALLY AN NFL OFFICIAL

Over the Labor Day weekend, I finally had a chance to catch my breath and decompress with an adult beverage in one hand and the TV remote in the other. If I wasn't channel surfing sports program, I was listening to sports talk shows on the radio. From what I could find, the reviews for the replacement officials around the country were overall good. The only criticism by some beat writers was the lack of penalties. Was that good or bad? That depends if your team won or lost.

All I know was that there were no controversial calls that questioned the competency and ability of the replacement crews. That wasn't just good; that was great. For sure, there were some minor missed calls, but nothing that impacted the outcome of the game. If the NFL was happy, the replacement officials were ecstatic.

On Monday, I watched and critiqued the replay of Friday's game. There were a few minor miscues and missteps not obvious to the fans in the stands or in front of the TV, but the crew performed well. It was obvious that we had done our homework. The one play that I watched about ten times was the pass that I had initially called a catch and fumble before calling it incomplete. Larry Upson had my back on the play, and I was grateful. More accurately, he had the angle, and I didn't. I was in the right position at the right time, but my view was partially blocked. That's part of the game, and that's why teamwork was important for crews.

I spent the rest of the day sequestered in my house waiting for a call from the NFL. I was certain the league office would soon be telling me politely and professionally that I had screwed up. If not that, then the caller would say the lockout was over. Either way, I didn't want to hear phones ringing in my house. Football officials live to make calls on the field and die from phone calls made off the field.

Back at work on Tuesday, I was the office hero for the day. In the lunchroom, the game was being replayed on the television non-stop. Coworkers huddled around the screen and cheered whenever number 59 came into view. Well-wishers stopped by my desk all morning to ask me about the game and any future games. "Just a one-shot deal. Most likely the regular crews will be back this weekend. Too much money involved," I replied nonchalantly, hoping that was a lie. Throughout the morning, I checked the news to see if there was a settlement. It appeared neither side was going to blink or budge. I paced around the office like a lion in a cage.

At 10:20 a.m., I called the league office on the private officiating line. "No word on any agreements. Right now, we're working on this week's assignments. Should have them completed this afternoon," Neely Dunn assured me. I put down the phone and took a deep breath. I didn't want to get my hopes up too high, but it looked like we were going to open the NFL regular season. I suppressed a grin and went back to work, but

I couldn't concentrate. I watched the clock and stared at the phone. Seconds passed like hours. "Ring, damn it," I muttered to myself.

Later that day, Larry Upson called me back. "Pack your bags, Lou. You're going to Cincinnati for the Bengals-Patriots game. Focus on the line judge because that will be your position on Sunday," he announced cheerfully.

That evening American Express Travel, travel agent for the NFL, called. It would be another whirlwind weekend of getting from point A to B, proving that nothing good comes easy. My college game was at the University of Rhode Island on Saturday afternoon. I planned to fly to Providence on Friday afternoon and rent a car to get me to the game and back to the airport. That meant I had to fly out of Providence to Cincinnati on Saturday evening, and after the game fly back to Baltimore on Sunday.

"You have to get me to Cincinnati on time. I can't afford any delays or overbookings," I pleaded nervously as I pictured myself standing at the Providence airport on Sunday afternoon like a homeless waif from a Charles Dickens novel.

"No problem. We're travel pros. We'll have all of your travel documents safely in your hands on Thursday," the agent said assuredly. I wanted to reach through the phone and kiss this woman. *Nothing like dealing with the pro in any business*, I thought. I easily related to the kind of professional attitude.

On Thursday, I received a package from the NFL containing a rulebook, a casebook, the *Week One* bulletin, and a game-day operations manual. Now I wondered and worried about my airline tickets.

Minutes later, I signed for my travel documents from American Express. My biggest challenge wasn't going to be working the games, it was packing for them. That evening I packed and repacked, checked, and rechecked both college and pro uniforms. "Lou, don't forget your socks," I mumbled repeatedly. Luckily, I was able to cram both uniforms in one bag for a carry-on. Due to league rules, officials were not allowed to check their uniform bags through regular baggage en route to a game. They had to keep the bag in their possession in case the flight was canceled or the plane was switched. On the way back, it wouldn't be a problem. There was a whole week for the airline to find your bag.

◆ ◆ ◆

The breaking news that afternoon was music to my ears. In a telephone conference, the NFL made a counteroffer to the executive board of the NFLRA. The board voted immediately and, as expected, the counteroffer was unanimously rejected. Neither side commented on any future talks. That meant that I had the game on Sunday. It was time to celebrate.

That evening on our way to dinner at a local restaurant, Kelly and I listened to a sports talk show hosted by veteran sportscaster Tom Davis. His special guest to kickoff the NFL season was none other than Johnny U. When the conversation shifted to the replacement officials, John had nothing but praise for the crews that worked last week. When John spoke, you listened, and I did with sense of pride.

"Hon, you should call in and tell them your side of the story," Kelly suggested. I knew she was proud of her hubby, but it was out of the question.

"Great idea, but I can't. Officials should be seen and heard on the field, not off of it. That's NFL policy," I replied sheepishly.

Back home, John Smith, referee for Sunday's game, called with updates. He had a college game at the University of Miami on Saturday night and could not get a flight out until Sunday morning. For the rest of the crew, there was going to be a police escort from the airport in Cincinnati to the stadium. He would meet us in the locker room. I worked on a crew with John during his first year in DIV I and was looking forward to working with him again. I always considered him one of the best in the business. The game would be well officiated.

◆ ◆ ◆

On Friday afternoon, I touched down in Providence and picked up my rental car. At the hotel, I met the crew and headed out for dinner that included clam chowder, Rhode Island spicy calamari, and stuffed lobster. Seafood, not *see-food*, was one of the job perks when working in New England, and I never failed to take advantage of the situation. As expected, the dinner conversation focused on my NFL experience. "Guys, just another football game," I exclaimed after detailing my debut. "Not by a long shot," I added after a pause. The crew cheered and whistled. They knew exactly where I was coming from.

After dinner, we retired to the hotel conference room to view game films from the previous week. Following the film session, I met with head linesman Matt Fitzgerald who provided me with study materials for Sunday's game. Matt was not a replacement official but worked in the NFL Europe. He had some great stories about football life overseas, namely the cultural gaffes. "There were more fumbles in the locker room than on the field," he joked. I laughed along with him. With my Baltimore accent, I knew exactly what he was talking about. Speaking *Bawlmerese* could be socially awkward, if not downright embarrassing at times.

Saturday's game between the URI Rams and the Hofstra Pride was a great tune-up for Sunday. It had everything a field crew could want: a first half rout, a fourth-quarter rally, long touchdown passes, and long touchdown runs. After a 21-0 halftime lead by URI, the Pride rallied to pull within 21-20 on three touchdowns passes in the third quarter. The Rams pulled ahead 28-21 in the fourth quarter, but the Pride wasn't finished. With less than two minutes, they marched down the field to make it 28-26. On their next possession, the Rams iced the game with a 44-yard touchdown run.

In the locker room, we received good reports from our observer George Cullen and our on-field boss Jack Winter. I felt that I had an excellent game. I was focused and properly positioned in a game that was an emotional roller coaster for coaches, players, and fans. I was peaking at the right time. I was ready for tomorrow's game.

Having a flight to catch, I quickly showered and changed into street clothes. I dropped the rental at the Providence airport then jogged to the departure gate for a flight to Pittsburgh. From there, I caught a connecting flight to Cincinnati. A long day had just gotten longer. I was bouncing from airport to airport like a pinball, spending more time in airplanes than football fields. Trying to unwind in flight with my game materials was impossible. I kept thinking about tomorrow's kickoff. My countdown to kickoff had officially begun.

Finally arriving in Cincinnati, I took a seat on the Marriott shuttle and plucked a bottle of water from the on-board cooler. The ice-cold water was refreshing, but I would have paid a king's ransom for a gin and tonic. However, officials were not allowed to consume alcohol prior to game day. At the hotel, I handed the driver a twenty-dollar bill and grabbed my bags. One thing Larry Upson impressed upon us at the mini-clinic was the NFL tipped generously for good service. It felt good to throw money around like a first-round draft choice on a replacement's salary.

That night I roomed with Paul Vargo. Paul worked in the Southern Conference as a back judge, but the next day he was working as a head linesman. We talked a little about our football backgrounds. By 10:30, both of us had turned in for the night totally exhausted.

After another restless night of sleep, I was up at sunrise, once again staring anxiously out the window. It was Sunday morning in the NFL, the first game of the regular season. Why would I possibly be nervous?

At 8 a.m., the crew convened for breakfast in the hotel dining room. After filling our plates, we headed to the conference room to discuss and review game-day procedures. While waiting in the lobby for the ten o'clock shuttle to Paul Brown Stadium, Larry Upson handed each of us two tickets for the game and our first NFL game check. With gigantic smiles, NFL security escorted us to the shuttle.

The shuttle was part of a four-bus, police-escorted caravan for the New England Patriots. As we approached the stadium, a police SUV pulled ahead and blocked traffic from a travel ramp. The NFL did not like to hurry up and wait.

At 10:30 a.m., we pulled into the service entrance, grabbed our bags, and headed for the locker room. Unlike last week, there were no TV cameras waiting for our arrival. Any stories about replacement officials would have to wait until after the game.

When we entered the small locker room, our referee, John Smith, was waiting. His game last night had a two-hour delay for a hurricane warning. Now you know why the University of Miami teams are known as the Hurricanes. His flight didn't leave Miami until 6:30 that morning. As we dressed for the game, a worker delivered box lunches for the crew. "Guess the chain gang got the deli platter," someone quipped. All I could do was shake my head and laugh when I thought about last week's spread at PSINet. *There's no place like home*, I thought. Other members of the crew were Paul Frerking, umpire; Bob Powell, field judge; Dick Bell, side judge; and Lex Baxter, back judge.

Following last week's procedure, I dropped off my uniform bag and headed to the CBS production truck. Once again, my mission was to get the exact time of day from the producer. "Who's the referee for the game?" he asked.

"John Smith from New York," I replied.

"Then I guess your name must be Jones," he chuckled in reference to the TV Western *Alias Smith and Jones* from the early '70s. We both laughed, and I formally introduced myself. Before I left, he gave me seven CBS Sports hats for the crew. At least, the crew would have one souvenir from our time in the NFL.

Back in our locker room, Larry checked with me about my official NFL game watch. The official time was kept on the field, and the scoreboard clock was adjusted as necessary during the game. For some reason, possibly nerves, I couldn't get my watch to work properly. There were just too many functions to decipher. In addition to timing the game, there was a function to time TV commercials, team timeouts, on-field injury timeouts, and the halftime intermission. I was thinking that I needed at least two watches on each wrist.

As I hopelessly fiddled with the watch and mumbled under my breath about watch technology, an exasperated Larry saved the day.

"Lou, just use your own watch," he uttered in disbelief at my antics. My college watch was a good luck charm that returned me to my comfort zone. When the clock operators entered the room to review timing procedures for the game, I was ready.

After the room emptied, the crew pitched in to scrub the game balls. News balls have a sheen that needs to be removed for a better grip. The ball boys dropped off a case of Wilson NFL footballs, which we scrubbed with water and dried with towels. Since there was no rain in the forecast, we scrubbed or prepped about a dozen balls. On a rainy day, it's not uncommon to have to have fifty footballs ready before the game.

At 11:32, I left the locker room to meet with Dick LeBeau, head coach for the Cincinnati Bengals. Once again, it was the same routine as the previous week with Coach Billick. "Have a good game today," he said cordially as I turned to leave.

"You too coach, and by the way Happy Birthday," I replied cheerfully. Coach was celebrating his sixty-fourth birthday.

"A win today would be a great birthday gift," he chuckled.

"That's up to your team. They make the right plays, and I'll make the right calls," I razzed. Coach LeBeau struck me as a quiet, measured man with a confident demeanor. As his players milled around the locker room and conversed in hushed tones, they reflected the same business-like attitude. Although I was inside that space for only seconds, I felt the emotions of the players. This was the proverbial calm before the storm.

Back in the officials' locker room, I shared the information from Coach LeBeau with the crew. Before heading out to inspect the field at 12:19 p.m., Robert Kraft, the owner of the New England Patriots stopped by and told us that we had the full support of the owners going forward. I was tempted to ask him how long is going forward—one game, two games, or the entire season?

◆ ◆ ◆

On the field, I gazed at the stands bathed in glorious sunshine. The temperature was in the low eighties with a slight breeze, almost identical to my NFL debut last Friday. The stadium looked a lot like PSINet Stadium on the inside, which looked like every other football stadium. Unlike baseball where the ballpark is part of the game, football requires a venue that maximizes capacity and comfort. While each football stadium has its distinctive features and trademarks, architects were limited in creating a revolutionary oval.

"New turf this year. Kentucky Blue Grass. Best four-season grass for strength and durability. Best grass money can buy," said the supervisor of field operations as he walked next to me. Rambling on, he sounded like a salesman for a grass company.

"Last year's field didn't seem to hold up when I was here. Can't wait to see what it looks like next year," I wisecracked as the crew chuckled. The joke went right over his head. None of us were here last year, and we certainly wouldn't be here next year.

As I looked over the field, I couldn't help but notice one of the Patriots warming up. He stood nearly 6 feet 5 inches and was effortlessly throwing tight spirals like laser-guided missiles. As he continued his routine, he exuded the quiet, confident, business-like demeanor that I had seen in Coach LeBeau. More accurately, his mannerisms reminded me of Johnny Unitas during his heyday with the Colts. "Who is that guy?" I asked one of the ball boys, pointing to the player.

"This year's backup, Tom Brady. Hopefully, he'll stay the backup," he replied dryly. In his rookie season the previous year, Tom was 1-3 in passing for a grand total of six yards. There wasn't a lot of praise being heaped on the six-round draft pick from Michigan. Like the replacement officials, he was just waiting for his chance.

"I'll have to remember that guy. He looks to be a strapper," I quipped. Over the years, I had seen a lot of quarterbacks at every level of play and considered myself to be adept at spotting talent. With the right team and the right coach, Tom Brady could be the real deal.

At 1 p.m., team captains and the crew met at midfield for the coin toss. Whimsically, we looked to the heavens for our cue. Actually we looked at the video screens high above the crowd. Today President Bush was the honorary captain for all NFL games.

Seconds later, the president magically appeared to the masses, standing in the White House Rose Garden surrounded by a contingent of Pop Warner players from the DC area. Just before the president flipped the coin, The Bengals called tails. The Bengals won the coin toss and elected to receive.

As the teams lined up for the kickoff, I thought, *It's official. I'm an official in the NFL.* There was no sweeter thought in the universe. I had reached football nirvana. With one game under my belt in the NFL, I was less nervous, but I also realized today's game was the first step to the Super Bowl. *Concentrate, concentrate, concentrate. Don't get caught up in the hype*, I reminded myself as Adam Vinatieri's kick bounced out of the end zone for a touchback. "First and ten for the Bengals at their twenty-yard line," a voice boomed from the PA system. Game on!

◆ ◆ ◆

On the first play of the game, the Bengals bruising running back Cory Dillon ran for nine yards. The crew was off and running with him. Both teams punted on their first possessions. When the Bengals got the ball for a second time, they moved downfield to the Patriots 24-yard line before QB Jon Kitna was sacked and fumbled. The Pats recovered the ball and drove downfield despite two false start penalties. The first quarter ended 0-0.

On the first play of the second quarter, Pats quarterback Drew Bledsoe threw a 14-yard touchdown pass to Troy Brown for a 7-0 lead. The scoring fuse had been lit. All I could think was, *Fasten your seatbelt, Sweet Lou.*

The Bengals Curtis Keaton returned the following kickoff 64 yards to set up a 36-yard field goal. The Pats lead was 7-3. The defensive offside on the play was declined. On the next possession, Drew Bledsoe had a 32-yard completion to David Patten to set up a 39-yard field goal by Adam Vinatieri. Patriots led 10-3. Seven plays later Corey Dillon ran off the right guard for five yards and a touchdown. At halftime, the score was 10-10. Both offenses and the weather were heating up.

As the crew jogged toward the locker room, I was thinking that football couldn't get any more exciting than this, and we still had another half to play. In the locker room, we recorded our first half fouls in our game report. We totaled three false starts, a clip, a defensive offside, and a delay of game. There was only one play we wanted back. Cincinnati had questioned the spot on a possible first down. When the referee went to the sideline to talk with Coach LeBeau, the Bengals should have been charged with a timeout because he was challenging the ruling on the field. We didn't catch it.

With the twelve-minute half time, the crew had only time to grab a cold drink and use the restroom. Since I kept time for the halftime, I gave the crew a five-minute warning. "Here we go, guys. Let's get the teams. Finish strong. Best team on the field," I exhorted my colleagues.

To the delight of the TV people, we had the teams on the field at the designated time to start the second half. The third quarter started with a three-and-out by the Pats. On their first possession of the half, the Bengals drive stalled, and Neil Rackers kicked a 47-yard field goal for a 13-10 Bengals lead.

After another three-and-out by the Pats, the Bengals marched downfield for a 33-yard field goal to extend the lead to 16-10. After a third three-and-out, the arm of Kitna and the legs of Dillon powered another drive that resulted in a 25-yard TD pass to Tony McGee. The lead was 23-10 at the end of the third quarter.

The Pats opened the fourth quarter with another three-and-out." Bengals fans were roaring with delight, but I knew the game was far from over. This was the NFL. With the best football players in the world, anything could happen on the field.

The Pats offense was built around the arm of Bledsoe and now that he had to pass, the lead could dwindle in a hurry. At 9:17, the Pats took over on their own six-yard line following a Bengals punt. Bledsoe wasted no time. Completing six of eight passes, he capped the scoring drive with an 8-yard TD pass to Jermaine Wiggins. The score was 23-17 with 5:37 left in the game. The Bengals challenged the scoring play, but the ruling was upheld.

After a three-and-out by the Bengals, the Pats got the ball back at their own 30-yard line with 3:57 left in the game. That was plenty of time for a game-winning drive. The Bengals defense stiffened. On fourth down and two at the Bengals 41-yard line, Bledsoe tried a quarterback sneak and came up short of a first down by inches. I ran to the pile along with the linesman to mark the spot of forward progress. This was a huge spot in a critical point of the game, but we nailed it.

Trying to milk the clock, the Bengals Dillon ran three times before Cincinnati had to punt. The Pats and Bledsoe got the ball back with 1:54 remaining. At the two-minute warning, the crew had convened at the line of scrimmage to review the number of timeouts each team had left in the game. We reminded ourselves about big fouls, and to let the teams decide the outcome of the game. There was still time for the Pats to score.

On the last Pats drive, the head linesman ruled a catch by the receiver near the sideline. The replay assistant challenged the play upstairs in the replay booth and the call on the field was overturned. I put five seconds back on the game clock. After three incomplete passes and a sack, the Bengals took possession and ran out the clock to preserve a hard-fought 23-17 victory. We jogged off the field to the cheers of the Bengals fans.

Back in the locker room, we hurriedly peeled off sweaty uniforms and headed for the showers. Everyone had a flight to catch, so we wasted no time in completing our game reports. We had worked a tough ball game. There was a total of seven penalties. We had kept the flags in our pockets and let the players play. That's what the fans and players wanted. A pool reporter asked John Smith why the fourth quarter pass play at the sideline was overturned. The answer was simple. The instant replay official told John the receiver did not get both feet down in bounds.

Back in civvies, we grabbed a box lunch and boarded the bus. Once again we were given a police escort to the airport. Larry Upson informed the crew that we'd be working in Chicago or Indianapolis next weekend. We were confident that we would have another game to officiate. Larry had no update on contract talks, but we knew the stalemate couldn't last too much longer.

Aboard the plane, I finally had a chance to relax and reflect on the weekend. With two close games in two days, I was stumbling to the finish line physically and emotionally drained. The days had passed in a blur. All I could do was go home and wait to see what would happen next.

UA Flight 175 hits South Tower. A new Day of Infamy.
Photo courtesy of Prints and Photographs Division, Library of Congress.

CHAPTER 27
AMERICA ATTACKED

On Monday, I wore my CBS Sports hat to work. Some people thought I had taken a job with the network. Once again, coworkers stopped by my desk for the game-day update. "Lou, I thought you said it was a one-time deal," one of my coworkers joked.

"Just déjà vu all over again," I kidded. "They say the third time is a charm, but I'll have to wait to see what happens this week." That was no lie. Based on hearsay, every sports talk show was reporting an imminent deal between the NFLRA and the NFL. That didn't bother me, but I was hoping to hear something official from the league. It was tough twisting in the wind from week to week.

On Tuesday morning at work, I expected my phone call. Instead, I got a wake-up call that forever changed the American way of life. A coworker was listening to the radio when she heard about the first plane crash. We gathered around her desk with grim faces as the horrific tragedy unfolded.

That morning at 8:46, American Airlines Flight 11 from Boston to Los Angeles crashed into the North Tower of the World Trade Center killing all aboard. At 9:03, United Airlines Flight 175 from Boston to Los Angeles crashed into the South Tower killing all aboard as the North Tower burned. Within an hour and half, both towers collapsed in a billowing cascade of steel and concrete that obliterated the Lower Manhattan financial district.

The news worsened. At 9:37 a.m., American Airlines Flight 77 from Washington to Los Angeles crashed into the west side of the Pentagon killing all aboard and one hundred and twenty-five people inside the building. I left my office and hurried to our power control center just a few blocks away. As the attacks were unfolding, utility companies around the country were implementing emergency plans to ensure the power grid did not black out.

The carnage ended at 10:03 that morning when United Airlines Flight 93 crashed into an empty field near Shanksville, Pennsylvania, killing all aboard. The passengers and crew had unsuccessfully attempted to retake control of the plane to prevent the hijackers from hitting another American landmark, reportedly the White House or the Capitol.

America had hit the pause button in a state of shock and disbelief. All planes around the country were immediately grounded. The Islamic terrorist group al-Qaeda had murdered nearly three thousand people. We were now fighting a war on terror. Words such as *terrorists* and *jihad* entered the lexicon with the name of Osama bin Laden. The commercial airliner had become a new weapon in the arsenal of our enemies, a guided inter-continental missile loaded with thousands of gallons of jet fuel and hundreds of people. We had new heroes: the crews and passengers aboard the ill-fated flights, firefighters, police officers, medical personnel, and everyday people on their way to work who suddenly found themselves caught in the apocalypse. They became the new face of America.

Kelly and I spent the evening glued to the television, not believing what we were seeing. Having spent the weekend in the air, all I could see were those doomed souls sitting in airplanes or at their desks. I wondered about their last seconds and their last thoughts on earth. All I could think was, *There but for the grace of God goes me.*

At 8:30 p.m., President Bush confidently and calmly addressed the nation. In his speech, he reminded us of the evil that we had witnessed and reaffirmed our resolve to stand united in defending our freedom. I believed this was his finest hour, maybe the finest hour of any president in history. I was ready to stand for freedom, but also worried that this war on terror would become another Vietnam? Would the country have to suffer like that again? What was the price that we would have to pay for freedom?

Throughout the evening, I channel surfed for updates. One reported called the attack a "new Day of Infamy and a second Pearl Harbor." That struck a nerve since my father was aboard a destroyer in the Pacific during WWII. Many other fathers in the neighborhood had served overseas, including one who had witnessed the Japanese attack. The hijacked planes exploding into the sides of the towers in blinding flashes of fire and smoke evoked the cataclysmic explosions along Battleship Row on the morning of December 7, 1941.

Images from both attacks were eerily similar. Sailors diving into the burning oil on the harbor's surface, civilians leaping from the towers to escape the white-hot flames; sailors trapped in the hulls of sunken and overturned ships, civilians trapped under tons of steel and concrete; sailors coated in smothering black oil, civilians cloaked in choking gray dust like living statues.

The iconic picture of first responders raising the American flag on an angled flagpole jutting from the rubble at Ground Zero was a ghostly portrait of the Marine flag raising on Mount Suribachi.

That evening before going to bed, I stepped outside to watch the sky. I was humbled by the view. Millions of stars flickered silently in the dark void like dying candles in a reverent tribute to the lives that were lost. In the ethereal solitude, I instinctively did some soul searching. What would I do if I knew that I had one last day to live? How would I like to be remembered? What were the priorities in my life? I went to bed with those horrific images of the day flashing in my head and said a silent prayer for all the 9/11 families. I hoped they would remember their fallen family members as American heroes who sacrificed their lives in the cause of freedom. That's exactly what they were.

"Doesn't one of your officiating buddies work near the Twin Towers?" Kelly asked solemnly at breakfast the next morning.

"Oh, my God, you're right. Tom Considine works only a few blocks from the plane crash," I gasped in horror. Frantically, I tried to call Tom on his cell phone, but the calls went directly to voicemail. Not a good sign. I then called Jack Winter and asked if he had an update on Flippy, the nickname that Jack had given to him. No luck there either.

A few days later, Flippy called with an unbelievable story. Barely able to see a few feet ahead, he stumbled blindly in a suffocating cloud of toxic dust and ash until he heard a voice. For a minute, he actually thought that he might be dead. Following the directions of a first responder, he was led to a safe space where medical personnel examined him. Covered in soot and debris, his $300 suit was shredded, and his $150 shoes scuffed and scraped. "Everything you saw on TV could not describe the conditions at Ground Zero. I literally walked through the valley of death. I looked like a ghost by the time they found me," Flippy responded grimly. It had taken him two days to get home across the bridge in New Jersey.

◆ ◆ ◆

When I arrived at work on Wednesday, there was a message on my voicemail from Larry Upson. "Lou, if we play football on Sunday, you're going to Chicago for the Bears game," he advised. In the wake of the tragedy, I had almost forgotten about football. Personally, I hoped the games would be rescheduled. I believed this was a time to mourn even though I knew the break would most likely end in an agreement between the NFL and the NFLRA. Football was no longer my priority.

On Thursday, the NFL announced all games were canceled to coincide with the decisions from every other sport. To his credit, Paul Tagliabue, Baltimore's nemesis and NFL Grinch who stole our football, secured a consensus from owners and players to postpone the season for a week. I applauded his hard-fought decision. There were those owners and players who wanted to keep playing, but Tagliabue stood firm with good reason. After the assassination of Present Kennedy in November 1963, NFL Commissioner Pete Rozelle decided to continue with the games. He later went on record to say that it was the biggest mistake during his tenure. To my relief, later that day I was informed that my game on Saturday at the University of Massachusetts was also canceled. This was not the time to be traveling anywhere by any means in America.

On Monday, September 17, the news media reported the NFL and NFLRA were close to an agreement. I knew from my contacts that meetings had been held over the weekend. Both sides were moving quickly to a resolution. I kept my fingers crossed that negotiations would continue for another week. I wanted one more game before I was fired.

That evening while watching Fox 45 news with Kelly, evening sports anchor Bruce Cunningham announced an agreement had been reached. Regular officials would be back on the field this weekend. I took a deep breath and exhaled. I told Kelly that I wasn't surprised. I knew my time on the field with the NFL would end, but it was quicker than I thought. I was dismayed that I hadn't heard the news from the NFL first. *Nothing personal, just business*, I reminded myself.

At work on Tuesday morning, my first call of the day jolted me from my musing mood like a lightning strike. Recognizing the number, I hesitantly picked it up to learn my fate. "Lou, Phil here from the NFL office. Pack your bag. You're going to Cleveland for the Browns and Lions game on Sunday," the voice announced.

"But what about the lockout? Last night, I heard on the news that a settlement had been reached," I asked warily.

"The report from Associated Press was false. We'll keep you posted. American Express Travel will be in touch," he said haltingly as if reading from a script.

At this point, I didn't know what to think. I should have been jubilant, but I had my doubts. Something was fishy here. Why didn't Larry call? Was he too busy arranging the return of the regulars? After talking with Phil, I impulsively checked ESPN News. They reported that a deal was close but not finalized. A new contract was being sent to the officials and would be voted on tomorrow. Maybe I was going to Cleveland this week after all. I crossed my fingers once again, but I knew that time was quickly running out for the replacements.

On Wednesday, I received my plane tickets and travel instructions in the mail from American Express. Also, there was a notice from the league that three random crews would be tested for drugs and alcohol on Saturday. No problem with that. I just hoped to be around on Saturday to be tested. So far, so good, I thought until I turned on the radio. The headline story reported that the NFL had extended the deadline from 10 a.m. to 10 p.m. for the regular officials to ratify the latest contract. I kept my fingers crossed that somebody on either side would blink and call a timeout. Hey, guys, please think about this over the weekend.

Later that day, I pursed my lips in contentment and breathed a huge sigh of relief. The time had come to uncross my fingers. The NFLRA voted 2-1 to accept an offer from the NFL that was almost identical to the one before the lockout. The deal was basically the same in total monetary value with a 50 percent increase in salary the first year and a 100 percent increase by the fourth year of a six-year deal.

Under the previous agreement, which was signed in 1994, a fifth-year official was making $42,295, and a ten-year veteran $64,215. Even though the contract didn't come close to the original demands of the union, it appeared to be a generous package. At the press conference, both sides said the right things on cue with forced smiles. I had a strange feeling this wouldn't be the last showdown.

The NFLRA didn't want to say it for the sake of public opinion, but those numbers were merely crumbs from the banquet table of the penurious owners. That was common knowledge among officials. The NFL was a global juggernaut with the Midas touch. While the average team value doesn't reveal the complete financial picture, such as total revenue and operating income, it reflects the exponential growth of the NFL. In 2001, the average team value was $400 to $500 million; twenty years later it was $3 billion to $5 billion. That's a lot of bread on the banquet table. There should have been enough crumbs to satisfy any appetite, but it wasn't going to be at this meal.

As usual, there was a story behind the headline. Following the tumultuous days after 9/11, the NFLRA was in danger of losing favor with the American public. Squabbling over money during an unprecedented national crisis was petty and unpatriotic. Both sides knew it. Only this time the owners leveraged the advantage. Tom Condon, union negotiator, acknowledged the terrorist attacks were a major incentive in returning to work. Reading between the lines of his statement, he was saying that we've only just begun to fight. The settlement was only a truce. Every official knew it.

With my NFL career officially over, I was pleased the dark cloud of uncertainty had vanished. Not knowing from day to day if I was working was nerve racking. Instead of being sullen, I was grateful. I had lived my dream.

Of course, I was pleased to see the regular officials get a substantial raise. After all I was part of the brotherhood, at heart an underpaid and overworked football official. While both sides played the patriotic card, one of the main reasons for the settlement was the excellent performance of the replacement officials. To our credit, we threw a scare into the NFLRA. It was something to be proud of.

To my utter delight, the reputation of the 2001 replacement crews was enhanced with the second NFL referee lockout in 2012. What did I say about the truce in 2001? The circumstances were similar to the 2001 lockout. On June 4, 2012, the NFL announced it would hire replacement officials for the upcoming season after a stalemate on a new contract. This time the issues were salaries and pensions. Once again, it was about the money and who gets it. The NFLRA wanted a piece of the pie, not just the crumbs.

True to form, NFL owners boldly declared they were willing to play the season with replacements. However, this time the NFL forgot to hire NFL caliber officials. The new hires were from lower college DIVs, other professional leagues, and high schools. A small contingent of scabs from 2001 also joined the motley crew. Most DIV I officials were barred from crossing the picket line after conferences banned moonlighting. That left a limited supply of qualified officials.

This time I watched the drama unfold in front of my TV. While I rooted for the replacements, I saw a disaster waiting to happen. There were a number of minor mishaps and miscues during the preseason that were glossed over by the owners and the media. To the average fan, they meant nothing. To a football official, they were a harbinger of events to come during the regular season. To me, it already appeared the replacements were in over their heads. With poker faces, the owners declared the replacements would get better with time. "They're improving from week to week," was the popular refrain. What else could they say? All they could do was cross their fingers and hope for the best once the regular season started.

♦ ♦ ♦

Sadly, the replacements wilted under the NFL spotlight as soon as they stepped on the big stage. During the Seahawks-Cardinals game of week one, an extra timeout was awarded to the Seahawks. During week two, a side judge was pulled from his game after his Facebook page showed he was a fan of one of the teams. During the Broncos-Falcons game, three plays were overturned after replay reviews. Numerous scuffles broke out between the teams, and players and coaches left the sidelines to yell at the officials on the field. The last infraction broke two NFL commandments: "Thou shall not trespass on the field of play" and "Thou shall not bear false witness against thy official." For their egregious sins, the coaches were levied sizable fines for verbal abuse of the officials. The NFL was trying its best to keep law and order on the field. Maybe, the officials should have been issued badges and guns.

During week three, the NFL pressure cooker literally exploded. During the 49ers-Vikings game, two extra replay challenges were mistakenly awarded. During the Titans-Lions game, the officials erred in spotting the ball after a penalty, increasing the penalty from fifteen to twenty-seven yards. They had marked the penalty from the wrong side of the field.

The relentless heat on the officials was getting white hot. It increased throughout the day and peaked that evening during the *Sunday Night Football* broadcast. During the fourth quarter of the Patriots-Ravens game, multiple penalties, viewed by many as questionable, were called against the Ravens on subsequent plays. Ravens Head Coach John Harbaugh was flagged for unsportsmanlike conduct after yelling at the officials. He had broken another NFL commandment: "Thou shall not take the name of thy official in vain." After the game, he claimed he was yelling for a timeout.

If the coaches were incensed about the officiating that evening, the hometown crowd was apoplectic. Over the next minute, they chanted "bullshit" until it reached a crescendo over the airwaves. Play-by-play commentator Al Michaels called it "the loudest manure chant I've ever heard." And who ever said that Baltimore wasn't passionate about its football team? Baltimore *uncensored* was a beautiful place.

On the final play of the game, the Ravens Justin Tucker nailed a 27-yard game-winning field goal that sailed high over the right upright. On replay, the ball was inches from being outside the upright, but the officials under the goal posts were in the proper position and made the right call. At the time, I was working in the press box as the coach-to-player cutoff operator (more on that job later) and listened to the drama unfold. Sorry, Pats fans, but the officials made the right call.

The fans agreed, but not the Patriots. Players danced wildly around the field as if their feet and heads were on fire, waving off the play. Helmets and hands filled the air! What a joyous sight for Ravens fans. It was the first time they had beaten the Patriots in the regular season.

The play was nothing new to me. The frenzied ending was reminiscent of the 1965 Colts-Packers game. The outraged Patriots head coach Bill Belichick wanted a review of the play and grabbed the arm of an official who was running off the field. Bill lost on both counts. The play was unreviewable, and he was fined $50,000 for physical contact with an official. Another sacrosanct commandment had been broken: "Thou shall not defile the presence of an official with an uncleansed hand." You don't touch the officials, no matter what. Around the league, NFL commandments were falling like rookie quarterbacks.

The excitement for fans and replacement officials was far from over. There was still the *Monday Night Football* game between the Packers and Seahawks in front of another national audience. Football fans were catching their breath, the NFL was holding its breath, and the replacements were hoping for the next breath. "Expect the unexpected" was the buzz phrase before the game. The replacements didn't disappoint.

On the last play of the game, Seahawks quarterback Russell Wilson threw a 24-yard Hail Mary pass to Golden Tate for a 14-12 win. Or did he? The Packers safety appeared to have intercepted the pass prior to Tate getting his hands on the football. As the players tumbled to the ground in the end zone, two officials rushed to the spot. One signaled touchdown; the other signaled touchback on the interception. The final ruling of a touchdown was confirmed by instant replay.

That solved only half of the problem. Prior to the catch, Tate had shoved Packer cornerback Sam Shields with both hands. Offensive pass interference was not called. Still the game was not officially over.

With no time left on the clock, the replacements weren't finished. The Packers who had left the field were forced to return ten minutes later so the Seahawks could kick the mandatory extra point.

I felt sorry for the officials. It had to be the longest ten minutes of their lives. The play would go down in NFL history as the *Fail Mary*. Following the game, the NFL released a statement defending the touchdown ruling but admitting that pass interference had occurred. The NFL was in the hot seat. The press and fans were calling for action, actually the heads of the officials.

Finally, after three weeks of substandard officiating, the NFL had seen enough of their new hires. On Tuesday, Commissioner Goodell issued an apology to the fans. On Wednesday, the NFL and NFLRA announced an agreement to end the lockout. Although the agreement still had to be ratified, regular crews would work the *Thursday Night Football* game. This time the NFLRA had the leverage and got the deal they wanted. Who could blame them?

There was a bright spot for the replacement officials. On August 9, 2022, Shannon Eastin became the first female official in the NFL when she worked as the line judge for the San Diego Chargers-Green Bay Packers preseason game. I was rooting for her all the way, and she didn't disappoint. Like me, she had diligently worked her way through the college ranks and bravely endured all the slings and arrows from the press, the players, coaches, and regular officials as a replacement.

I watched her games on TV and was impressed with her mechanics and composure. If anybody deserved a shot at becoming a full-time official, it was Shannon. Shame on the NFLRA for not supporting her and labeling her the "Lady Scab." In the end, she had the last laugh. Her game cap and whistle were sent to the NFL Hall of Fame for display.

◆ ◆ ◆

Looking back on the 2001 agreement, it could best be described as an uneasy ten-year truce. While the regular officials grudgingly accepted their contract, I was overjoyed with my severance package. I had worked two games and was paid for four and received a $500 bonus, which I donated to the NFL Disaster Relief Fund, which the NFL matched. There was no more worthy cause in the universe than 9/11.

Also, the NFL was going to give me a satellite dish and pay for the NFL Sunday Ticket and NCAA Game Plan for two years. In October, I received a letter from Mike Pereira, director of football officiating, thanking me for my service during the lockout. My only disappointment was that I never got a call from Larry Upson or the NFL office informing me of the settlement. This was surprising because of our constant communication throughout my tenure as an official.

For me, life in the NFL had been a dream come true. However, that dream would always be associated with the events of 9/11, one of the darkest days in American history. Reconciling those two events in my life would always be a bittersweet memory.

Still in the game at a different level.
Working my fingers as the coach-to-player cutoff operator.

CHAPTER 28
PUSH BUTTON, PRESS BOX

On October 7, 2001, I was back on the field at PSINet Stadium for the Ravens-Tennessee Titans game. Once again, I was in uniform, and once again I was standing on the sideline as the penalty recorder. Except for the chain crew and game-day assistants, nobody knew where I had been and what I was doing. It felt good to be back with the guys on the crew. They welcomed me with hugs, handshakes, and pats on the back. The dream was over, but the football journey continued.

There were a thousand questions from the chain gang, and I was more than glad to answer all of them. When I was first selected to be a replacement, I realized that I was living their dream also. I was the mystical zebra who changed stripes. I only wished that they had the chance to be in my shoes for one of the games.

As we dressed, the surprising question was, "Did you get paid yet?" There was no mention about how much I got paid, only if I got paid. Maybe, some of my colleagues were thinking that I would be double-crossed by the union or the NFL. Perhaps, they were thinking, *Lou, take the money and run before they change their minds.* Other questions concerned the stadium, the locker room, the food, the picket lines, the phone calls, and the perks. I tried to stay humble and not sound like a braggart, but the crew wanted to know every detail about my NFL journey. I felt like Cinderella trying to describe what it was like at the NFL ball.

As was customary, the head linesman came into the locker room an hour and a half before the game. He introduced himself and shook everyone's hand. "I heard one of you guys worked as a replacement," he said offhandedly.

"Yeah, Sweet Lou worked in Cincinnati," one of crew piped up.

"How did you do?" the linesman quipped. "Did you fuck up?"

"No, just a normal day at the office," I snickered. "You know how it is."

He laughed with everyone in the room and then began instructing the crew. "Wait a minute. Why don't you go over our pregame review?" he kidded.

"I'd love too, but you know how it is. Can't break union rules or they'll be looking for me in the basement of some stadium," I quipped, referring to the disappearance of mobster Jimmy Hoffa who was rumored to be buried at Giants Stadium. The room exploded in laughter. No one laughed harder than the head linesman. Here was one official that had no animosity toward me. I stubbornly kept repeating the phrase "you know how it is" to show that I wasn't going to be intimidated by any of the regular officials. I had proven to the football world that I had the right stuff to officiate in the NFL.

◆ ◆ ◆

As the season progressed, I discovered a few regular officials, who I considered friends, did not feel the same way. When near them, I learned to keep to myself and only speak when spoken to. The caste system was alive and well in officiating. They considered themselves princes, and I was a pauper who had the audacity to crash the party. To be honest, this handful of bigots didn't bother me. What hurt was the rejection from my brotherhood. There were two officials from my college days who refuse to speak with me to this day. We had worked for a number of years together on the field and had each other's back, or so I thought. For them, loyalty was a one-way street, so be it.

If the caste system in football was still alive, so was karma. *"Work hard and believe in yourself and good things will happen,"* I was always told myself. Maybe not all the time, but at the time you least expect it. In 2010, I was still working on the chain gang and officiating college games. I was completely satisfied with my football career. After my NFL experience in 2001, I wasn't searching for the next career highlight.

However, the football gods of fate had their own game plan. That year I was fortunate enough to be promoted from the backup to the primary coach-to player (C2P) cutoff operator at M&T Bank Stadium, formerly PSINet Stadium. Bill Ryan, who had a long stint in the NFL as a clock operator with the Baltimore Colts and later as the C2P for the Ravens, retired for health concerns. Bill was an all-around good guy who lived and breathed football. His main hobby was keeping a list of everybody who had officiated in the NFL. He always delighted in showing me my name on his rolls.

Once again, it was a phone call that got the ball rolling. This time it was Johnny Grier, supervisor of NFL officials, asking me if I was interested in the full-time position. For those football fans unfamiliar with the name, take a minute for some research because Johnny is an NFL legend. In 1988, he became the first

African American referee in the history of the NFL. Prior to that, he became the first African American to officiate (field judge) a championship game, Super Bowl XXII. That game saw Doug Williams become the first African American quarterback to win a Super Bowl.

Johnny was a personable and humble man who stayed connected to his roots. Like myself, he began officiating high school basketball and football games at the age of eighteen and persevered to rise to the ranks of the NFL. Johnny was born to make the calls. Thank goodness, he made that call to me.

Without hesitation, I accepted Johnny's offer on the spot. Instead of being employed by the Ravens on the chain gang, I would be an employee of the NFL. The money was better and so were the working conditions, especially for an older official. I wasn't going to miss the freezing cold in December and January, or the boiling heat and humidity in August and early September. What I would miss was the beautiful autumn afternoons and the sights and sounds of the game on the field. While I loved being where the action was, I realized the aches and pains of age were catching up with me. Once again, I ascended into football heaven, well, at least as high as the press level.

Adjusting to the friendly confines of the press box was effortless. Although we kept the windows closed, we were steps away from the cafeteria and restrooms. The Ravens were noted for having one of the best catering facilities in the league. Thick, meaty crab cakes were a favorite of local and visiting media. And the price for this football feast? Nothing! Who said there's no such thing as a free lunch? Certainly, not the NFL.

Press levels in the NFL stadiums are expansive. They usually run from one 10-yard line to the other alongside one side of the stadium. They are some of the best seats just below the luxury suites. While it's a lot of floor space, it can get cramped. Vying for space are the printed media, the scoreboard operations center, radio and television personnel, medical observation teams, assistant coaches from both teams, the copy center, the instant replay booth, and finally my office, the clock management booth. My booth also housed the game clock operator, play clock operator, and the coach to player audio equipment.

The job of the C2P is simply to hold and release a button that cuts off communication between designated players on the field. During a game, one offensive player (the quarterback) and one defensive player (usually a linebacker or defensive back) have receivers inside their helmets. Those designated players, the ones with the green dot on the back of the helmet, can only receive information from coaches. They cannot transmit.

In 1993, the NFL reduced the play clock from forty-five to forty seconds. Coaches complained they had to burn timeouts to send in plays. It was time to tweak the system. In 1994, the league implemented a radio communication system between the coach and quarterback to save time between plays. Fourteen years later, a defensive player was afforded the same opportunity. For security reasons, such as tampering and play stealing, radio frequencies are encrypted. Rumors about plays being broadcast over commercial radio are urban myths.

Along with the play and game clock operators, I arrive at our booth three hours before kickoff. Our first priority is to test the equipment. If there's a malfunction, we immediately notify the stadium management staff. Within minutes, technicians, repairmen when I was growing up, will be inspecting the booth from top to bottom to troubleshoot the problem. Two hours before game time, we meet with the back judge and side judge in the officials' locker room to review our responsibilities for the game. We tell them if the equipment was working properly and if there are any malfunctions with the clocks or audio equipment. We also discuss the pace of the game being controlled by the officiating crew, scenarios during the game when the clock should be running, and disabling radio communication from the coaches.

What appears to be an easy job (after all, who can't push and hold a button?) actually requires a great deal of attentiveness and concentration. Communication between the coach and player is disabled with fifteen seconds on the play clock or when the ball is snapped, whichever occurs first. I have a box with two sets of buttons and red and green lights. When the play clock hits fifteen seconds, I push down on the primary button. The red light comes on, and communication between coach and player is blocked. When the play ends, I release the button and the green light appears. For my manual dexterity, I have been rewarded with playoff games in New England, Tampa Bay, Philadelphia, Washington, and Los Angeles.

Forget the money, food, and the press box, the best part of the job is the people. Arriving early at the stadium provides numerous opportunities to mix and mingle with football people in a relaxed atmosphere. On the press level, the cafeteria is the crossroad to meet-and-greet. You never know who is going to cross your path in the chow line.

One morning Art Rooney II, owner of the Pittsburgh Steelers, sat down at the table next to me with a cup of coffee and a Danish.

"Good morning, Mr. Rooney and welcome back to Baltimore," I chirped with a smile. A lot of fans wouldn't have recognized him, but I had seen him every year when the Steelers were in town.

"Nice to see you, Lou," he replied, covertly glancing at my NFL credential. "Glad to be back in Baltimore. Maybe, I can find a decent crab cake this year." I didn't know if he was bullshitting me or what. In 1995, his father, Dan, was one of two owners who voted against the Cleveland Browns moving to Baltimore. From a business standpoint, his decision made sense because Cleveland was his biggest rival at the time.

After chatting about the fierce rivalry between the Ravens

and the Steelers since the move, he asked me about my job. I politely explained my game-day routine. He seemed genuinely interested and asked a number of questions about the technology involved in the process. Unlike his grandfather Art, a Damon Runyon type character who was the original founder of the franchise in 1933, Art II was the prototype of the modern NFL owner. Impeccably dressed in a two-piece as if he just posed for Forbes magazine, he was personable and soft-spoken, seemingly comfortable in the boardroom or locker room. Despite being a Steeler, I liked the man. That could spell trouble for me in Gardenville.

Another memorable meeting occurred with sportscaster Jim Nantz, the iconic voice of CBS Sports. He had stopped by the cafeteria to grab a soft drink and a sandwich before the production meeting of his pregame show. I was also grabbing a quick bit to eat when I saw him sitting alone at a table. Since he was by himself, I took the opportunity to politely introduce myself. To my surprise he invited me to sit at his table. As expected, the ensuing casual conversation focused on sports. When I mentioned his book *Always by My Side*, the conversation became more somber. His sports memoir, providing an insider's look into his unprecedented stretch of broadcasts from February through April 2007 that included the Super Bowl, was actually a loving tribute to his father.

The values instilled by his father, who later in life battled Alzheimer's, were the driving force behind his successful career. Every step in his career, Jim's father was by his side offering encouragement. His father would often accompany him on his road trips as my father did. Teary-eyed, we talked about the passing of our dads in 2008. At times, I felt self-conscious asking Jim personal questions, but we shared a common bond. I readily saw that he enjoyed talking about his father, so I kept asking questions about their relationship. That meeting was a lesson in compassion and character that has stayed with me until this day.

❖❖❖

Unlike Jim, who treated people like family, there were other personalities who weren't so approachable in the press box. The *Sunday Night Football* broadcasting team of Al Michaels and John Madden immediately comes to mind. They only rode the elevator by themselves. No one dared to squeeze in at the last second, and definitely no small talk in the hallways or press box. Now I realize John was a big guy, but the elevator had room for more than two John Maddens. As soon as the game ended, the elevator operator had to hold the elevator until the duo finished their postgame wrap up. Likewise, they never appeared in the cafeteria. Instead, they had an assistant run the food errand. No doubt, they had their reasons.

Some people you meet and like; some you don't. That's life! Either way, the key to a successful career in any field is networking. In the world of officiating as with any endeavor, it's a combination of what and who you know. I never missed an opportunity to engage people who might advance my career.

While writing this book, I was asked if my latest job in the press box was a reward for my service as a replacement official. Although, I had never thought about it, it very well could have been. On my behalf, the decision to become a replacement official involved some courage. I was sailing into uncharted waters and had no idea what the league was thinking. However, to their credit, owners don't forget favors. For the players, NFL stands for *Not For Long* due to the length of an average career. For me, perhaps, NFL stood for Never Forget Lou. Who knows? I simply embrace the mystery.

Sharing a smile with John Unitas, childhood hero and fellow HOF member.

CHAPTER 29
MY FAVORITES

When I moved up to the NFL press box, I felt like I stumbled into the studio of a sports roundtable. Some of my favorites wandering around the hallways were the Ravens radio team of Scott Garceau and old Colt Tom Matte, talk show host Keith Mills, former Washington Redskins general manager Vinny Cerrato, the dean of Baltimore sports Vince Bagley, local TV sports anchor Bruce Cunningham, and newspaper reporter Mike Preston. There were a lot of opinions on a variety of sports, most notably football. Since these guys had inside sources, I always enjoyed eavesdropping on the conversations that were strictly off the record. After all it was just a bunch of guys bullshitting about sports. They should have sold tickets. It was that entertaining.

In addition to the press box encounters, I had the distinct pleasure of meeting a number of sports celebrities. Hanging around a sport for fifty years presents a lot of opportunities. In no particular order, here's my short list of my favorites:

John Unitas: The most famous person I met off the football field was my childhood hero. We first met at the airport in

Pittsburgh while both of us were waiting to catch a connecting flight to Baltimore. That was ironic considering John's journey from the sandlot to professional football. John was returning home from working an NFL game as a CBS analyst, and I was returning from a college game. I politely introduced myself, and we immediately started talking about the Baltimore Colts. Even though he was tired from working the game, he took the time to talk with a fan. That was a lasting memory.

When I worked on the Ravens chain gang, we talked during each game on a first-name basis. Forget football, we now talked about family. His daughter has recently graduated from St. Paul's School for Girls, and my daughter was considering attending. From his smile and the warmth in his voice, I could see he enjoyed the break from the football roundtable.

At Ravens games, he would stand in his spot at the 20-yard line and watch the game while greeting an endless stream of well-wishers. Like Larry Yocum, I always kept root beer barrels in one pocket and something to sign before the game in the other. When John passed away, his spot on the sideline was roped off as a memorial for the rest of the season. Inside the rope was a pair of his patented high-top football cleats.

Cal Ripken, Jr.: I met baseball's Iron Man after my daughter decided to attend St. Paul's. His daughter was a year behind Kathleen. We had the opportunity to chat at many of the school's social functions and sporting events. In person, Cal was genial but rather reserved in his demeanor. He enjoyed being around people but didn't enjoy talking baseball out of uniform. That was easy to understand. Other than Babe Ruth, there's probably no player that's been asked more baseball questions than Cal. One thing I learned in my travels was never talk shop with celebrities, especially sports figures. Instead of baseball, we once again talked about families and schools, namely how our children were doing in school and where they might be headed for college.

Brooks Robinson: If Johnny U is Mr. Football in Baltimore, then Brooks is Mr. Baseball. I met the Hall of Fame third baseman for the Baltimore Orioles at a charity golf tournament. It was a highlight in my life that still brings a smile to my face. There simply aren't enough words to describe Brooks. Just call him a true Southern gentleman and leave it at that. At the awards luncheon, I was fortunate to find a seat at his table. Brooks talked about growing up in Arkansas, his path to the Orioles, and his favorite golf courses. He amiably posed for pictures and signed autographs until the room emptied, all the time with a sincere smile of gratitude. Brooks baseball, and Baltimore—simply inseparable!

Gene Steratore: You probably recognize Gene's name as the CBS rules analyst for the NFL, college football, and basketball's March Madness. What you probably don't know is that in addition to officiating in college and the NFL (fifteen years and Super Bowl LII), Gene was also a basketball referee for NCAA DIV I games. The man has been there and done that, so listen when he speaks. During the first week of the 2010 NFL season, he ruled a touchdown reception incomplete after the receiver failed to maintain possession while going to the ground. The controversial instant-reply call became known as the *Calvin Johnson rule* after receiver Calvin Johnson. To officials, it was the *Gene Steratore* rule.

Gene was resourceful and always determined to get it right. In 2017, during a game between the Dallas Cowboys and the Oakland Raiders, he gained notoriety for wedging his game card between the ball and a front stick marker to decide if the Cowboys converted on a fourth-and-one quarterback sneak. They did and went on to win the game 20-17 on a late field goal.

Not only was Gene knowledgeable about football, he was innovative. When I officiated on a crew with Gene at the start of his college career in the Yankee Conference, he showed just how resourceful he could be. As a field judge, Gene wore an *F* on the back of his shirt. One game, he filled in as a side judge and did not have a shirt with an *S*. At the hotel the night before the game, he managed to sew an *S* over the *F* using black-and-white cloth.

Another time we were traveling to our game at the University of Rhode Island. Since Gene had never been to Rhode Island, we took him along the scenic coastline to see the mansions in Newport. When we arrived at the stadium ten minutes late, Charlie Calais, supervisor of officials, was waiting for us in the doorway to the locker room, looking at his watch and shaking his head. "It was my fault boss," Gene blurted without a word from anybody. "I left the video projector back at the hotel and we had to go back to get it." Gene is a likable, outgoing guy who rolls with punches and thinks fast on his feet. It's no wonder he had a successful career in officiating. I always felt that Gene could have a successful career in the broadcast booth.

David Crosby: You're thinking the name sounds familiar but can't remember where or when he played. Think Super Bowl of rock music; think Woodstock 1969. Think legendary singer, songwriter, guitarist, and co-founder of The Byrds, and Crosby, Stills and Nash.

In 1997, I met David at the hotel bar in New Haven, CT, while attending a football clinic. People in the bar, mostly football officials, didn't recognize him. Over the years, he had put on a few pounds and his hairline was receding. But being a fan of CSN, I recognized him the minute he sat beside me at the bar.

Typical bar talk followed. "I can't believe nobody recognizes you," I said casually, slightly turning my head to get a better look at the music legend.

"That's a good thing," he responded nonchalantly. "Tonight I just want to have a couple of beers and relax."

"What brings you to New Haven?" I then asked.

"I'm working with Phil Collins on a few things," he said quietly, so as not to be overheard. Occasionally from the late 1980s to the late 1990s, he worked with Collins as a songwriter and backup vocalist. I had a million questions to ask him about his career but left him alone. I doubted if he wanted to talk shop with a stranger. Like me, the man just wanted to have a beer and relax. "Thanks, man. I appreciate it," he said before getting up and leaving the bar unnoticed. I knew exactly what he meant.

"Who were you were talking to?" one of my crew asked after David had left.

"That was my brother," I kidded.

"Well, he did look like you with that bushy mustache. He even had the same hair, just longer."

I never revealed the identity of the stranger. I doubt if anyone would have recognized the name or the music. I was just glad no one in the bar asked us if we were the Oak Ridge Boys. Then again, it was fun daydreaming about singing a duet with David.

Ron Luciano: Known for his flamboyant style and witticism, the MLB umpire from 1960 to 1979 was famous for his long-running feud with Orioles manager Earl Weaver. Over eight seasons, he ejected Earl eight times. One time, Earl was ejected from both games of a doubleheader, the second ejection coming when Earl brought out the lineup card.

My fortuitous meeting with Ron started in Baltimore when I was working a semipro playoff game. The referee for the game was from Binghamton, New York, where Ron owned a sporting goods store. He was a good friend of my umpiring idol. Before the game, we talked about Ron and his dislike for Earl Weaver. When he returned home, he had Ron send me a couple of souvenirs. One was a calendar from his store that read: "To Lou, my only friend in Baltimore." The other was an autographed baseball inscribed: "To Lou, the best line judge ever."

One morning while listening to WBAL radio, Charlie Eckman announced that Ron would be a guest on his show that evening.

Ron was in town promoting his latest book *The Umpire Strikes Back*, so I stopped by the studio. We shared some laughs as he talked about his philosophy on baseball, his start in the game, and his dislike of Earl Weaver. Before leaving, I thanked Ron for his gifts and finally got my book autographed. The inscription read: "Lou, great to see you're reading my book. Still my only Baltimore friend." Hey, that's what friends are for.

Al Davis: "Although I had the pleasure of meeting the owner of the Oakland Raiders only once, he's my all-time favorite football character. We met at Memorial Stadium on September 1, 1996, the day the NFL returned to Baltimore. Always one of the first people on the field, Al approached me as I was walking the field prior to the game. Dressed in matching slacks and open-collar shirt, he looked like he just stepped off the set of *The Sopranos* or was heading to Vegas to spend a weekend with The Rat Pack. With his slicked back black hair, actually an Elvis pompadour in his younger days, and bling that included a pinky ring, Super Bowl ring, and a silver wrist bracelet, he wasn't hard to pick out in the crowd.

"Great day for a game. Glad to be back in Baltimore. Lot of great memories here," he cheerfully announced as he shook my hand. I instinctively knew that he was referring to the 1977 AFC playoff game won by the Raiders in double overtime.

"Al, if you're glad, we're delirious. Let's hope we see you for a long time," I replied earnestly.

"Should have never happened the way it did. Baltimore was too good of a football town," he said in a somber tone, referring to Bob Irsay's midnight move. I was somewhat startled to hear this comment from an owner who moved his team from Oakland to Los Angeles and back to Oakland. I guess in Al's mind, he did it the right way.

Before he left, he talked glowingly about Art Modell and his accomplishments in the NFL, such as *Monday Night Football*.

"You guys are lucky to have Art. He's a good man," Al said before turning to leave.

I watched as Al circled the stands greeting fans, shaking hands, and signing autographs. I overheard him trading friendly barbs and one-liners with fans about their respective cities and teams. He seemed to know more about Baltimore than most Baltimoreans. Fans flocked to him like he was their long-lost favorite uncle. I could have sworn at one time he lived down the street from me in Gardenville.

Al was a hit in Baltimore. The carefully cultivated tough-guy, sinister façade was nowhere to be found around the fans. Too bad Al didn't move his franchise to Baltimore. He would have fit nicely with Baltimore's cast of blue-collar characters such as Charlie Eckman. They would have had one heck of a sports talk show. Despite his lawsuits against the NFL and his long-running feud with Commissioner Pete Rozelle, he was elected to the NFL HOF in 1992. "Just win, baby", was his mantra, and he did just that on and off the field.

George Young: The most influential person I met in football was Baltimore native George Young. A star player at Calvert Hall and Bucknell, George found a home in the coaching ranks. After eight successful years at City College, where he also taught history and political science, he became an assistant coach with the Baltimore Colts. Later in his career as the general manager and vice president of the New York Giants, he led the franchise to two Super Bowl victories. The five-time NFL Executive of the Year was inducted into the NFL Hall of Fame in 2020. Coach Young never forgot his roots.

When he returned home to be the guest speaker at a sports banquet, I had the opportunity to talk with him about his years as the head football coach at City College. That never happened. With George, you couldn't talk about football on the field without talking about its potential off the field. To him, football was a character builder that developed young men to be mentors and role models in their community. On his teams, if you didn't make the grade, you didn't play football. If you were on the team, you wore a coat and tie on game days. Football wasn't an extracurricular activity; it was a commitment to better your life. George was an old-school coach who believed what worked in the past would work in the future. To him, the issues facing our youth today were nothing new. He had seen them during his childhood and teaching days. In his eyes, the challenge to instill a value system was the same. He believed the paramount problem in today's society was the breakdown of the family unit. He espoused traditional family values as the keys to success. We could use more people like George in our classrooms and on our playing fields today.

Being a fixture at Baltimore's football venues since the early '70s, I was now a minor celebrity, often recognized by the fans, stadium workers, and the media. Unofficially, the Lou Who fan club had expanded from my wife and daughter. Conversations that followed these chance encounters usually involved my career as an official. Following the examples of gentlemen Jim Nantz and Vince Bagley, I always responded in a friendly tone with a smile.

Eat Your Wheaties and Follow Your Dream!

CHAPTER 30
FINDING YOUR CALLING

Invariably, people wanted to know how to get started as an official and what I would do differently if I had the chance.

Think you might like to be a football official? As the old Nike campaign said, "Just do it!" Start early and stay late. Get involved with sandlot teams (Pop Warner, etc.) and advance through your expertise and experience. I actually started my field career at the tender age of twelve. On Saturdays, my friend Johnny DiBattista, fellow bottle cap hunter, and I would pedal our bicycles for the four-mile round trip to man the chains at Archbishop Curley High School. We did it for free because we loved being on the field and close to the action. We were hooked on football.

Another venue for fledging officials is intramural sports, such as flag and touch football in high school and college. Likewise, there are a number of opportunities to get your foot in the door off the field, such as volunteer positions, internships, and game-day staff. You never know what could happen. In

2011, I worked a game as the clock operator for the Baltimore Charm of the Lingerie Football League. While the MTV2 producer kept reminding me it was strictly entertainment and not to worry about cutting seconds or minutes to fit the time slot, I saw it differently.

The ladies on the field took the game seriously and played with an intensity that rivaled any level of football. Dressed in bikinis, hockey style helmets with plastic visors, and jerseys that covered only the shoulder pads, they didn't feel exploited as eye candy for a TV audience. At heart, they were football players who loved the game and wanted a chance to play and prove themselves.

While you're at it, don't limit yourself to just football. Maybe you'll find your calling with another sport. Diversify your sports portfolio but always remember that to successfully officiate in any sport, you'll need certain skills.

To make the calls, you need a take-charge personality, communication skills, decision-making abilities, and a thick skin. Be fair, be impartial, and be honest at all times. Don't be afraid to make the call and don't be afraid to admit that you blew it. Maintain your integrity and character.

Who was responsible for my value system? My father, of course. During a youth baseball game, I rounded third, missed the bag, and scampered back to touch it before scoring. After the game, I asked my father, the home plate umpire, if he would have called me out if I hadn't touched the bag. "I didn't see my son. I saw a ball player," he responded thoughtfully. "Rules of the game, like the rules of life, are made to be followed. Break the rules and be ready to suffer the consequences," he added warmly with a pat on my shoulder. That advice was seared into my memory and guided me throughout my career.

If officiating is not for you, don't worry. There are other ways to stay connected to the sport that you love. Remember, failure is not succeeding; it's not trying. You don't want to look back on your life and say that I could have done that if only I tried. Once again, the bottom line is that it has to be fun.

So if you have decided that football is your sport, *now* is the time to give it your best shot. Be committed; be dedicated. Eat, live, and breathe football. Be willing to attend training classes every week from July to November. Work scrimmages a couple days a week in August. Watch veteran officials during the football season. Hold the chains at high school games. Be willing to travel at a moment's notice.

Early in my career, I sent a letter to Charlie Eckman, former NBA coach and official who I highlighted earlier in the book, asking for advice. He wrote back and gave me contacts for the Baltimore City Recreation and Parks and local Pop Warner Football Leagues. I followed his advice and joined the ranks of these groups. "Call'em as you see'em, Lou," he exhorted in the closing line of his letter. There was no better advice on the subject of officiating.

Some of the best advice I can impart is to network; and that means volunteering.

One of the biggest boosts in my football network occurred in 1985 when I became a member of the National Football Foundation and College Football Hall of Fame, Greater Baltimore Chapter (GBC). Their mission was to promote and develop the power of amateur football in developing leadership, sportsmanship, competitive zeal, and the drive for academic excellence in America's young people. Sounds something like John Carrigan would have written, but there was a lot of truth in those words.

Each year the GBC honors high school and college scholar athletes at an awards banquet. The event, one of the largest in the country, includes 1,200 attendees from sixty-five schools and features the big names in football as guest speakers.

In 1990, I became president after serving on the board of directors. This opportunity allowed me to meet and greet a number of influential people. The board of directors and the board of advisers were a variable Who's Who of coaches, businessmen, politicians, sportswriters, and football people from around the country.

During my tenure, I was able to interact with different coaches and learn what characteristics they desired in an official. Foremost, they looked for consistency. If there was a holding foul, pass interference, or personal foul this week, it should be the same next week. That doesn't always happen. That's why officials attend clinics, watch film, and have evaluators for every game. Coaches also look for officials who are in shape, positioned to make the calls (mechanics), and communicate effectively with them on the sidelines. I found that if you get coaches away from the field, they will openly discuss their concerns about officiating. We provided those opportunities.

Through the GBC, I became friends with Gordy Combs, Towson University head football coach for seventeen years. Unfortunately for Coach Combs, I called an unsportsmanlike conduct foul on him after he ran on the field to protest a call. After a review of the game film, he was right about the call but still wrong about coming onto the field.

The following year, Gordy and I were on the cover of Towson's official football program. He said that my call was his first penalty during his coaching career. His wife said differently. Sorry Coach, but I'm sure fans will side with your wife. When he retired from coaching, he became an analyst for TU sports radio and television. Over the years, we kept in touch on and off the field, discussing everything about football and our personal lives. That's how I discovered that Gordy was a Gardenville Guy like me. We grew up together and never knew it until we both finished our careers on the field.

The lesson here is to be bold and brave. Don't be intimidated in following your dream. Inspiration abounds all around you. When I was president of the Maryland Board of Football Officials (MBFO) in 1987, I received a letter from our first female applicant, Debbie Weinberg. She had written a letter to the NFL asking how she could become a football official and work in the NFL. Coincidentally, the supervisor of officials at the time was a former member of the MBFO. He advised her to contact me.

Debbie subsequently joined our group and eventually worked as a high school official. The road was bumpy, but she preserved. When she first started, she had to make her own pants and customize her shirts. Unfortunately, the officiating world was not ready for a female official in the college ranks. But that didn't stop her. She later became a clock operator for college games. Debbie had the dedication, desire, and skill set but not the opportunity. An unsung hero, she was trailblazer for women in football.

Is there a place for women as football officials? Unequivocally and absolutely, yes! You've seen Shannon Eastin. Now take a look at Sarah Thomas. She rose through the ranks of high school and college to become the first permanent female NFL official in 2015. In 2021, she was selected as the down judge for Super Bowl LV. She credits her success on understanding the spirit of the rules, her communication skills, and the courage to make the call. She reminds me a lot of Debbie Weinberg.

◆ ◆ ◆

The most important women in my life have been my wife, Kelly, and our beloved daughter, Kathleen. I have, largely because of Kelly's support, lived my dream. And if I have one regret, it is that we didn't meet earlier in life. She is an amazing woman who has supported me every step of the way.

When we first met, she knew nothing about football but still managed to develop an appreciation for the game. After watching a few games together on TV, we took the bold step and attended our first live game. "I am having difficulty finding the yellow line on the field," she exclaimed, referring to the yellow line on the TV to mark a first down. "The magic of television, hon," I responded, gently explaining the nuances of a football broadcast.

I met Kelly at Baltimore Gas and Electric in 1994. We both worked in the same department and would occasionally go out to lunch as a group. Our first date was a Christmas concert by the Baltimore Symphony Orchestra. Kelly had an extra ticket and was looking for a date. Well, not really a date, just someone to accompany her because she wasn't going to go by herself. Coworker John McGee suggested that I graciously accept the invitation. "You won't be disappointed," he exhorted. I wasn't disappointed; I was smitten with this charming and caring woman.

After dating for more than a year, I decided that it was time to settle down. After years of roaming lounges and barrooms in vain, I had found my soulmate. During our engagement, Kelly was introduced to the life of a football wife. She was not deterred. To give Kelly a taste of life during the football season, we flew to Harvard University for a game where I was officiating. It was her first college football game. Although not a sports person, she quickly embraced the aura of college football. Much to my relief, she had fun despite not having a rooting interest on the field other than me. That was the time that she met US Senator Ted Kennedy who was tailgating in the parking lot.

Our wedding day, December 5, 1996, was after the football season to accommodate my football family. At the reception, my father presented Kelly with a football official's shirt, a referee's white cap to let me know who's the boss, and a gold penalty flag in case I got out of line. Through the years, we mixed business with pleasure. Football became a romantic getaway weekend that included shopping and dining. That was something I didn't have to worry about as a bachelor. Kelly still loves to visit William and Mary College in Williamsburg, Virginia, Cornell University in the Finger Lakes of New York, and Georgetown University in Washington, DC. Being able to spend time with this remarkable woman whom I love and the sport that I love has been a blessing.

I have always enjoyed being called Sweet Lou. The moniker is music to my ears and my calling card. Those words always remind me what a sweet ride my life has been on and off the field. From Radecke Park to the NFL, there has been a mountain of cherished memories. I sincerely hope that you enjoyed this trip down memory lane with me. For without you, the fans, none of it would have been possible.

ACKNOWLEDGMENTS

To chase a dream, you need a team of compassionate and caring people who believe in you. Over the course of your journey, they provide the insight and wisdom to be successful. They cheer you to greater heights because they love you, and as we have learned over the course of our lives if you grew up in the '60s, love is all you need. A sincere and special thank you to the following members of my dream team:

Paul Travers, one of the Gardenville Guys that I have known for over sixty years. For two years, he dedicated himself to researching and documenting, my story. Over his career, he has written numerous books on a variety of subjects, including a bestseller. Where did a Gardenville Guy learn to write like that? Had to be the fairy dust at Radecke Park.

Jimmy "Jimmy Mac" Maconaghy, who gave me the opportunity to advance my officiating career at the collegiate level. He taught me how to manage the game on the field and on the sidelines. Without his mentorship, my six NCAA DIV I playoff assignments and the classic college rivalries, Harvard-Yale, Lehigh-Lafayette, William and Mary-Richmond, and Villanova-Delaware would have never happened.

John "The Chief" Carrigan, dear friend, football confident/collaborator, and crew chief who nominated me for the Minor League Football Hall of Fame. Without his phone calls, my career would have never advanced beyond the sandlots.

John made football an adventure to be savored. I'll always remember our work in establishing the USFL as one of the most satisfying experiences in my career.

Tom Armstrong and Frank City, who gave me my start in sandlot and Pop Warner. They recognized potential in a young man and convinced him to take the next step in his career wearing the proper shoes.

My BGE cadre, Ron Daiker, Dick Rosenberger, and Buzz Stallings, who unselfishly honed my football skills while I progressed through the ranks.

Norm Brewer, Commissioner of the MBFO who developed me as a high school football official and assigned me my first state championship game. Also instrumental in guiding my career was the MBFO connection that included Jimmy Diggs, Leon Jones, and Steve Smith.

Gordy Combs, former head football coach for Towson University, for getting my picture on the cover of the Towson University game day program. Even though I had to escort him back to the coaching box after a fifteen-yard penalty, we've remained friends over the years.

Tom Beck, dear friend and referee in my first college game. With an encyclopedic knowledge about football, he readily had the answers to my questions. And, over the years, I had a lot.

Jack Winter, the brother I never had. I had the privilege of being the head linesman for Jack's first DIV I game. Since that day, our families have become close friends. Jack was the referee of my DIV I crew for many years. On and off the field, we taught each other about the game of life.

Lance Garth and the entire Garth family who became part of my extended family. Lance was the first person to call and congratulate me on my promotion to DIV I. During my first year on a DIV I crew, he taught me the skills to survive at that level.

He was also responsible from my nickname. The Garth family, like the Winter clan, holds a special place in my heart.

My crew of many years, John Shigo, Brian Thomas, Ed Mokus, Jack O'Keefe, Chris Garth, Rusty Acree, Gary Powers, John Swartz, and our leader Jack Winter. We perfected our craft and had fun in the process. After the game, we always enjoyed an adult beverage or two together. Why the waiting list to join our crew? We had a beer distributor among our ranks. Maybe, that's the only reason we had a waiting list.

Larry Upson, NFL supervisor of officials, who gave me a chance to work in the NFL. He ensured that every replacement official received a game ball.

Bill Ryan, former NFL clock operator, who recommended me as his backup. When he retired, I was named primary coach-to player cutoff operator.

Gardenville guys and gals, who sprinkled Radecke Park with fairy dust and created memories that still bring a smile to my face. You were some of the most memorable characters that Baltimore has ever produced.

Butch Hensel and my former bandmates, who taught me about teamwork and show business. We reached for the stars (Ed Sullivan Show) and landed on the moon (Kerby Scott Show). Along the way, we became a legendary rock band, at least in our minds and in Gardenville.

Mark Canham, childhood friend since the Cub Scouts, who generously donated his time and talent as the official photographer for Team Hammond.

Larry Yocum, who gave me the opportunity to work my first chain crew assignment over fifty years ago at the University of Maryland. Larry continues to assign me game day duties at the university when I'm available.

www.ingramcontent.com/pod-product-compliance
Lightning Source LLC
LaVergne TN
LVHW041749060526
838201LV00046B/956